# The New Way to Compete

# The New Way to Compete

## How to Discover Your Personal Competitive Style and Make It Work for You

by

### HARRY A. OLSON

Lexington Books

D.C. Heath and Company · Lexington, Massachusetts · Toronto

*Library of Congress Cataloging-in-Publication Data*

Olson, Harry A., 1944–
The new way to compete : how to discover your personal competitive
style and make it work for you / Harry A. Olson.
p.   cm.
Includes index.
Bibliography: p.
ISBN 0–669–21406–X (alk. paper)
1. Employee competitive behavior.   I. Title.
HF5549.5.C7047   1989

650.1—dc20                                                      89–8271
                                                                CIP

Published simultaneously in Canada
Printed in the United States of America
International Standard Book Number: 0–669–21406–X
Library of Congress Catalog Card Number: 89–8271

The paper used in this publication meets
the minimum requirements of American National Standard
for Information Sciences—Permanence of Paper
for Printed Library Materials, ANSI Z39.48–1984.

Year and number of this printing:

89 90 91 92 8 7 6 5 4 3 2 1

# Contents

# List of Figures, Tables, and Boxes

## Figures

## Tables

## Boxes

*This book is dedicated to*
*my son, Dave,*
*who, at age 15, in several important ways, is a natural Healthy*
*Competitor, possessing depth, sensitivity, and understanding*
*beyond his years,*
*and to my wife, Carol,*
*the love of my life, who is an ideal blend of strength and caring.*

# Acknowledgments

I wish to thank, first and foremost, my wife and son for sharing me with this project. Their love and patience, and sometimes their impatience, helped me get through the task of writing. I also owe a deep debt of gratitude to my wife for the countless hours she spent typing this manuscript.

Two consultants and special friends deserve credit for their help and advice: Gordon Shea, who in so many ways over the years helped me target my thoughts, and Jeffrey Davidson, who, with Gordon, helped me develop and polish my original proposal for this book. I thank these two also, as published authors themselves, for being an inspiration to my writing endeavors.

Special thanks to Paul Kelly, my publicity agent, who has worked closely with me and has encouraged me as we have attempted to raise consciousness on this vital issue of healthy competition.

I wish to express deep appreciation to my friend, Arnold "Nick" Carter, of Nightingale-Conant Corporation, who has guided me, shared with me, bucked me up, and been more of a friend to me over the miles than he'll ever know. I wish also to thank some of my other friends from the National Speakers Association and elsewhere for their caring, support, and encouragement: Peter Johnson, Nat Starr, Jack Cohen, Bill Brooks, Dottie and Lillet Walters, Joe Charbonneau, David Alan Yoho, Ed and Cynthia Helvey, Ira Westreich, Stu Crump, Anne Boe, Jeanne Robertson, and Robert Henry. I also wish to thank my Swedish colleagues, Dr. Lars-Eric Unestahl, and Sven Atterhed and Gustaf Delin of the ForeSight Group for their friendship and input.

In special ways, both large and small, each of these friends has touched my life, inspired me, and helped me along, not only in my career, but also in my personal life. And that's what friendship— and "Healthy Competition"—are all about!

# Introduction

COMPETE or DIE! That's the harsh reality of today's world.

We're living in the midst of a global competition explosion! In every profession, in every area of life, the competition is getting stiffer and fiercer. The number of competitors has increased faster than the number of jobs, resources, and opportunities. The pressure is on! To become a "winner" today is an ever more demanding task, demanding more talent, more guts, more preparation, more savvy . . . and causing alarming increases in stress and burnout.

You want to be a winner. You're "going for the gold" in your chosen field. Are you prepared?

It's not enough to be technically competent, or to be bright, or to be talented and motivated. Those things are essential, but there's more. To maximize the opportunity and speed of your success you must master the basic skills of competition itself. You need to understand how competition affects you, how to recognize and protect yourself from hidden competitive ploys. You need to know how and where to channel your energy to increase your edge, and at the same time reduce competitive stress. You need to identify and polish your competitive style and make the most of your power of positive impact.

In short, you can benefit from competition training. If Olympians are taught to cope with the heat of athletic competition, shouldn't you have the same advantage in the type of competition you face?

Competition in America is relentless. We're first faced with competing in some form or other in our early preschool years, and it continues with increased pressure and consequence throughout our lives. Not to compete is impossible in our society.

But here's the rub. While America is competitive to the core, our models of competing are mostly poor and our methods often destructive. Yet because competitiveness is an American sacred cow, its worth, values, and methods have been passed down from generation to generation without being seriously questioned. Until now. The latest research has stripped the veil (and the halo) from competition, revealing it as it is. Competition is far from being the great motivator. Rather, its iron jaws have chewed up and spit out many promising careers, and even lives.

But what about free enterprise? The Olympics? Doesn't competition bring out the best in us? Yes, it can. *It all depends on how, when, and where you use it.*

That's what's so confusing about competition. It's not a simple concept that can easily be written off as good or bad. In fact, those who have praised competition in the popular literature as well as those who are now beginning to pan it are often guilty of oversimplification. And that confuses people even more.

Much is being said and written today about win-win relations, cooperation, and team-building. And it's about time! Yet the implication is that once people know the skills of communication, negotiation, and cooperation, they will naturally stop competing. That makes sense in theory, but have you seen any organization naturally drift toward mutual cooperation just because of skill training? Neither have I.

Which brings us to the first of three basic, underlying facts about healthy competition:

> You cannot have maximum cooperation until you can understand and control the dynamics of competition within your organization.

Ever try to build a team out of a group of would-be superstars? How about when a task group comes up with an important solution or suggestion: which member of the group gets the most credit? Even the peace talks that ended the Vietnam War were hung up for several days because the delegates were jockeying about where to sit! You see, competition is everywhere. The healthy competitor who would maximize his or her effectiveness must learn how to cope with it.

The second fact has been mentioned earlier:

> While competitiveness is not a biological drive, in our advanced society it is a cultural imperative. You can't not compete.

Let's get real! Competition is here to stay. It is no more possible for the achiever—you—to stop competing than it is for America to drop out of the arms race (which is also a form of competition). Yet paradoxically, while survival demands we compete, cardiologists and others are saying that competition is one of America's greatest killers!

What's the answer?

Competition *is not* one of America's greatest killers; *misdirected* competitiveness is! The answer is not to stop competing, but to learn how to do it in a healthy manner.

There *is* a healthy way to compete, one that produces minimum stress and maximum productivity. One that can restore the positive thrill to the competitive process. One that will give you a competitive edge without power jockeying and backbiting.

The current way we compete is often energy disbursive. We put our efforts into defeating our opponents, protecting our egos, etc. This drives down productivity while driving up the cost of doing business, and of doing anything else worthwhile. The new model is energy intensive. The effort is concentrated in just the right place, in just the right way, to maximize impact and results.

Here's the third fact, also a paradox, about healthy competition:

> Healthy competition is rooted squarely in solid cooperation and contribution.

This fact eludes most competitors. It is ignorance or disbelief in this principle that leads to competition's dark, destructive side.

This book lays it all out. *The New Way to Compete* has taken competition into surgery. The disease has been cut out and the healthy aspects strengthened. The new model and methods presented in this book are not a panacea, but they will prepare you to be your best in high-level competition and help you to improve your productivity and relations with colleagues and coworkers.

This book will enlighten and, I hope, challenge you. To be a healthy competitor may mean casting aside some of your most cherished beliefs and strongly held myths about competing and cooperating. You'll come face to face with your own value system about competition and cooperation. While the path of growth may be arduous at times, you'll experience a new freshness, freedom, and joy in competing. You'll streamline your own competitive endeavors and gain a significant, positive competitive edge.

But first, you need to understand what competition in our society is all about and how to sort the wheat from the chaff. Here is where our journey begins.

# The New Way to Compete

# 1

# The Competition Explosion

How well America enters the twenty-first century depends on what we do today. Will we be strong, or a second-rate power? Will we give our children a legacy of war or peace? Will America solve its internal problems, or will our nation be riddled with domestic strife? Will the planet survive to see the twenty-second century? This is the scope of the competitiveness issue. It cannot be ignored.

As an economic power, the United States has its back to the wall. With mounting trade and budget deficits and the fluctuating dollar, the U.S. hasn't been cutting it in the world market. Nineteen eighty-six closed with a more than $170 billion trade deficit, a national all-time high. Our shrinking economic competitiveness abroad has escalated to crisis proportions. President Ronald Reagan highlighted competitiveness as a national priority in his 1987 State of the Union address. Since then we have seen a stock market crash second only to the Great Depression.

## The Tragic Irony

We're in trouble! What went wrong? America is one of the most competitive nations in the world. We have always felt that we can compete and win—anywhere, anytime.

The problem isn't that America can't compete. Rather, while we are relentlessly competitive, *we don't know how to compete prop-*

*erly and effectively!* More precisely, we don't know where and when to stop competing.

The Japanese compete with other companies and nations with fierce finesse, while we're busy competing internally, with ourselves. A few years ago a large U.S. aerospace company was developing a new plane. The company needed a special part and put it out to aerospace suppliers to bid. A prominent American and a Japanese firm responded. While the developers wanted to "buy American," they accepted the Japanese bid. Why? The Japanese firm could guarantee delivery on time, the U.S. firm could not; it could not be certain its employees wouldn't strike!

There has been a flurry of analysis and proposed solutions, but there is one aspect of our competitiveness plight that the business analysts have overlooked: how we as individuals compete.

While the whole is greater that the sum of its parts, the "corporation" as an entity apart from the persons who comprise it is a myth. You cannot achieve corporate excellence until individual excellence is attained. Likewise, you cannot improve the long-term competitive position of the corporation in the marketplace without improving the attitude and behavior of the employees.

The bottom line for improved corporate competitiveness in the outside world is maximal cooperation and contribution internally. But *you cannot have maximum cooperation until you are able to control the dynamics of competition within your organization.*

Why? The ability to cooperate and contribute depends directly upon, and is limited by, our attitudes and values regarding competition. While cooperation produces better, longer lasting results than competition, cooperation is fragile. If in a cooperative work group one person starts to compete, the group quickly turns competitive. Unless, of course, the other group members are trained enough, savvy enough, and strong enough to recognize negative competitive behavior when it first occurs and head it off at the pass.

Let's get one thing straight. When we're talking about problems relating to competition, we're not suggesting that we just need new competitive tactics. New tactics in the hands of people with the traditional attitudes and values is like putting a Band-Aid on a third-degree burn, or a scalpel in the hands of a butcher! The problem isn't just with tactics. The rot lies within traditional competition itself.

As indicated in the introduction, the problem isn't necessarily with competition per se, but with how it is used. Competition can put you over the top or under the sod, depending on how you play the game. The healthy way to compete bears little resemblance to the cutthroat, dog-eat-dog, traditional competition we currently practice in our society.

Some have suggested that we stop competing. But how can we? To get a highly competitive person or organization to give up competing just by touting the advantages of cooperation or instituting team-building or Quality Circles is like attempting to build a bridge across the Grand Canyon. It can't be done just by trying to span from one side to the other. The gulf is too wide. To build such a bridge, you must first go down into the abyss, smooth rough spots, and build a solid foundation and support structure upon which you can erect the bridge. This foundation is a solid understanding of the complexities of competition, a knowledge of how to recognize and cope with the competition you currently face, and a recognition and adoption of values and strategies of healthy competition which actually promote cooperation, contribution, and excellence.

But before we get to bridge-building, we need to answer this: Who made America great? Daniel Boone or *Little House on the Prairie?*

America has always had a remarkable pioneering spirit. That spirit is part of the backbone of our whole culture and world view. Daniel Boone, Davy Crockett, Lewis and Clark, and our other pioneers are folk heroes, full of courage and tenacity. They exemplify the "rugged individualism" that we so identify with "the American way." Sure, they charted unexplored territory and opened the path toward western expansion. We owe all of our explorers, from Christopher Columbus to the astronauts, a tremendous respect and debt of gratitude. Yet we must not delude ourselves as to where our nations's true greatness lies.

The qualitites exemplified by *Little House on the Prairie* form the foundation for our true greatness: true grit and determination, blended with a strong group identification and cooperation. The early settlers were raided out, starved out, droughted out—but they came back, again and again. They rebuilt, working together. They all pitched in to build one man's barn. Mutual harvesting and husking bees were commonplace. When work had to be done, they banded together, and petty quarrels were cast aside.

But in the "me-ism" of modern society, "rugged individualism" is deified, while cooperation is overshadowed. So many people want to "do it on their own." In all of America's history, it has never been harder to cooperate and to form commitments than today. And "rugged individualism" is a solid foundation for unhealthy competition.

Many individuals feel embarrassed about asking for help. They see receiving help as weakness, as inability to "do it on my own." When any of my consulting clients tell me that, I ask, "Will you invite me out to your farm to see your sheep and cows?" After the client stops looking at me as if I'm crazy, I explain that I'd like to see how he raises his sheep and shears them all by himself, and see the loom on which he weaves the wool into the cloth from which he sews his own clothes. By then the light dawns. No man is an island. We are all interdependent. As the Beatles put it: we get by with a little help from our friends.

All mankind is socially embedded. Even our personal freedom demands responsibility back to the society at large. All of our actions make sense only in a social context. No one can escape his neighbor. There are always strings attached. Even the hermit trapper had to come to town to exchange his pelts for knives and gunpowder.

True freedom begins with our acceptance of our social embeddedness. True independence, therefore, is comprised of (a) the courage and ability to make choices and take action and (b) the ability to *use the network without feeling threatened*. Only the insecure bolster their weak egos by insisting on going it alone. The emotionally mature and truly free individual uses all the appropriate resources available to achieve her goals, and gladly gives back in return as payment for what she has received.

What has all this to do with competition? Everything! Look at the following quote:

> There have been counter-suggestions, there have been criticisms by special-interest groups. But the most heartening reaction was the

surge of national confidence, the reaffirmation of our competitive spirit, the willingness to make personal sacrifices in the pursuit of worthy goals. . . . Let the detractors of America, the doubters of the American spirit, take note. America's competitive spirit, the work ethic of this people, is alive and well on Labor Day 1971. The dignity of work, the value of achievement, the morality of self-reliance, none of these is going out of style.

Richard M. Nixon[1]

What was Nixon really saying? Is "America's competitive spirit" the same as "the work ethic of this people?" Is it identical with "the willingness to make personal sacrifices in the pursuit of worthy goals"? He seemed to think so. But if he did, he was confused. So are most of us. We each look at "competition" from our private perspectives and biases, and come out with different evaluations. On the one hand, we see positive benefits: price stabilization, innovation, rapid growth, personal excellence. We look again and find increased stress and burnout, undermining of productivity, imitation and conformity, even warfare. Figure 1-1 shows some of the actual outcomes of competition. When we stop and think about it, competition is all-pervasive and pretty mysterious.

Our competitiveness is a mystery precisely because we're immersed in it every day. We involuntarily participate in it. We see its good and bad effects, but because we live it and our cultural values support it, we take it for granted. Some of us seem to thrive on it while others are crushed by it. We value it without understanding how it can work for us, and how it works against us. As individuals and as a society, we have failed to analyze competition and its effects.

Sociologist Thurston Veblen dubbed the postwar era "The Age of Anxiety." The age of anxiety has become "The Age of Competition." Competition is on the rise in all quarters of society. It is more open, on more people's lips. As we look around we notice numerous socio-cultural and business factors that have contributed to the rise in competitiveness. Here are a few of them:

Sociocultural

- The baby boom and declining death rate, with more of a scramble for existing jobs and resources.

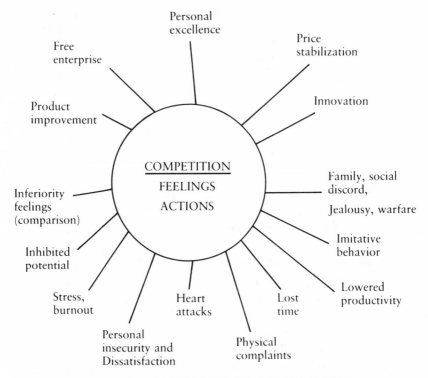

Figure 1-1. OUTCOMES OF COMPETITION

- The "tenderizing" of the postwar generation. Psychiatrist Rudolf Dreikurs called the "pampered child syndrome" the greatest psychiatric problem of our time. We have raised proportionately more spoiled children than ever before.

- The "me" decade of the seventies—the epitome of the "do your own thing" philosophy.

- Greater social consciousness of the sixties and the eighties, notably the Women's and the Civil Rights movements.

- A widening gap between the haves and have-nots within our society. A new millionaire is created in America every seventeen minutes. At the same time, one out of five Americans is functionally illiterate.

- Threat of nuclear war. Escalating of defense projects and budgets to maintain an increasingly precarious balance of power.

- Increased child and spouse abuse, and substance abuse.

- Increased demands on existing resources as Third World nations develop.

Business

- Deregulation, with mad scrambles to enter and capture market share.

- Economic development of Japan, South Korea, Taiwan, China, Western Europe, and other areas.

- Shift at home from a product-driven to a market-driven economy.

- Rapid mergers, acquisitions, buyouts and takeovers—hostile or not—along with increasing in-company restructuring.

- Similar rapid increase of entrepreneurialism, cottage industry, and "intrapreneurial" projects in large corporations.

- Rapid advance of technology, often occurring faster than our ability to keep up.

- Increased job stress and substance abuse, especially at high corporate levels.

- A trend toward "militarization" of business. Ads tell us "Business is War." Books on warfare and military strategy become "must reading" for corporate executives. Military language pervades the boardroom. Language conditions us. The more we use warlike words, the quicker we develop warlike attitudes.

By now many people recognize that competition can be destructive, but they don't know what to do about it. It's like trying to control handguns. How do you do it in a serious, effective way when over half the homes in America possess at least one firearm? Even worse, as many people are beginning seriously to question our business ethics, they feel dishonorable about competing, yet feel that they must continue to compete to carry out business day to day. What's really going on?

# Get Out Your Knives and Cleavers; It's Time to Butcher the Sacred Cow!

Boil down the various social theories regarding competition and you come to this practical definition: to vie with an opponent whom you are trying to beat, or against an external or internal standard, to achieve a particular goal.

When opponents are involved, the implication is that the goal cannot be shared equally among all contestants. Therefore, the closer your opponent gets to the goal, the worse your chances become of achieving it. This aspect is critical! If you both are competing for a goal you can't share, your opponent's behavior is linked to yours in a negative way. Your chances of achieving the goal are out of your direct control because they depend not only on what you do, but also on what your opponent does.

You have two ways, then, of improving your chances to win: (a) improving your performance or advantage (honestly or by cheating), or (b) undercutting or impeding your opponent's progress. You can use either or both methods. And, theoretically, in a competition in which your chances of success are directly related to your opponent's actions, either option (a) or (b) will work equally well. Unfortunately, it is usually easier (and often more fun) to trip up your opponent than to be consistently excellent.

The more scarce or limited the goal, the stiffer the competition usually becomes. In a limited competition, there are only one or a few prizes. In baseball's World Series, for example, there is only one winner. Compare this to an unlimited contest where anyone who meets a certain criterion "wins" a prize. Theoretically every contestant could walk away with a reward. Some sales contests are like this; everyone who meets the quota gets a prize. The Million Dollar Roundtable in the insurance industry operates this way, as do admissions to some colleages. A semi-limited competition is like an unlimited one except that there is some cutoff to the number of spaces or prizes available.

In an unlimited competition, contestants may even help each other. At one time in Switzerland, to become an MD you had to pass two state examinations. There were no limits as to how many could pass. Swiss medical students would help each other prepare. Because all could pass there was no individual threat, no reason for the students to undercut each other. Compare that to the cutthroat behavior that exists in some of our colleges and graduate schools.

People will often behave according to how the system is set up. If it is competitive, they will compete. If the system rewards cooperation, cooperative behavior is more likely, provided people can move beyond the imperatives of their culturally ingrained competitiveness. This can be difficult. Psychiatrist Theodore Rubin, who studied medicine in Switzerland, indicated that the American medical students studying in the Swiss system did not cooperate. They undercut each other, and distrusted the Swiss faculty and system, thinking that the examination requirement had to have some trick behind it. They formed competitive cliques and spied on the other students.[2]

Every relationship is an opportunity to assert personal power and status vis-à-vis another person. We are early taught to compare ourselves with others, and comparison breeds competition. Comparison and competition are actually cyclical: comparison creates competition, which in turn breeds more comparison, and so on. This cycle is what fuels jealousy and the desire to "keep up with the Joneses."

Americans also have a penchant for putting contests where they were never meant to be. Look at our schools. Kids are supposed to be there to get an education, but they often end up jockeying for grades. Parents many times do a child's homework, or overly assist, so the child will get an A. "Curving" grades, so that there are a set number of A's, B's, and so on, may sometimes pit students against each other. I can't help but ask, what are our children really learning—about life, about relationships, about the relative value of education itself?

Husbands and wives jockey for power, parents and children vie over authority. Many people even believe that competition is innate, that it is human nature, genetically determined. When we speak of "competitive drive," the implication is that there is an internal "need" to compete, longing for expression.

Nothing is further from the truth. Sociological analyses show that some societies, such as the Zuni and Hopi Indians, the Bathonga in South Africa, and the Tangu in New Guinea, avoid competition, preferring cooperative relationships. It is a sad commentary that there is no technologically advanced society in which cooperation reigns. Competition is culturally, not genetically, determined.

The bottom line of all of this is that competition is a highly complex process. Either to support it in total, or to degrade it totally, is an oversimplification. Competition has spawned greatness, and also great evil!

Today there are serious problems with how competition is used. Like power and gambling, competing is an addiction, especially in America.

We identify competition with the American spirit, the "American Way." We are convinced that it is the greatest motivator ever. Want to motivate people for peak performance? Just create a contest! We think that this is a simple thing to do, and that we know how. Actually it is quite difficult to implant competition without actually *de*motivating people! The only ones motivated are the ones most likely to win. It's really quite discouraging to be locked into a contest where you feel you have no hope of winning! The "losers" often continue to perform below par, and may even subvert the organization.

The fact is, traditional competition, especially at the interpersonal level, has failed miserably to achieve positive results. Most of the problems occur in the realm of social, everyday competition, but structured competition also is often destructive. Sport psychologists Ogilvie and Tutko studied approximately fifteen thousand athletes and could find no evidence that competitive sports builds character. In fact, they found that "athletic competition limits growth in some areas." The competitors they studied showed higher levels of stress, depression, and shallow interpersonal relationships. Many players with strong character strengths avoid competitive sports, preferring more individual athletic outlets.[3]

Another sports psychologist, Terry Orlick, noted that:

For many children, competitive sports operate as a failure factory that not only effectively eliminates the "bad ones," but also turns off many of the 'good ones.' In North America it is not uncommon to lose from 80 to 90 percent of our registered organized sports participants by fifteen years of age.[4]

Nelson and Kagan found that:

> The American competitive spirit may be alive and well, but it has produced a culture whose children are systematically irrational. Ten-year-olds in Los Angeles who participated in our experiments repeatedly failed to get rewards for which they were striving because they competed in games that required cooperation. In other situations, these children worked hard and even sacrificed their own rewards to reduce the rewards of their peers. Among children the tendency toward irrational competition increases with age. And we can easily find adults whose drive to compete overrides self-interest in academia, athletics, business, politics, and Vietnam.[5]

How about business? Hasn't competition been effective in improving quality? Since when is competition necessary for excellence! In fact, competition has brought price stability in some areas, and has spurred certain innovations, but this has occurred at the broad, inter-group level. What about the price we have to pay for that improvement? Because of our obsession with traditional competing at all levels, we have not explored other options that would produce even greater achievement with less stress. All too often, winning and excellence have very little in common.

Has competition been good for business? Quality expert, W. Edwards Deming, states:

> Management has failed in this country. The emphasis is on the quick buck. . . . The emphasis in Japan is to plan decades ahead. . . . There must be constancy of purpose toward an aim. That aim could be anything, but there must be a consistency of purpose, which does not exist in this country. . . . The Japanese government intervenes to break up competition and help people work together. Washington promotes competition, which creates waste. Competition is not the answer today for quality and price. . . . When you have eight or ten companies working on the same thing and all going in different ways, you have waste. . . . We're in a new economic age. The methods that made this country wealthy don't work anymore.[6]

The examples that support Deming's assertion that competition produces waste are legion if we're willing to look at things as they really are. Here are a few salient ones:

- U.S. Olympic chances are undermined by infighting. In January 1988, U.S. Olympic Committee Executive Director, Harvey W. Schiller, quit after holding office for nineteen days, complaining of internal squabbling. Some observers insist that this infighting is overflowing onto the playing field. After decades of stellar U.S. Olympic victories, our Olympic athletes appear to have fallen behind their foreign counterparts. "Since 1984 the USOC has deteriorated into a democratic nightmare, rife with conflict and turmoil, 'It's a national embarrassment,' says John P. Bevilaqua, a sports marketing consultant."[7]

- AIDS research is hindered by infighting. "So intense is infighting at viral research laboratories in the AIDS program that experts have sabotaged each others' experiments and suppressed research aimed at combatting the disease."[8]

- A problem encountered in some Quality Circles is sabotage from above. Some supervisors, not understanding the role of QC, become competitive. They make sure the group fails because they see the ideas generated as criticism of themselves, or because they don't get full credit.[9]

- Airline competition up—airline safety down. Since deregulation, airlines are fighting more for financial survival. Many are cutting safety expenditures. In the face of tough competition, some airlines are making pilots fly more hours than federal laws permit. The pilots, more fatigued, are not "safe."[10]

- Because of vastly increased medical malpractice suits and higher judgments awarded, the cost of medical malpractice insurance has skyrocketed. This adversarial process has forced many physicians to treat significantly more patients each week to meet expenses. The result: reduction in quality of care.

- Four vice presidents of a large firm are so busy jockeying for individual power that their employees are suspicious and insecure, and vital information that should flow across departmental lines for the overall good of the company is held back for fear of giving another division VP an advantage. Relationships are strained at the top and the stress filters down through the ranks.

How about competition where *you* work? Box 1-1 gives you a questionnaire to help you assess the situation. Take a few minutes to fill in the questionnaire before reading further.

Box 1-1

---

### TWENTY QUESTIONS

Please indicate the degree to which you find each of these factors occurring in your organization, on the following scale:

5—Very frequently
4—Frequently
3—Moderately
2—Less Frequently
1—Very infrequently

The words "group" and "team" in the statements below can apply at any level appropriate to your situation, from a project team to a department or office, to the company as a whole.

1 Increased rivalry when one person or group gets closer to a common goal.
2 One person or group obstructs or sabotages the progress of another person or group.
3 More of "each one doing it on his own."
4 More criticism, put-downs—individuals and their contributions are not valued highly enough.
5 More *self*-conflict within group, team, or department members.
6 Less coordination of efforts, less teamwork.
7 More similarity and imitation of amount and type of work activities among members (less productive diversity and creativity).
8 Less group solidarity and loyalty among members.
9 More organizational rigidity in the face of changing circumstances.
10 Direction of energy and activity in group is more scattered and diverse, less organized.
11 Greater communication breakdowns among group members.
12 Fewer mutual agreements, more conflict, bickering, insistence on being "right."
13 Higher anonymity and isolation among members.
14 More personal striving outside of work group (therefore, less energy available for work).
15 Group or company products or goals are not valued highly enough by members.
16 Less friendliness, more suspicion. People often feel on their guard for vague reasons they can't define.
17 More goofing off or working on personal business during available work time.
18 Greater emphasis on responsibility to self and one's territory, even at others' or company's expense.
19 Greater expectation of receiving hostility or rejection from others in the work setting.
20 Greater difficulty in reaching consensus and moving on toward goals.

If you scored high, you have plenty of company. In our New Way To Compete™ seminars, over 80 percent of attendees so far have had average, per-item responses between 3.5 to 4, and many were significantly higher. A total low score was rare. What these questions describe are twenty items found by research to be symptoms of misdirected competition within a group. If your score was moderate to high, your organization has a problem with internal competition, and so do you insofar as you work there and are affected by the corporate culture.

Competitiveness in business can work to your personal detriment. In a series of studies of Ph.D. scientists and successful business people, Helmreich and Spence discovered that "achievement motivation" is actually composed of four traits:

1. Work—desire to work hard and keep busy
2. Mastery—preference for difficult, challenging tasks that meet internal criteria of excellence
3. Competitiveness—desire to beat others
4. Personal Unconcern—little worry about other people's negative reactions to one's accomplishments.

They found that those who achieved greatest success scored high on Work, Mastery, and Personal Unconcern, and notably lower on Competitiveness. They discovered that "a high degree of 'Competitiveness' tended to have deleterious effects on the production of influential work among otherwise motivated scientists." And regarding their business sample, they found "the highest income was received by those high in Work/Mastery and low in Competitiveness."[11] Competition, therefore, may boost production in the short term, but long-term competitiveness, or operating with a highly competitive life-style, actually hinders excellence.

The above conclusion is true not only for business. Johnson & Johnson analyzed 122 studies on classroom achievement from 1924 through 1980. Of that number, 65 found that cooperation produces higher achievement than competition, while only 8 showed the reverse results. Thirty-six found no significant difference.[12] Numerous other studies in academia, business, and even athletics came to the same conclusion:

Traditional competition impedes performance! It diverts the energy needed for optimal learning and production into extraneous endeavors such as beating your opponent. You have only so much energy; where should you direct it for maximal benefit?

## What Is the Fallout on Us Personally?

At the personal level, competition can poison relationships. When we feel competitive toward another person we feel an increased tension and distrust. We can't feel totally at ease. If this happens often and keeps up, we may even come to view the person as a rival, or worse, an enemy. Then, instead of relating as equals, we look to gain the last word or the upper hand. We build walls instead of bridges!

Competitiveness also has a direct effect on wellness. Friedman and Rosenman discovered the cardiac-prone "Type A personality" is twice as likely to develop coronary artery disease and have heart attacks as the rest of the population (Type B). One of the key traits of the Type A personality is "competitiveness." Their conclusion: highly hurry-oriented, competitive people are at twice the coronary risk as their less competitive counterparts.[13]

Is competitiveness per se the culprit? Later research on Type A found that people who are *hostile* have a much higher rate of heart disease and its danger signals than people who are not hostile. Also, repressed anger has been related to high heartdisease risk. Hostile, angry people tend to be "hot reactors," who have very intense physical reactions to stress, which may lead to heart disease. Redford Williams, Jr., of Duke University Medical School, investigated this area and concluded that the real culprit is not Type A behavior, but a cynical, mistrusting attitude.[14] This is precisely the type of attitude exhibited by highly traditionally competitive people!

Psychologist M. W. Buckalew studied the effects of Type A and Type B attitudes on the benefits of exercise. He found after years of research that men who work out in a compulsive, competitive Type A way aren't doing their hearts as much good as those who approach exercise in a more cheerful and less competitive way.

Type A's can make anything competitive. . . . The true Type A is fully capable of competing intensely against himself. He'll feel compelled to be forever excelling in his performance levels. . . . My studies leave little doubt that overly aggressive and competitive people do themselves a disservice to approach their fitness routines with the same vengeance they approach their careers.[15]

America has a love-hate relationship with competition. We have never fully made up our minds whether or not we completely approve of it. We both fear it and revere it, and as a result we promulgate some significant mixed messages.

We have confused process with purpose, winning with achieving, and competing with surviving. We have expanded the limited nature of specific competitive activities such as sports and games into the total fabric of how we do business, run our families, and live our lives. As my pastor, Dixon Yaste, once said in a sermon, "We worship our work, we work at our play, and we play at our worship."

Wellness expert, Dr. Ken Dychtwald, states an ironic truth: It's not microbes that are killing us today. Our major killers are life-style-related disorders![16] Misdirected competition is, in a variety of ways, America's Number 1 killer, yet we are embedded in a competitive morass. We *can't not* compete. Pogo was right: We have met the enemy, and he is us! Is there hope?

The winds of change are sweeping across Corporate America. The corporation of the future will be leaner, and will place higher value upon the human side of business—upon caring, respect, and personal concern for workers' needs and interests.

Traditional internal competitive practices must be transformed if the future corporation is to succeed. If the total human potential demanded by tomorrow's business is to be realized, "Healthy Competition" and cooperation must characterize the corporate culture. Starting now!

---

# Notes

If you are interested in the research behind traditional competitiveness, you can't overlook the following two books. In some ways they disagree with each other, but both are landmark works.

Kohn, A. *No contest: The case against competition*. Boston: Houghton Mifflin, 1986.

Ruben, H. *Competing*. New York: Lippincott & Crowell, 1980.

# Chapter 1

1. Nixon, R. M. Quoted in L. L. Nelson and S. Kagan. "Competition, the star-spangled scramble." *Psychology Today*. September 1972, 53–56, 90, 91.
2. Rubin, T. I. *Reconciliations: Inner peace in an age of anxiety*. New York: Viking, 1980, 38–40.
3. Kohn, A. "No contest: A case against competition." *New Age Journal*. September-October 1986, 18–20.
4. Ibid.
5. Nelson, L. L. and Kagan, S. "Competition, the star-spangled scramble." *Psychology Today*. September 1972, 53–56, 90,91.
6. "Japan's rebuilder grim on U.S. biz." *American Business*. February 1982.
7. Ivey, M. "If there were a gold medal for bickering, the U.S. would win." *Business Week*. March 21, 1988.
8. "Infighting at federal lab hindering work on AIDS." *Baltimore Sun,* August 31, 1986, 106, 108.
9. Shea, G. Personal communication. Gordon Shea is the author of several books on trust and employee effectiveness.
10. Stephani, S. A. "Aviation safety . . . a necessary professional concern." *Speak Out,* December 1987, 8.
11. Helmreich, R. L., et al. "Achievement motivation and scientific attainment." *Personality and Social Psychology Bulletin*. 4, 1978, 222–226.
12. Kohn, A. "No contest: A case against competition." *New Age Journal*. September-October 1986, 18–20.
13. Friedman, M. and Rosenman, R. H. *Type A behavior and your heart*. New York: Fawcett Crest, 1974.
14. Fischman, J. "Type A On Trial." *Psychology Today*. February 1987, 42–50.
15. "Are you a Type A exerciser?" *Men's Health*. August 1987.
16. Dychtwald, K. "Peak Performance." Audiocassette distributed by National Speakers Association, Phoenix, AZ.

# 2

# Behind the Mystique

I N order to achieve, you don't have to compete. It is fully possible to start a project and carry it to a stunningly successful conclusion without having to compete with anyone. This does not imply that others won't compete with you, however. Competition becomes involved when the element of a contest, of winning, enters the picture. Then the issue becomes beating out the opponent. When that occurs, the achievement often becomes secondary.

In our society, once we perceive we are in a contest, it becomes very difficult to proceed as if the contest doesn't matter. We get hooked into competing, even if we had not intended to do so when we began. But competition is a red herring—so often it sidetracks our energy, taking us away from the goal of achieving for its own sake, into a mistaken realm of "winning."

Not only can misdirected competition divert our energy, it can lead us into several traps:

1. *The Ego Trap.* It is very easy to get hooked into competing. But *what* gets hooked? Our egos, that's what! When our egos get involved, we think our personal worth also rides on the outcome. We can fall into the trap of taking things too personally. Then we become defensive and lose our objectivity. If we succeed, we're worthwhile; if we fail, we're not much good. This faulty thinking puts on added competitive pressure, which fuels a "win at all costs" attitude.

2. *The Jealousy Trap.* Once our egos are involved, jealousy is quick to follow. When we're jealous of someone, that person becomes our adversary by definition. We may be cordial on

the surface, but in our hearts we harbor enmity. Not only can this poison our relationship with that person, but we may end up making improper decisions because our jealous hearts overcame our rational heads!

3. *The Imitation Trap.* While competition has occasionally spurred creativity, more often it creates imitation. When we perceive that someone is "winning," we tend to emulate his or her style and action in hopes that we also will have a greater chance at winning. For example, much "dressing for success" is actually an exercise in conformity. We loosely talk about "keeping up with the Joneses," but this is actually imitation. Competition often is little more than a number of people or groups trying to beat each other *at the same thing!* When competing, there is little room for creative individuality. We're too busy marching to someone else's drumbeat.

4. *The Speed Trap.* Competitive pressure often narrows our time frame. When the main goal is edging out the competition, speed is often of the essence. When we rush we often don't think things through well enough, we miscalculate and jump to unwarranted conclusions. While speed can be important in certain circumstances, it is only in a race that it becomes primary.

5. *The Shortsightedness Trap.* In competition it is often easy to lose long-range perspective, to focus narrowly on the demands of the moment. American management has long been criticized for neglecting the fact that "the big picture" is long as well as broad. While the Japanese may look at twenty-year goals, many American firms can't see past the next couple of years, or even past the next quarter's balance sheet. In our rush to beat out the competition, we have sacrificed quality on the altar of the fast buck.

6. *The Misdirected Vision Trap.* By focusing so much on the opponent we can quickly lose sight of where we need to be going, where we need to be putting our energy to our best advantage. When we focus on the opponent we are getting sidetracked and hung up on nonessentials. We can even be led to shoot for the wrong goal, which wastes precious time and resources.

7. *The Indecisiveness Trap.* This comes from getting side-tracked. When our goals and directions become confused we can often fall down on follow-through. We readily spin our wheels rather than sort out the issues and move on.

Individuals, and even whole organizations, can get caught in these traps. A healthy perspective about competition and cooperation can help you avoid them.

# Why Do We Compete?

If competition causes such problems, why do we compete?

First of all, when contests are a part of everyday life, its nigh on impossible to avoid thinking in win-lose terms. Television game shows are competitive by definition, and so are sports. Kids' cartoon shows, sitcoms, and soap operas also involve the ultimate contest between Good and Evil, or people contending with each other over their differences, which, hopefully, get resolved. Competing comes naturally. Creating win-win situations is much more difficult.

But more deeply, competition is rooted in our personal insecurity, which manifests itself in a desperate desire to prove our worth and capabilities as much to ourselves as to others. We have the mistaken notion that through competing we might earn love and approval. This rarely occurs on any permanent basis, however, and more often a winner faces envy from his or her opponents. Winning is transitory; it's always up for grabs. As author Alfie Kohn says:

> King of the Mountain is more than a child's game; it is the prototype for all competition, since winning promptly establishes one as the target for one's rivals. In any case, the euphoria of victory fades quickly. Both winners and losers find they need more, much like someone who has developed a tolerance to a drug.

This is the insidiousness of traditional competition. Once you're "into the system" it is very difficult to break free. Psychiatrist Theodore Rubin states:

I believe that society is unfortunately becoming more competitive, more glory-seeking, and more pride-oriented. This is happening despite the fact that cooperative relating becomes mandatory for survival as populations increase and natural resources must be cherished and shared on a mutual basis. I believe that an increase in paranoia born of competition and pride in a world of ever-increasing technological advance is the greatest menace to our survival on the planet.[2]

"Pride" and "glory" help keep us locked in. We have the mistaken notion that through vying with others we can boost our pride. And we identify glory with "winning" in the traditional sense. The belief that feelings of pride and the glory of achieving need to come through competing is a mistake, and one that can be fatal. If you want lasting glory and something to feel proud about, you *can't achieve it through traditional competing!* "Healthy competition," however, can lead you there.

Society forces us into competitive situations. The social rewards for competing are strong. Likewise, social degradation falls upon the shoulders of the noncompetitive. They are seen as "wimps"; thus, it's hard to buck the flow. But it can be done. In spite of its love-hate relationship with competition, our society does not make education in noncompetitive alternatives readily available. In fact, many people who would try to establish a cooperative environment are hard put even to know how to attempt it, let alone make it work!

There is another delusion, however, that may be even more insidious. That is, that traditional competition is fun. For some—mostly the winners—it is. As indicated in chapter 1, competition demotivates people more often than it motivates them. Yet we are taught to believe that competition is enjoyable, in spite of the fact that we usually lose much more often than we win. The fact is, many people who say they enjoy competitive activities find that their "fun level" in contending diminishes quickly once they have had the chance to try out cooperative, no-lose games.

Ironically, contests can be fun, but the fun increases as the *competitive* aspect decreases! The most fun occurs when the competition is short-term, nonrepetitive, and sufficiently divorced from one's ego needs that it is seen as "only a game." In this context the significance of winning or losing is greatly diminished, and all "opponents" are friends before the contest. An example would be a three-legged race at a church picnic. As the contest becomes more "important," the pressure mounts.

## SUBLIMINAL RULES

When a computer is programmed, data are not the only things entered. Actually data themselves are the minor part. Of vital significance are the "rules" that are programmed in to tell the computer what to do with the data being entered. These rules themselves, however, never appear on the screen. Unless you're a computer whiz, you don't even know what the rules are. The computer does its thing, and you just punch in or access data, oblivious to the rules, which you take for granted.

Our minds operate much like an elaborate computer. While we have a certain degree of free will, and can make decisions and choices, most of our daily behavior follows an elaborate set of "subliminal" rules which were "programmed in" at a very early age. While some of the subliminal rules are genetic patterning, the vast majority have been absorbed through our early experiences.

These rules are so complex, and have been learned so subtly, that they escape our conscious awareness. The subconscious mind organizes and stores them for us all by itself, without bothering us with the details; hence, their "subliminal" quality. They operate behind the scenes, forming the basis of our habits of thinking, feeling, and acting, but only become recognized when we consciously call them into question. This, however, is likely to occur only when a specific behavior "doesn't work" or gets us into trouble. Even then the actual "rule" is rarely examined or questioned.

Yet awareness of these rules is vital for understanding our actions and reactions. Our "gut feelings" and attitudes always follow these rules, and so our resultant actions reflect them as well. In fact, they operate so well that they can even color or limit the options we perceive to be available to us!

There was once a highly qualified and bright hospital chief of social work who was chronically unhappy on her job. She was continually being sabotaged and undercut by her boss, who outwardly disliked her. She had worked in that unit for seven years, and had boss problems almost from day one. She was employed by the state, and at that time the state system was crying for more social workers. One day she was asked, "If you can't be effective here, and you're so unhappy, why don't you transfer? There are plenty of openings." Her response: "It never occurred to me to leave!"

Notice that she didn't mention salary, benefits, or other working conditions. Rather, it never occurred to her to leave. She was operating according to an inner imperative that must have said, "Stick it out, no matter what." With that kind of subliminal rule, a conflicting option wasn't even recognized, let alone considered. And here's the postscript: the social worker continued in that unit, under the same boss, for six years thereafter. Luckily for her, the boss finally left.

Such is the power of our subliminal rules. But in spite of their controlling influence, the rules are often irrational and mistaken. While they may have been learned in a time and place where they made sense, many of them have since been generalized to the point where they are no longer appropriate. In fact, when confronted with subliminal rules brought to light, many people would state that they disagree with the rule as stated.

Since we have subliminal rules covering every important aspect of life, it goes without saying that we have numerous ones about competing. Box 2-1 lists several common ones. Look at the list and do the exercise in the box before reading further.

Now let's review what has just happened. These rules actually foster *destructive* competition. Therefore it's highly likely that you agree with very few, or perhaps none of them—at a conscious level. As stated, they are irrational, particularly with the use of such words as "always," "only," and "must."

But what do you do at the behavioral level? If you were honest, you probably checked a lot more of them. Let's look at what this means.

Take number 10, for example. Probably you would not consciously agree with that rule as stated. It doesn't sound like a positive or flattering statement to admit to oneself. But if you become the least bit nervous, uptight, or concerned when you perceive that someone is getting ahead of you in some way, then you are accepting that rule, or some variant of it, at the emotional level. And if you accept the rule at the emotional level, you will probably act

Box 2-1

---

### THE BAKERS DOZEN

Subliminal rules which foster competition.

*Exercise:* Under Column "A" place a check next to those rules with which you comfortably agree.

A  B

____  ____  (1) Winning isn't the most important thing . . . it's the *ONLY* thing.

____  ____  (2) I must measure my personal worth by what others have, do, or are.

____  ____  (3) The best things in life are scarce.

____  ____  (4) I can only feel significant when I am the first or the best. (Watch out, Joneses! Here I come!)

____  ____  (5) My image is the key to my success.

____  ____  (6) The outcome of my efforts determines the meaning and satisfaction I derive from my actions.

____  ____  (7) It's a dog-eat-dog world, so I must constantly compete.

____  ____  (8) I must constantly prove myself to others.

____  ____  (9) I must always strive to impress others, and must always be held in high esteem by them.

____  ____  (10) I feel insecure when others get ahead; I can't let them get the advantage.

____  ____  (11) Everyone is basically competitive, so I must keep my guard up at all times.

____  ____  (12) My happiness is directly related to the quality and quantity of material goods I possess. ("The one with the most toys wins!")

____  ____  (13) The opponent is "the enemy".

Now, under Column "B", place a check next to those you find yourself *acting* as if you believed. Think this through carefully, look at your everyday actions, and be honest with yourself. When you have completed this exercise, return to the text.

---

accordingly in some way, even though you may temper your behavior with ethics and other positive values. It is even possible to act out the rule in subtle, undercutting ways that not even you are aware of, justifying your actions so well that even you are fooled. Such is often the nature of hidden competition.

## FEAR OF FAILURE, FEAR OF SUCCESS

Misdirected competition is in large part responsible for two major fears that so often affect business and sales people: fear of failure and fear of success.

We often see people with great promise who seem paralyzed on their climb up the ladder of success. All too often we assume that they are afraid of failing. But if this is so, why do they seem to court so closely the thing they fear? Actually they are afraid of success.

Isn't success desirable? Of course it is, in some ways. But it can also have its drawbacks, especially if it comes upon us rapidly. It can propel us into new and greater responsibilities that we may be unsure we can handle. Also, it may make our individual decisions more weighty, with more severe consequences if we're wrong. A false move may kick us out the door.

Success often pushes us into new arenas in which we face tougher competition. It's easy to be a big fish in a little pond, but when we have to swim in the ocean, we might run into sharks. Success also may push us into a new social set with which we are uncomfortable, and we may incur the envy of our former friends and associates.

Competitive personalities and highly traditionally competitive people often have a harder time with fear of success than their less competitive brothers and sisters precisely because striving for success is so important to them. The closer one's self-esteem is attached to being "a success," the more one defines his or her worth on the basis of performance, the more vulnerable the person actually is.

Fear of failure is based on the same misconceptions, but those who fear failure the most are the highly driven ones who often appear to be in a race with life. They can't take it easy, lest someone else get ahead. It is as if they feel the hot breath of the wolf on their backs. It is the drivenness of their behavior that distinguishes them from non-fearful high achievers.

---

# Competition Itself

Now let's look at competition itself.

When do we compete? Any time we are involved with another person and we are not cooperating. Psychiatrist Karen Horney stated that there are three ways of dealing with others: moving toward them, moving against them (aggression), and moving away from them (withdrawal). From our perspective, there are only two options for involvement: cooperative, corresponding to Horney's "moving toward," and competitive, corresponding to her "moving against" and "moving away."

Moving against is plainly competing, but you may wonder how moving away qualifies as competitive. It is passive competition. The person moving away refuses to give—robs you of the benefits of—his or her contribution. It's a matter of attitude as well as behavior. The person who moves away is at odds in some way. He or she may not feel significant, or may otherwise feel ill-disposed toward the group. The underlying attitude of a person who copes through withdrawal is one of hostility, or in psychiatric parlance, passive-aggressive.

I am not talking here about the simple act of walking away from another person. Sometimes this is the best strategy. Rather I mean withdrawal as a common tactic, a habitual response when pressed to interact with certain others.

Given our paradigm, then, those who are closely involved with you can't remain neutral very long. Whoever is not cooperating with you is competing.

Cooperation implies relating as equals. This can be called the "horizontal" dimension, two people coming together on a horizontal plane. Competition, by definition, is a "vertical" orientation. It implies vertical thinking: who is above, who is below, how do I rate in relation to others? True equality and traditional competitiveness do not coexist!

Part of the reason competition is so confusing, and so difficult to change, is that it is deeply tied to "attitude." An attitude is made up of three components: belief, which is the underlying "rationale"; emotion, which fires a person up or triggers a reaction; and behavior, the direct (or indirect) action that the person takes. (see figure 2-1). These three components are indelibly interlocked, support each other, and shore up resistance to change. New, or "experimental," behaviors are more easy to alter because they haven't been adopted as "attitude" yet. But when a behavior transcends the threshold of attitude, it is defended with all sorts of reasons and justifications, and is bolstered by the power of emotion.

This is a vitally important practical concept. Since competition is deeply attitudinally ingrained, sweeping change in a person's behavior is extremely unlikely. You can't easily make a competitive person become noncompetitive, but you can help her redirect com-

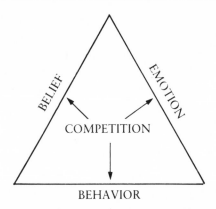

Figure 2-1. COMPONENTS OF THE COMPETITIVE ATTITUDE

petitive drive, balance it with cooperative strategies, and train her in healthy competitive methods, fostering the growth of positive competitive and cooperative values. In other words, managers, giving your overly competitive employees "shape up or ship out" lectures will be like steering your car with your horn—pretty darned ineffective!

## FORMS, MODES, AND LEVELS OF COMPETITION

"Natural competition" is that form of competing required for physical survival. Fighting on a battlefield or fighting off a mugger or rapist when your life is in danger or when you need to protect someone else are examples. When one's back is to the wall, even a relatively noncompetitive person will engage in natural competition, and when the threat is over, may return to his or her more noncompetitive stance.

Games, sports, contests of all kinds fall under the category of "structured competition." Structured competition is planned, circumscribed, specific, and time-limited, such as a tennis match, the Olympic Games, a courtroom trial, or a sales contest. Ideally, in this form of competition, we can turn our competitive behavior on for the contest and turn it off afterward, although turning off often is not easy.

"Social competition," on the other hand, is the competitiveness we see in everyday life, that which spontaneously occurs as part of the daily flow of activity. The attitudes and interpersonal relations that occur in social and structured competition may be precisely the same. In structured competition, to some degree, competitive behavior is triggered by the contest itself. In social competition this is less true, with one's social competitiveness being more a function of one's life-style.

Social competition is virtually limitless. It is not bound by time, space, or circumstance. It can superimpose itself on structured and natural competition, and often does. When we speak of a "highly competitive" person, and refer to competition in the context of the aim of this book, we are dealing mostly with social competitiveness. Social competition is based on the individual's particular biases, attitudes, and life-style. Such a person may never enter formal contests and may not even enjoy them as an observer. Yet he or she may still be competitive to the core. This is important. Many competitive people don't view themselves that way. They deny being competitive, and when you ask them how they know this about themselves, they say, "I don't like sports!"

In its most subtle forms, competition is present in virtually every situation in which one is consciously—or even subconsciously— trying to influence someone else. Competition exists in three modes and at four levels, as indicated in figure 2-2.

The three modes are Open, Veiled, and Hidden: *Open* behavior is openly identifiable as competitive by all concerned. Often, overt

|  |  | MODES | | |
|  |  | Open | Veiled | Hidden |
|---|---|---|---|---|
| L | Inter-group |  |  |  |
| E |  |  |  |  |
| V | In-group |  |  |  |
| E | Inter-personal |  |  |  |
| L |  |  |  |  |
| S | Internal |  |  |  |

Figure 2-2. MODES AND LEVELS OF COMPETITION

competitive behavior falls into the category of structured competition, narrowly defined, such as individual or team sports, or two attorneys battling it out in court. In such situations there are usually more contestants than prizes.

*Veiled* behavior has strong competitive elements when analyzed as such, but is generally identified in other categories, such as getting ahead, assertiveness, beautifying the neighborhood, keeping up with the Joneses, etc. Examples include subtle put-downs, the salesman who works night and day to become a field manager, and the neighborhood where ten patios appear soon after one person adds a patio to his house. While this behavior is competitive, it is often mislabeled because it occurs in other primary context and is often indirect.

*Hidden* behavior, as which is often acted out subconsciously, goes unrecognized by the competitor. This behavior is indirect and may include such things as manner of dress, manner of speech, and everyday methods of social interaction such as looks. gestures, and humor.

To make the distinction between Open and Veiled/Hidden competition clearer we can use the example of the American and European method of racing. In the American method, all the contestants line up together at the starting line, gun goes off, and the racers run off toward the finish line. Whoever crosses the line first is the winner. In the European style, used in some cross-country skiing races, for example, only one racer starts at a time. The officials start timing her when she begins to run and record her time at the finish line. Then the next racer starts. The winner is the one with the fastest time. Now suppose that you turn on your television and are flicking channels and you stop at the scene of the race while it is in progress, but due to technical difficulties you hear no sound on your set. If you tuned in to the American race in the middle, without explanation, you could tell it was a race. The runners are all visible, vying for the lead. But if you tuned in to our European style example under the same circumstances, all you would see is one person skiing across a field. You would not know it was a competition unless you could observe what was going on behind the scenes.

Open competition is like the American race. Not all overt competition is sports or games, i.e., structured competition; much of it is social competition. Yet it is plain and open for all to see. The behavior is easily recognizable as competition. Veiled and Hidden competition are much like the European style race. It is not labeled as competition on the surface, but upon closer analysis, the competitive aspects of the behavior become apparent.

Think about *your* workplace. What examples of Open, Veiled, and Hidden competition exist there?

Now let's examine the four levels of competition. People can act on several levels and modes simultaneously. By creating an analysis in terms of mode (Open, Veiled, and Hidden) and level, we can much more precisely understand and cope with what is going on.

The levels, shown in figure 2-2 are Intergroup, In-group, Interpersonal, Internal:

At the *Intergroup* level two or more groups or teams are competing in some way. Examples can include anything from baseball games to companies, such as Ford and General Motors, vying for market share, to all-out international war. On the positive side, intergroup competition is what holds prices relatively stable in a society whose economy is *not* based on economic self-restraint and social interest. Intergroup competition can also lead to product improvement, innovation, and personal and team excellence. Often the "common enemy" mentality helps group members band together. On the negative side, intergroup competition often manifests itself within larger units or companies and results in sabotage, slowdowns, and even strikes.

As the name implies, *In-group* competition exists among members of a particular group, team, division, company, or family. Structured in-group competition refers to competitive situations established formally and/or consciously to achieve a particular result. For example, members of a football team scrimmage against one another so all improve their skills. Or the sales force for a particular company sets up quotas and individuals compete for prizes and the title of Salesperson of the Month. The idea behind such in-group competition is that it should provide incentive so that the team or the sales force as a whole is more productive. Social in-group competition just happens. It is not formally or consciously established, and it often occurs for quite a while before anyone is aware of what is going on. Sometimes the results can be positive but far more often they are destructive. For example, the one basketball player who wants to be an all-star may try to out-perform and even subvert his own teammates so he can stand out to the scouts. Or how about the secretaries in the word processing center who have formed cliques and produce a frigid psychological climate in the office which hampers productivity.

Some *Interpersonal* competition is involved in the above levels because competition can only occur between persons. But at this level the focus is not upon groups but upon individuals. Here, as above, the categories of structured and social apply. Structured interpersonal competition would include such individual sports as tennis and marathon running, and the individual salesperson competing against others for top monthly sales in a formal competitive structure. Social interpersonal competition often occurs simultaneously within the structured competitive setup when the competitors take the situation overly seriously or overly personally.

It also occurs apart from formal competitive situations. The battling and power jockeying of brother and sister, husband and wife, boss and secretary, and teacher and pupil are prime examples of negative social interpersonal competition. Usually, social interpersonal competition is negative.

At the *Internal* level, the person competes against himself or herself. This may be an effort to surpass a previous performance, such as one's last golf score, or to create an even tastier soufflé. Or it may involve needing to meet or surpass internalized goals, such as "be best," "be perfect," "be strong," etc., for which we have been heavily trained in childhood. Depending how it is used, internal competition may produce high excellence or deep anxiety.

We have dealt with behavior, and with competition, in general. Now let's get specific. How do *you* compete? What is *your* competitive style? In the next chapter you will find out.

---

# References

Kohn, A. "No Contest. A case against competition." *New Age Journal.* September-October, 1986, pp. 18-20.

O'Connel, W. Personal Communication.

Rubin, T, I. *Reconciliation.* New York: Viking. 1980.

# 3

# How Do You Compete?

How do you compete? What are your attitudes and values about competition?

Your answers to this question will determine:

- Whom and how far you can trust

- How well you can love, and how you will use sex and relationships with the opposite sex

- How true a friend you can be

- How well you can cooperate

- The degree of ethics you will use in doing business

- Your ability to negotiate, to network, to be a mentor or to accept advice or criticism

- Your ability to accept outside help

- Your ability to help others succeed

In the last chapter we stated that you have a "competitive style," whether you're aware of it or not. Here is your opportunity to discover that style and to determine whether it is a stepping stone or stumbling block on your path to success. This chapter will present you with several diverse exercises and ways of assessing your competitive style. By going through them one by one, giving them serious and thoughtful attention, you will be able to put together the various pieces of that complex characteristic we call competitiveness.

Fundamental to any personal style, and underlying it, are your values and belief system. The opening question to this chapter is not an easy one. Maybe you never thought about it before. You can't just rattle off a few time-worn clichés and expect to do justice to your value system on this or any other complex issue. I spent over two years studying and researching competition and fifteen years working with achievers in sports, business, and sales, with couples in rocky and sound marriages, and with parents and children in conflict and harmony before I firmed up my values of competition. This book is the result of that search. Your path, therefore, will be much easier.

Also, you don't need to know all there is to know about competition. However, what you *do* need to know, first and foremost, to become a healthier competitor is *yourself*. Models and methods of healthy competition follow, and must fit into your own personality and willingness to expand your skills.

Isn't it great? You don't have to be sick to get better. So let's get going.

---

# Questions of Values

A value is a belief with a plus or minus sign attached. Values determine our judgment of what is good, bad, right, wrong, or neutral. We all have them by the hundreds. Our values are operating when, for example, upon seeing the way another person is dressed, or the way we act, or a particular car, we say, "Yeah!", "Yuch!", or "Ho hum."

We have values about almost everything, including competition. We've absorbed most of our values through "osmosis" from our parents, friends, the media, school, church or synagogue, and the culture in general. Our values determine who and what we idolize, and those idols in turn shape our values even more.

In truth, we cannot avoid making a "value judgment" about anything that we care about, be it a person, product, or an experience. It is about as difficult to stop making value judgments as it is to stop breathing. In fact, the former ceases only when the latter occurs.

Throughout our lives we question many of our values, but most of them we have accepted lock, stock, and barrel. Somehow our subconscious mind puts our values into a "system," and the stronger or narrower these values are the more rigid and inflexible we become. This has nothing to do with conservative or liberal. You and I have seen rigid liberals and flexible conservatives.

Generally speaking, the more people who appear to hold similar values, or the greater the cultural support for certain values, the less likely they are to be called into question. We just act them out in our daily lives without ever thinking of our actions as stemming from a value system. So it is with our values regarding competition.

Yet any examination of our competitiveness must begin at the values level. Are your values about competition clear and consistent? If not,—which is the case for ninety-nine and forty-four one-hundredths percent of us,—here are some questions that should help clarify things:

- How competitive are you?

- Are you a dove or a hawk?

- Do you enjoy competing? If so, what aspects bring pleasure? If not, what aspects turn you off?

- Does competing bring you happiness? If so, under what circumstances? If not, why not?

- How important is it for you or your team to win:
    a game with your young child?
    a football or baseball game?
    a business or sales contest?
    a business deal or negotiation?
    a bigger market share for your company's product or service?
    a war?

- Which is more important: whether you win or lose, or how you play the game?

- Do the ends justify the means?

- How far will you go in competing before you:
    stop because it's inconvenient to continue?

stop for ethical reasons?

stop because someone else's rights, respect, or dignity is being threatened or violated?

throw in the towel because you can't take it any more?

- Which do you feel gets better results: competition or cooperation?

- Do you agree with the following statements? If so, why? If not, why not?

    "Business is war."

    "It's a dog-eat-dog world."

    "Winning is not the most important thing, it's the only thing."

    "The most important thing for success is keeping ahead of the pack."

- How do you compete when the chips are down?

- If your answers to any of the above were, "It depends upon the circumstances," what circumstances?

You might also go back to box 2-1 on subliminal rules in the last chapter. These are actually values statements. How you responded to those will also help you to clarify what you actually believe about competition.

The point of this exercise is to help you *specify* as well as clarify. It's easy to judge competitiveness as all good or all bad, but competition is too complex for that. Hopefully, as you answered these questions you began to sort out specific issues and circumstances where you enjoyed competing or where it caused you difficulty. As you saw in the last chapter, competition is a very broad activity, that can be done in almost any human interaction, from a boxing match, to making love, to doing business day to day. In fact, most "office politics" is an exercise in competition. Therefore, to know your competitive values and style is fundamental to understanding your daily interactions.

## YOUR PRIOR EXPERIENCE

Let's see where your values are formed. Earlier I said that you "inherited" your values, absorbing them from the world around you. This is only partly true, however. You are not just the product of your experience, but rather your life-style is developed on the basis of *your interpretation* of that experience,—what you made of the experience through your emotional and behavioral reactions.

As we look back at early experiences we see not only how our values came into being, but also the rudiments of our competitive style.

Here's another exercise.

Sometime in your past, perhaps yesterday or long ago, you wanted to achieve something very badly. But you were not alone going for it; you had to face one or more competitors. You gave it your all, but you lost and you didn't reach the goal. How did you feel? (Check all that apply.)

_____ It hurt
_____ I wanted to hide and cry
_____ I wanted to get even
_____ I was angry and resentful, perhaps even furious
_____ I lost confidence in myself
_____ I felt defeated, felt like a loser
_____ I was embarrassed, ashamed
_____ I felt like I let important people down
_____ It wasn't fun anymore
_____ I rationalized that I didn't care
_____ (Other) _____

What did you do?

_____ I harbored resentment
_____ I got even
_____ I gave up
_____ I disparaged the winner and/or the contest
_____ I tried again, desperately hard, fueled by my anger
_____ I began to doubt myself and my abilities
_____ I was more hesitant the next time I tried
_____ I redoubled my efforts; I was more determined the next time
_____ (Other) _____

Now, would you have responded the same way, about a different type of competition, or one that was more important, or less important? Let's take this exercise even further.

## EARLY RECOLLECTIONS

Think back to your very earliest memories involving competition. Perhaps you were competing yourself in some way, or maybe you were an observer of what others were doing.

Take six pieces of paper and jot down the first six of these separate memories that you can recall, as far back as you can remember. Try to remember each instance from beginning to end, and write each down as you remember it. The accounts needn't be long or excessively detailed, but should cover the sequence of events. To aid your recall, close your eyes and visualize it as it took place. This will make the memory come alive. (Complete this step before reading on.)

Now it's time to review your recollections. Reread them in order, one through six. For each, underline that part of the recollection which stands out the most in your mind, which is the most vivid part as you recall the incident. Next, jot down how you felt at the time, as best you can recall. Were you happy, sad, scared, let down? Did you feel warm and affirmed, or cold and rejected? Whatever you felt, try to capture that feeling in a couple words or phrases.

Next, pretend that each recollection is a local newspaper story in search of a headline. Look over the story and think up a "headline" that captures the gist of the incident. For example, "Christine wins spelling bee; embarrassed as parents gloat with pride," or "Phil passed over again; vows to get even." Attaching a headline helps you to crystalize the experience at an emotional, attitudinal, and behavioral level, capturing its significance.

Now that you have your headlines, look over the recollections for consistencies and patterns.

- Did you tend to feel a similar way when dealing with certain people, or in certain situations?

- Did you respond the same way in different competitive situations? or vice versa?

- Did you mostly recall situations in which you won, or those in which you lost?

- How did you react to winning? To losing?

- Is there any consistency with how you felt in each memory, or with what part of the memories stood out as most vivid to you?

- Did your memories about competition deal mostly with games, sports, or contests, or did you recall other, informal forms of competition, such as fighting, arguing, or some other way in which you felt you had to be the best? This is a telling question. As stated earlier, many people think of competition strictly in terms of games and sports, and if they don't participate in these activities they think they are noncompetitive.

As you compare and contrast your early recollections, you may or may not see similarities with how you respond today, but either way, these early incidents colored your current style.

What patterns did you see? Was there a common thread that ran through some or most of the recollections? If so, what was it? If there were a common thread, especially if it appeared across highly different or varied experiences, then you have a handle on a significant characteristic of your competitive style.

Your style includes not only how you initiate or respond to competition, but also how you interpret and feel about your experiences of it. This brings in your emotions, attitudes, and values. These underly your actions and serve to make your outward behavior more consistent. The common thread may have been one of action, or one involving feelings, or both.

If you did not discover a common thread, it may mean that your responses to competition are more varied, more situationally determined. It does not mean, however, that you don't have a relatively consistent competitive style. Your style may simply be more flexible or more subtle.

Of what value are early recollections, especially if the memory may not be completely accurate?

It doesn't matter if the memories are accurate. You remembered the incidents: (a) as you *perceived* them to be, and (b) as they reflect your attitudes and values today.

Memory isn't "recall," it is "reconstruction." We "remember" those incidents that support our current attitudes and values, that support our life-style. They are the "evidence" which serves as the foundation for our current conclusions. The early recollections act as a guide or warning, like a little voice inside that says, "Do it this way," or "Go ahead,"or "Watch our—remember when. . . ."

Not only do we subconsciously select *which* incidents to remember, we also remember them *in the way* that most supports our life-style. In other words, we remember it in the way that most suits our purpose, whether that's how it really happened or not. In fact, the whole recollection may never have happened. It's fascinating to observe, when working with clients in psychotherapy, that, as they make progress, their early recollections often change. They remember the incidents differently later in therapy than they did in the beginning of their treatment. The changes in the recollections reflect the life-style changes that have occurred in therapy.

Let's come back to the present.

---

# The Competitive Quadrant

To get a more specific handle on your competitive style at work, fill out the following questionnaire. Please do it three times, each time checking in the appropriate column every statement that applies.

The first time through, think in terms of what you do in a specific, important competition or contest, such as a sales contest.

The second time through, consider what you do in the day-to-day social competition you face at work, e.g., the office politics, daily power jockeying, etc. We dealt with what is involved in social competition in the last chapter.

The third time through, respond for your company. As you perceive it, what is the prevailing corporate culture? What are the competitive methods most of the people you work with use in the day-to-day politics of doing business. You may answer in terms of your department, or the company as a whole. Record your answers under the "Prevailing" heading.

Please answer the questionnaire now before reading further.

## WHAT'S YOUR COMPETITIVE STYLE?

When involved in a competitive situation at work, I . . .

*Contest*  *Social*  *Prevailing*

1. ___ ___ ___ Act aggressively, barrelling my way through
2. ___ ___ ___ Engage in a bold display of competitive behavior
3. ___ ___ ___ Boast of my past achievements
4. ___ ___ ___ Try to intimidate others into backing off, or losing confidence
5. ___ ___ ___ Act angrily or become sullen if I'm not in the lead
6. ___ ___ ___ Challenge or confront others
7. ___ ___ ___ Sometimes move so quickly to gain the advantage that I don't think through my actions
8. ___ ___ ___ Resort to insults, abuse, or harrassment
9. ___ ___ ___ Withhold vital, advantageous information from others
10. ___ ___ ___ Pretend I'm not competing, but behind the scenes I work very hard to win
11. ___ ___ ___ Trick other competitors in some way
12. ___ ___ ___ Sabotage others' work or progress
13. ___ ___ ___ Smooth-talk my way into an advantage
14. ___ ___ ___ Lie or use cunning or deceit, falsify information
15. ___ ___ ___ Generally act superior, "above all that political stuff"
16. ___ ___ ___ Resort to verbal put-downs and sarcastic humor
17. ___ ___ ___ Hang in there, working hard at my job
18. ___ ___ ___ Look for new and creative, honest ways to achieve

19. ___ ___ ___ Proceed slowly and carefully, but keep on going
20. ___ ___ ___ Study my past accomplishments to give me ideas on how to proceed
21. ___ ___ ___ Look to my inner strengths to give me courage
22. ___ ___ ___ Become enthusiastic
23. ___ ___ ___ Am a good sport about it, demonstrate loyalty
24. ___ ___ ___ Compete ethically
25. ___ ___ ___ Go about my business quietly
26. ___ ___ ___ Charm my way into an advantageous position
27. ___ ___ ___ Act with patience and forebearance
28. ___ ___ ___ Pretend I'm weak or act the martyr ("look how I'm suffering")
29. ___ ___ ___ Try to make others feel guilty for competing with me
30. ___ ___ ___ Act very diplomatically
31. ___ ___ ___ Act as if the situation is humorous or funny
32. ___ ___ ___ Butter up others, curry favor

Now tally your scores. Here's how. This questionnaire actually measures four competitive styles with eight responses for each style. To make scoring easier, draw a horizontal line between responses 8 and 9, 16 and 17, and 24 and 25. Count the number of checks you placed in the Contest column on responses 1 through 8, and write that number on the "1–8" line under "Contest, # Checks" on Table 3-1. Then tally up the number of checks in the Contest column on responses 9–16 and enter that number on the "9–16"

Table 3-1
COMPETITIVE STYLE TALLY SHEET

|  | Contest (C) | Social (S) | Prevailing (P) |  |
|---|---|---|---|---|
|  | # checks | # checks | # checks |  |
| 1–8 | _____ | _____ | _____ | LION |
| 9–16 | _____ | _____ | _____ | FOX |
| 17–24 | _____ | _____ | _____ | BULLDOG |
| 25–32 | _____ | _____ | _____ | CHAMELION |

line under "Contest, # Checks." Do the same for items 17–24 and 25–32. Then repeat the process for the Social column and Prevailing column.

You now have a twelve-number matrix, which reflects scores for four styles across three competitive situations: (a) How you react in a specific, important contest (your C behavior); (b) how you compete in general at work (your S behavior); and (c) the prevailing competitive style in your department or organization, with which you must interact every day (the P behavior).

What are the four styles? Dr. Harvey Ruben[1] analyzed competition in terms of two dimensions, Aggressive-Nonaggressive and Direct-Indirect. Aggressive actions are those which could be physically and/or psychologically harmful to an opponent, while Nonaggressive responses basically are not harmful. If you are familiar with Assertiveness Training, Ruben's aggressive side would include aggressive, hostile responses, while his nonaggressive side would encompass both assertive and nonassertive behavior. His Aggressive-Nonaggressive dimension refers primarily to actions themselves.

The Direct-Indirect dimension corresponds to our Open-Veiled-Hidden paradigm in the last chapter. Direct maneuvers are open and straightforward, for all to see, while Indirect actions are disguised or done behind people's backs. The Direct-Indirect dimension refers primarily to the approach taken by the competitor, be it you or an opponent.

The two dimensions cross, yielding the four styles shown in figure 3-1.

If you wish to see how your scores come out graphically, you can plot them on the Competitive Quadrant, figure 3-2. This graph provides a quick visual comparison of how you behave in a specific competition as opposed to your style in coping with everyday social competition and office politics. You can also see how closely your own style matches your perception of the prevailing style in your organization.

Transferring your scores from table 3-1, put a C on the diagonal Lion line on the number that corresponds to the number of checks you had on the Contest 1–8 line. Put a C on the Fox line at the number of checks you had under Contest 9–16, a C on the Bulldog line for your Contest 17–24 score, and a C on the Chamelion line for your score on Contest 25–32. Do the same for Social scores

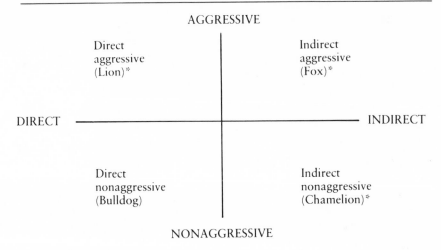

AGGRESSIVE

Direct
aggressive
(Lion)*

Indirect
aggressive
(Fox)*

DIRECT                                                                  INDIRECT

Direct
nonaggressive
(Bulldog)

Indirect
nonaggressive
(Chamelion)*

NONAGGRESSIVE

*These names applied by the author

Figure 3-1. FOUR COMPETITIVE STYLES

using an S and for Prevailing using a P. (Box 3-1 at the end of this chapter gives you an example of scoring and an interpretation of the results. To best understand the interpretation, however, please first read the following description of the styles.)

Now that you have plotted your scores, what do they mean? Scores from 0 to 2 are low, while scores from 6 to 8 are high. The higher your score in any one quadrant, the more likely you are to behave according to the description for that quadrant. Here are the interpretations of the four styles, à la Ruben:

*Direct Aggressives (Lions)* are the easiest to spot. They are forthright and up-front in their competing, and usually you know where you stand with them. They are tough and often uncomplicated in their approach.

Lions can be good guys—two-fisted and honest, a direct go-getter like John Wayne. They are selective as to *how* they win and, while zealous, generally are not obsessed with having to win. But when they become obsessed with winning, they can become bullies, and at the extreme, sociopaths. That kind of Lion is not above using brute strength, ruthlessness, and physical violence to attain his ends.

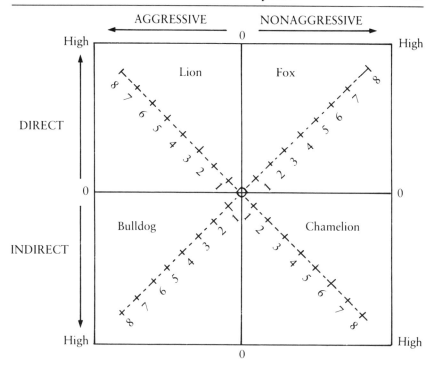

Source: Adapted from H. Ruben, *Competing*, Lippincott & Crowell, 1980.

Figure 3-2. COMPETITIVE QUADRANT

Good guy or bad guy, a Lion is hard to defeat. Lions are determined and forceful yet they generally possess a chink in their armor. They often rush ahead without thinking through the
ramifications of their actions. Sometimes, too, they can become so
unbending in their approach that they can't change their strategy,
even if they are headed for failure. The more forceful—and especially the more despotic—the Lion, the less likely he is to get necessary feedback on how he is doing. The best way to defeat a Lion,
therefore, is with a strategy of careful caution.

It's hard to detect when *Indirect Aggressives (Foxes)* are competing because they are masters at disguising how vital winning is
to them. They are often just as aggressive as Lions, but are adept
at hiding that fact. They are great foggers, skilled at Veiled and
Hidden competitive tactics.

A key to their ability to win is their apparent nonchalance. The Fox, outwardly, doesn't seem to care about winning. He's unconcerned, and displays an "It's only a game" attitude. By adopting this attitude he hopes to lull you off your guard. If the Lion will punch you in the face, the Fox will stab you in the back, while observers think he is giving you a pat of praise.

Foxes use cunning, flamboyance, lying, cheating, deceit, even feigned ignorance to achieve their goals. When a Fox competes with you, you've lost almost before you know you are playing the game. "Win at all cost" is the motto, and the ends justify the means. He will stop at nothing to win. J. R. Ewing on Dallas is a prime example of a Fox. Watch out, especially for the witty, hail-fellow-well-met opponent. Humor, which is often a nonaggressive action, is frequently used by the Fox as a way to throw you off guard.

Snobbishness and a haughty air of superiority characterize some Foxes. Their game plan is to appear "above all this political stuff." They appear not to care about winning because the contest is beneath them.

When having to compete with a Fox, early detection is the key, as well as being very careful not to let down your guard or to slip up. Keep your own ethics pure. If you stoop to the Fox's level or begin to compete like he does it may well backfire. After all, the Fox is master of his own game; play on his turf and he has the advantage.

It's hard to beat *Direct Nonaggressives (Bulldogs)* even though they may appear quiet and unassuming on the surface. Why? Because their key characteristic is tenacity. They're open about the fact that they're competing, but they dig in and hold on. They endure, have the patience of Job, and if knocked down, come back for more. They have a high tolerance for disappointment and do not need the reassurance of continued success to keep them motivated. They will hang in there long after less patient contestants have given up. For this reason, they are good long-range competitors.

Bulldogs have no interest in hurting their opponents, as Foxes do, and therefore easily keep their attention on their own performance rather than getting sidetracked into undercutting other's progress. This is another reason they're hard to defeat. They set their eyes on their goals and pursue them with dogged determination. They are stable and forceful. When faced with defeat, they entrench themselves and try harder.

As we shall see later, this style is closely parallel to our Healthy Competitor. Churchill, FDR, and Gandhi were Bulldog types. The prime weakness of the Bulldogs is that while they use tenacity very well, quick wit and cunning are underdeveloped. They win through their stamina and endurance, not through cleverness. This is not to say that Bulldogs aren't creative or clever; many are. The point is that these traits are not their main avenue of competing. When you compete against a Bulldog, then, a direct frontal approach is not likely to give you the win. Innovation, surprise, and quick-witted methods usually work best. If the contest calls for these behaviors, the Bulldog is generally at a disadvantage, but if persistance and industriousness are what will win the day, the Bulldog has the clear lead.

Ruben considers *Indirect Nonaggressives (Chamelions)* the trickiest competitors to deal with. They use some of the same indirect tactics as the Foxes, but they do so in an elusive and nonhostile manner. They seem to be the least competitive of the four types, but this is not necessarily so. Rather they have developed more roundabout ways of achieving their goals.

Chamelions can use a broad repertoire of nonaggressive behaviors to get their way. They may be talkative or shy, charming or reserved. The common denominator for Chamelions is that they do not appear to be competing at all. This makes them exceptionally difficult to spot. Lucille Ball in the "I Love Lucy" series was a prime example of the Chamelion. She bungled her way around so that others became sympathetic and let down their guard. They lost before they knew it, and Lucy got her way.

Chamelions are not necessarily inept, however. Charm, tact, and diplomacy are superb Chamelion tactics, and are highly prized in the business world today. A salesperson who can win customers with charm and effective listening is more highly regarded than one who browbeats or high-pressures customers.

Another common Chamelion tactic, however, is to instill sympathy, consideration, and even guilt, in an opponent. The game plan is to get the competitors to feel sorry for, or feel bad about competing with, the Chamelion who, after all, really does not appear to be competing. If the Chamelion is successful in this strategy, the opponent lets his guard down or backs off, opening to the Chamelion the path to victory.

I recall a client of mine who became tearful whenever I confronted her on a given topic. Yet the nature of the topic was not sad. Even so, I found myself backing off when the tears came. Finally I figured out what was going on and confronted her on the purpose of the tearfulness. Only then was she able to make progress. Up to that point she had kept me at bay.

It's really tough to spot a Chamelion, but one key to detection is your own feelings. When you find yourself feeling overly sympathetic or even guilty about competing with a certain opponent, you might be competing with a Chamelion.

Are you a Lion, a Fox, a Bulldog, or a Chamelion? The sector on the Competitive Quadrant in which you had your highest number of checks indicates your primary style. You actually have *two* primary competitive styles, one for Contest behavior and one for everyday Social behavior. Because your Social style is much more general, it is the more important of the two. Your C style and your S style may be identical or very different. Your corporation also has a primary competitive style (the Prevailing style). As indicated earlier in the chapter, the first two styles deal with how you operate, while the P style is that with which you feel you must contend.

Naturally there is no such thing as a "pure" type. While your highest C and S scores reflect your primary styles, your C and S scores on the other three sectors indicate your "competitive flexibility," or the degree to which you "borrow" tactics from the other styles. Your other three P scores reflect the "competitive diversity" with which you perceive you must cope at work.

The particular "degree of fit" between your C, S, and P styles can be very important for your career. The closer your personal style fits the corporate style, the easier it may be for you to get ahead or be "in with the crowd." The more divergent your style is from the prevailing one, the more resistance you may expect. This is especially true if your S style is direct and the P style is indirect.

Is your primary C style different from your primary S style? If so, then you probably alter your behavior and responses significantly for a formal contest. This is especially true if your primary

C style falls into the Direct side, and your primary S style lies on the Indirect side. If this is the case, you're likely to be a covert competitor in your everyday dealings, but you "come out" for a contest.

If the reverse score pattern is true of you (primary C Indirect, primary S Direct) then when faced with a contest situation you probably must win at all costs, using subterfuge to gain an advantage.

Another important comparison is between your primary S style and the primary "P" style. If these correspond, for better or worse, there is probably a "good fit" between your style and how others at your workplace compete. You may find that you fit in well and are able to understand and deal with the office politics you face.

If your primary S style differs significantly from the primary P style, then you may be out of sync. If your primary S style is Direct, say, a Lion, and the P style is Indirect, perhaps Chamelion, you may find yourself stepping on toes. Worse yet, you may be faced with veiled or hidden competition that you may not fully see, let alone comprehend. If your company environment is highly indirectly competitive, then watch out! You will have clandestine opponents. The techniques for detecting veiled and hidden opposition outlined in chapter 5 will be especially important for you.

If your primary S style is Indirect, and P style is Direct, you run the risk of being seen as a trickster, or even a subverter. Nothing can hurt your career more than having your coworkers feel they can't trust you.

Generally, people whose primary styles are Direct have a difficult time coping with Indirect competitors. Direct competitors, usually not as well schooled in subterfuge and innuendo, can get "hooked" before they realize it, or get lulled into indifference. While the Indirect competitors may appear to have the advantage, they often have difficulty in explaining themselves when confronted because they rely on covert tactics which they do not wish to admit openly. Direct competitors are more comfortable with confrontation because they are used to dealing up-front. A Direct competitor with a well-developed knack for behaviorally recognizing and labeling indirect competitive ploys is a rough person to beat.

The Direct competitor's chief advantage lies in directness, persistence, forcefulness, tenacity, and show of strength. The chief disadvantage, as stated above, is typical slowness and ineptitude in discerning devious tactics and labeling them for what they are. The chief advantage of Indirect competitors lies in indirectness—charm, trickery, and other veiled techniques. Their main disadvantage lies in the fact that they may spend more energy in attempting to outwit opponents than in the task at hand. They risk others' distrust or even worse feelings if they are found out.

Everyone is a master of his or her own style. When you have to compete and the stakes are high, beware of playing in someone else's ballpark. In other words, don't try to beat another competitor at her own game. She is bound to be better at her own strategy than you are. After all, she has been practicing it all her life! Your best bet for long-term advantage is to fine-tune the Healthy Competitor strategies spelled out later in this book. As you will see, often the best way to compete is not to.

# Putting It All Together

Go back over all the exercises. What common themes arose? Do your values and early recollection patterns fit well with your Competitive Quadrant C and S scores? How well does your value system fit with your Competitive Quadrant P score? This is another way of assessing degree of fit between you and your workplace. To what degree have you adapted your personal style to fit the prevailing corporate culture? What compromises did you make?

Can you summarize your findings in a few sentences? Doing so will give you sort of a competitive "character sketch." It will help you highlight your strengths and where you might be vulnerable. This is extremely useful information if you are locked into difficult or high-level competitive situations where careful self-protection is a must.

There is one added dimension that cuts across all the styles we've discussed so far. To be a Healthy Competitor, and also to be able to protect yourself to your best advantage, you must recognize and understand this dimension. You may or may not fall into this category yourself, but you will certainly have to deal with others who demonstrate this dimension. I'm talking about the Competitive Personality. Forewarned is forearmed! Get thee to the next chapter!

Box 3-1

## EXAMPLE OF A COMPETITIVE STYLE AT WORK

Edward—Middle manager in a manufacturing firm

| Numbers | Contest | Social | Prevailing | |
|---------|---------|--------|------------|-----------|
| 1–8 | 2 | 1 | 2 | Lion |
| 9–16 | 2 | 2 | 6 | Fox |
| 17–24 | 6 | 6 | 2 | Bulldog |
| 25–32 | 4 | 4 | 5 | Chamelion |

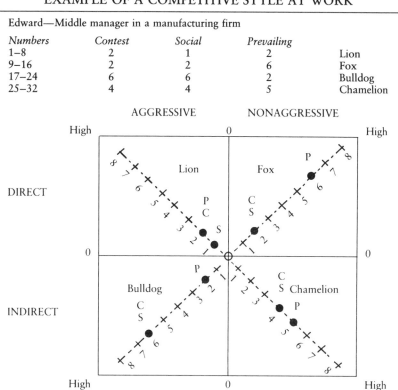

Edward is a Bulldog, with a close secondary Chamelion style. He's very congruent in that his C and S styles are virtually identical. When called on to directly compete, he exhibits the same persistence and tenacity that characterizes his everyday behavior, although in a contest he may persist more intensely. His high secondary score of Chamelion indicates that he has flexibility in the types of tactics he uses, yet he is basically nonaggressive, shown by his very low scores on the aggressive Lion and Fox scales.

Edward is straightforward most of the time, preferring to compete by working both hard and smart, and bolstering his own position without making waves. The items he answered on the Chamelion scale were those relating to charm and patience, not pretense or the provocation of guilt. Most people like him for his tact, honesty, and charming ways. As such, he is a tough competitor to beat.

The prevailing work pattern, at least as far as Edward perceives it, is quite different. Competitive interactions are primarily indirect, and quite often sneakily hostile. The political environment is characterized by non-follow-through, criticism, subtle put-downs, and undercutting. Much of this goes on at a subliminal level, under the guise of a friendly, hail-fellow-well-met atmosphere.

It may take an astute observer quite a while to discover covert patterns. Interestingly, Edward is such a savvy observer, possibly because he is also adept at playing the game on the indirect side.

The potential pitfall for Edward is the hostility in his work environment. Others will be out to get him, and the pressure upon him will increase to the degree he gets ahead. In fact, Edward discovered the hostile side through being stabbed in the back a few times. Fortunately, he did not respond in kind. He is now aware of the potential dangers and who his "enemies" are. He recognizes that his nonhostile ways are out of sync with the system and that protecting his position is just as important as doing his job.

An interesting but unanswerable question in Edward's case is whether his high Chamelion score reflects his actual personality or whether he has become more indirect in having to respond to a highly indirectly competitive work setting.

# Notes

1. Ruben, H. *Competing*. New York: Lippincott & Crowell, 1980, 29–39.

For more extensive information on the topics in this chapter, you may wish to consult the following:

Olson, H. A. *Early recollections: Their use in diagnosis and psychotherapy.* Springfield, Illinois: Charles Thomas, 1979.
Maccoby, M. *The gamesman: The new corporate leaders.* New York: Simon & Schuster, 1976.

# 4

# Forewarned Is Forearmed

S HARON was a hardworking if somewhat lackluster employee in
the accounting department of a large manufacturing firm. She
was dedicated and highly capable, working many hours overtime
and accepting any task without question. Yet she was quiet and
unassuming. Sharon, everyone thought, must eat, sleep, and even
breathe the company.

Sharon's loyal efficiency did not go without notice. When a va-
cancy arose at the head of the accounting department, Sharon was
immediately offered the position. She was directly responsible to
Bill Williams, Vice President of Finance.

Mr. Williams had always been supportive of Sharon. He often
commented on her excellent performance and company loyalty.
Sharon was unsure about accepting the position, but figured she'd
have a supporter and mentor in Mr. Williams. With his backing
and help, how could she lose?

After she accepted the position, Sharon seemed to blossom. She
began to dress in a more businesslike manner to befit her new
station. Even her posture improved. Sharon had quietly been preparing for this position. She read books and took courses on man-
aging the accounting function. She had a pleasing style and
maintained the loyalty of her now-subordinates.

At high level meetings with Mr. Williams and other key officers,
she began to speak out. She knew her operation inside-out and
suggested new ideas to improve efficiency and save money. Mr.
Williams was not only astonished at Sharon's new assertiveness;
he was perturbed.

Mr. Williams suggested that Sharon submit all new proposals through him, up the chain of command. When he received them, he put them aside. Sharon became increasingly frustrated as no action was being taken on her suggestions, and Mr. Williams was becoming increasingly cool. He began to criticize her for being too pushy and impatient. Rather than being the facilitator Sharon hoped he would be, Mr. Williams was now blocking her. He even began to make occasional remarks of a sexual nature. In their "mentor" sessions he was becoming increasingly critical and superior, backing his comments with his "long experience in the firm."

Sharon was disillusioned. More than that, she was confused. Her ideas were good. She had the support of her department. She backed up her proposals with hard dollars-and-cents evidence. What was she doing wrong?

Sharon's was a sin of omission; she failed to size up her new situation. Was this a case of "women shouldn't rise above a certain level," or was there something more personal at stake, something insidious in her relationship with Mr. Williams?

Two of the five corporate VP's were women. This company was forward-looking in its equal employment opportunity practices. This put the problem at the feet of Mr. Williams, or Sharon herself.

Williams had been Vice President of Finance for over fifteen years. His division was known for being accurate but uninventive. Over the years Williams had run the Finance Division as a little island within the company—always reliable, yet aloof and independent. He ran it on tradition and maintained the policies of his predecessor. Without the pressure of innovation, his job was easy, and he was the Grand Old Man of the vice-presidential cadre. But recently the company had put on a push for productivity and creativeness as its market share was becoming increasingly threatened.

Into this arena stepped Sharon, with new cost-cutting ideas. And Sharon, not Williams, was getting noticed. Williams was not only threatened, he was jealous.

What can Sharon do now? Publicly Williams is cordial, but she knows she has a tiger by the tail! What could she have done differently to prevent this all from happening?

Before we review this situation, first let's look at what's going on.

Sharon is dealing with a competitive personality, kind, laid-back Williams who is very supportive on the surface. Underneath, he is treacherous. Sooner or later, perhaps even now, *you* will have to deal with a Competitive Personality (CP), someone like Williams. Are you prepared? You can't defend yourself against something you can't see. Once you know how a CP thinks and behaves, then you can take effective action.

## Competitive Personalities

Is everyone who is "hard-driving and competitive" a candidate for the Competitive Personality label? No way. Many people have chosen to compete hard in order to survive and get ahead. You're probably one of them. But are you a Competitive Personality? Let's find out!

Take a moment to answer the following questionnaire. Respond as honestly as you can. Please score each statement to the degree it is true of you, on the following scale:

4 Almost always
3 More often
2 Less often
1 Rarely

_____ 1. Are you always competitive?

_____ 2. Must you always have the last word in a discussion with your spouse or associate?

_____ 3. Are you afraid of others stealing your ideas?

_____ 4. Are you always concerned about getting credit for what you do?

_____ 5. Is it important to you always to win?

_____ 6. Do you hold back from total effort for fear of criticism?

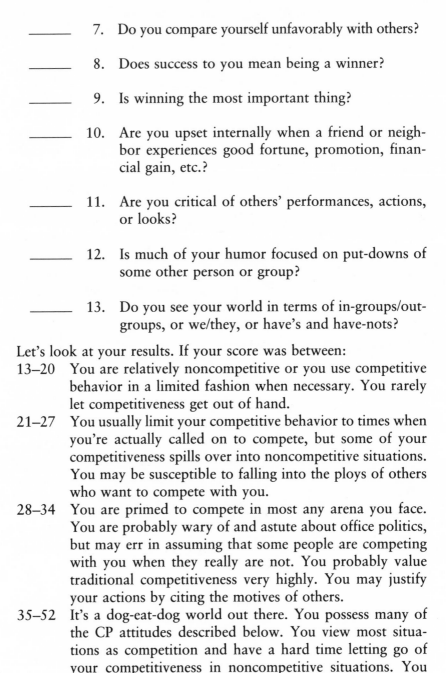

_____ 7. Do you compare yourself unfavorably with others?

_____ 8. Does success to you mean being a winner?

_____ 9. Is winning the most important thing?

_____ 10. Are you upset internally when a friend or neighbor experiences good fortune, promotion, financial gain, etc.?

_____ 11. Are you critical of others' performances, actions, or looks?

_____ 12. Is much of your humor focused on put-downs of some other person or group?

_____ 13. Do you see your world in terms of in-groups/out-groups, or we/they, or have's and have-nots?

Let's look at your results. If your score was between:

13–20  You are relatively noncompetitive or you use competitive behavior in a limited fashion when necessary. You rarely let competitiveness get out of hand.

21–27  You usually limit your competitive behavior to times when you're actually called on to compete, but some of your competitiveness spills over into noncompetitive situations. You may be susceptible to falling into the ploys of others who want to compete with you.

28–34  You are primed to compete in most any arena you face. You are probably wary of and astute about office politics, but may err in assuming that some people are competing with you when they really are not. You probably value traditional competitiveness very highly. You may justify your actions by citing the motives of others.

35–52  It's a dog-eat-dog world out there. You possess many of the CP attitudes described below. You view most situations as competition and have a hard time letting go of your competitiveness in noncompetitive situations. You may be very suspicious of noncompetitive people, seeing them as veiled or hidden competitors.

Before proceeding, let's clarify a couple of issues. First, this is *not* a questionnaire about being competitive per se, but rather about being competitive *in a particular way*. People who score low on this questionnaire may act very competitively when called upon to do so. The difference is that they are able to let go of their competitive behavior or feelings when the contest is over. These people are "situational competitors." Certain situations and contexts may call for competitive behavior and these people can respond accordingly. Many attorneys and Olympic and professional athletes fall into this category. They must compete as a demand of the job, but outside they can shift gears. The CP, on the other hand, is a "general competitor," likely to act or think competitively in most situations. The question here is not just one of degree, but also one of attitude. The high scorer—the CP–views his or her world in a fundamentally different way than low scorers, as we shall soon see.

The CP dimension cuts across, or "overlays," the four competitive styles we discussed in the last chapter. CP's may exhibit any of the four styles, although usually they will fall into the more aggressive categories (Lion or Fox). For example, one CP might express his or her driven competitiveness with direct brute force while another might use sly subterfuge, depending on the individual's personality. But the underlying mentality about competition would be basically the same for both.

Second, the CP is not necessarily "sick" or "crazy." Actually the relentless competitiveness that CP's often (but not always) display is highly rewarded and sought after by our society, especially in business and on the playing field. To the degree that the CP is willing to jump into the fray, he or she may actually be seen as a standard-bearer, a hero.

Upon closer inspection, however, we discover that, to the degree that CP's are successful, they succeed *in spite of* their competitive outlook, not because of it. In fact, the CP has certain liabilities and insecurities, based on a mistaken worldview of competing and cooperating, that actually undermine his or her effectiveness. Many of us mistakenly view hard-driven competitiveness as necessary for success. The CP confuses these issues to the extreme.

Third, the CP is not necessarily "evil." On television we see such good examples of the Competitive Personality as J. R. Ewing on "Dallas," Angela Channing on "Falcon Crest," and Alexis Colby on "Dynasty." In real life, however, CP's are often moral, upstanding citizens. Yet, as we shall see, they are motivated by fear, which, in a tight situation, may spur them to undercut others or compromise certain values.

Again, before passing judgment, let's remember that most of us possess some traits of the Competitive Personality to some degree. This is our cultural legacy. That fact may help you to understand and empathize with the pattern we are about to examine. For the sake of clarity and contrast, I will describe the pattern in the extreme. You may know some extreme cases; others may be more tempered.

# What Is the Competitive Personality Like?

Think for a moment about a boxer in the ring. Close your eyes and imagine what he must be thinking . . . feeling. Try to put yourself in the boxer's place; experience those thoughts, fears, concerns, feelings, physical sensations for yourself. Do this now for a couple of moments in silence before reading on.

What thoughts, emotions, and sensations did you discover? Was the boxer wary, tense, and suspicious? Did he feel he had to have eyes in the back of his head so his opponent couldn't sucker-punch him? Did he have a get-even attitude? Certainly he felt he had to win at all costs and to struggle hard. Naturally he felt he had to punch first to gain and maintain his advantage, and dodge and block to protect himself in every way possible from counterattack.

Take down the ring and make all of life the boxing match, and that's how CP's feel: always on guard, ready to compete, antennae up for the slightest threat. This is their basic mistake: they confuse the game with life itself, living their daily existence as if they were in cutthroat competition. In their own way, they think they thrive on competition and are excited by it. They often do not perceive the negative stress effects and interpersonal difficulties they may experience as arising from their own competitiveness. That their competitive outlook may be mistaken does not enter their minds. For they have to compete and win, and they often feel lost in low-competitive or noncompetitive situations (coworker beware!). Their competition may be subtle and/or overt. While they clearly recognize themselves as competitive, and usually pride themselves on it, much of their true motivation lies shrouded in the subconscious.

CP's usually share one basic conflict: high-flown ambition vs affection. On the one hand they want to dominate, to be *the* best, Number One. It's not enough just to be good, or even excellent. On the other hand, they want to be loved and approved of by others. To most of us this is not a conflict. You can be superb *and* be loved, even revered, for your excellent qualities. But because of their competitive outlook and their extreme thinking, CP's find these goals of ambition and affection mutually exclusive.

How does this happen? Let's look at the characteristics of the Competitive Personality.

1. *Dog-eat-dog world view.* CP's think in terms of "win-lose" and "survival of the fittest." They see their world in vertical terms, as if life were a ladder to be climbed. And we all know that there's no room on the ladder for two people to occupy the same rung. This makes other people potential competitors. When others are viewed in this manner, the basic ambition-affection conflict and the rest of the characteristics of the competitive personality begin to make sense.

2. *High-flown, comparative goals.* As mentioned above, the CP's goal is to be the BEST, to be FIRST. Since progress toward these goals is made in relation to others, the goals are often discussed in terms of being "better than." While CP's may talk in comparative terms, their actual goals lie in the superlative. Goals are often unrealistically high and CP's place stringent demands on themselves to be perfect, strong, all-knowing, etc. This leads to frequent frustration and self-doubt, and to viewing the world as a perpetual game of King-of-the-Hill, where the CP must protect his or her position and knock down opponents. Many times, CP's will talk about "competing with myself," but this is a thinly veiled rationalization. CP's are never far from feeling a need to

compete with others. Often, as we shall see from the rest of the characteristics, they make the wrong choice of opponents.

3. *Marketplace orientation.* CP's base their worth on what they can produce. Therefore they feel that their value as a person fluctuates in relation to their performance. Now we see, in part, why they have to be the absolute best: only then can they feel worthwhile about themselves as persons.

4. *Insecure about status.* Because their personal worth is never certain but continually up for grabs, they feel they must keep achieving and producing to impress and to prove themselves to others. What they do to impress others often causes them more stress than pleasure, because down deep they may not enjoy doing these things. The CP's insecurity affects not only his or her work, but also may carry over into family and community life as well. CP's may live in houses or buy possessions above their means, or live in "status" communities with neighbors with whom, down deep, they do not really care to associate. They may join organizations or clubs that they don't care about in order to rub elbows with "influential people." They may even join a church of a different denomination because the boss attends there.

Just because people do these things doesn't mean they are CP's. "Social climbing" is a common, highly supported activity in our society. In fact, many people believe that is what you must do if you want to be successful. I saw a bumper sticker recently that said: "He who has the most when he dies . . . wins!"

The key that distinguishes the CP from others who make these sacrifices for the image of success is their motivation. The CP operates from insecurity and fear, that down deep he or she is not enough. His or her worth is continually on the line. Other success-oriented people recognize social climbing as part of the strategy for getting ahead, and see sacrifices as part of the price to pay, without (as much of) the personal insecurity about one's worth.

5. *Suspicious of others.* CP's are continually looking over their shoulder to see who's gaining on them and to discover where they are on the ladder. Also they tend to distrust other peo-

ple's behavior or motives. Others' cooperative efforts come under particular scrutiny because they might actually be veiled competitive ploys.

6. *Insidious comparisons and worry.* Worry is the CP's constant companion,especially worry about his or her status relative to others. As a result, CP's continually compare themselves with others to see how they are doing. Their self-worth becomes fragile because their self-image is dependent on their perception of others' worth. Others, then, unwittingly become the standard-bearers for the CP's feelings and actions. This puts the CP's control of self-image and self-worth outside themselves. They can feel good and confident about themselves until they perceive that someone else has gotten ahead. Then their anxiety becomes aroused and they cannot rest until they have again, in their own minds, achieved a superior position. This is why Mr. Williams began to have difficulty with Sharon's new image.

   Here's the rub! it would be bad enough if the CP compared fairly. Alas, this is rarely the case. Most often CP's will compare some area of *weakness* in themselves against *strengths* they see in someone else. This tilts the shaky applecart of their self-esteem even more.

7. *Minding others' business.* In order to feel good about themselves, CP's must compare. In order to compare, they must know what's going on. These people are busybodies! They are a veritable gold mine of information about what those around them are up to, and especially about where others stand on the status hierarchy. In fact, they may watch what others are doing so much that their own performance suffers. As a rule they are excellent observers, but their anxiety and suspicion often will bias their interpretations of the information they glean.

8. *Jealousy and hostility.* Since others are seen as competitors, their advancement is considered a personal threat, even if no true threat actually exists. Remember how difficult it is for two people to occupy the same rung of a ladder. Is it any wonder, then, that someone else's upward movement can spark the flames of jealousy in a CP?

The Competitive Personality is jealous by definition. This jealousy is rarely far from the surface and increases in intensity the closer or more important the CP perceives the rival to be. For instance, if some unknown person in another town won big in the state lottery, the CP might not care. But if the big winner was his next door neighbor, his jealousy would be intense. While this may be true of most of us, since jealousy affects us all to some degree, the Competitive Personality, due to his or her defensiveness, experiences jealous feelings in spades! If you make a comment to him or her about a rival's good fortune, he or she will often return it with a sarcastic comparison or put-down. Jealousy can cause CP's to eat themselves out inside if another person, especially someone close to them, progresses too far. Needless to say such envy makes them formidable, and potentially treacherous, foes.

Their hostility may be open or veiled. It may come out seething in mild sarcasm and negativity, or may take the form of subtle subversion. In a work setting, especially at a professional level, you will rarely see it in all its raw, naked power. There is little opportunity in today's business environment for the direct expression of hostility. Therefore much of it goes underground, surfacing indirectly and/or in symptoms of stress disorders.

Often the hostility is free-floating, just under the surface. The CP may come on as the nicest person—until a competitive situation arises. Then you see the anger and wonder where it is coming from. For the CP, anger is never very far away. Anger and jealousy serve a strong need to dominate. While CP's may not necessarily want to boss others around openly, they need to be the first or best in their own minds. Anger is used when they feel that their self-conceived Number One position is slipping. They hope to regain the top slot by bullying or otherwise forcing others into submission. At the very least, their self-righteousness justifies their anger in the face of a situation they cannot control.

For example, consider the last time you had a fight with your spouse, child, or coworker. While jealousy may not have been involved, what were you trying to accomplish through your anger? You were attempting to win, to restore the balance of power in your favor, to get the other person to give in (often veiled as "getting them to understand" or to "see reason"). Anger is often difficult to understand, especially our own. When we view it in terms of the power and competition it expresses, its ultimate purposes become more clear.

9. *Imitative behavior.* Better known as "keeping up with the Joneses," this behavior is a result of the CP's need to compare. CP's must have the same kind of power, prestige, or kinds of possessions that those "above" them have, or they are personally dissatisfied and anxious. Again, it is the intensity of their insecurity and status-consciousness that separates them from the rest of us on this issue.

It's one thing to want the same kind of power, position, or possessions another person has. This does not necessarily imply any ill will toward that person. But if the jealousy is intense and the perceived stakes are high enough, the CP may view the other individual as an opponent to be defeated, and may attempt to undercut that person in some direct or indirect way.

When the CP determines who the winners are, or what style is rewarded, he or she will adopt that style and/or imitate the winners. CP's will often imitate competitors in order to beat them at their own game. Often in their desire to be "in" they imitate so relentlessly that they end up selling out their own basic values, desires, and preferences. Peer pressure and its results among teenagers is a classic example. Again, the greater the personal insecurity, the greater the imitation. While many people "grow out" of this behavior, for the CP imitation becomes a way of life.

10. *Hypersensitivity.* Because they derive status and self-worth from continually comparing themselves with others, it is important to CP's to be valued more than others by the people who count, e.g., the boss, supervisor, or influential contact. Therefore they are sensitive and very easily hurt by any perceived slights. They are also in need of frequent praise or compliments, even if on the surface this makes them uncom-

fortable. If you praise another person in a CP's presence, inwardly he or she will ask him or herself, "What does he or she think of *me?*" or "How do *I* rate?"or he or she will think "I wish he or she would say that about *me.*"or "Yes, but *I'm* better in this other skill." This sensitivity is there— you can count on it—whether or not its openly expressed. And this sensitivity adds to the CP's ultimate vulnerability!

11. *Ego-oriented.* When confronted with an unfamiliar task or challenge, the CP first asks, "Will I win or lose, succeed or fail?" This question becomes critical because of CP's marketplace orientation and insecurity regarding status. CP's egos and self-worth are so wrapped up in the outcome of their performance that they are likely to engage in excessive self-protective maneuvers, diverting too much of their time and energy from the task at hand.

    The Healthy Competitor, on the other hand, is task-oriented, focusing his or her initial attention on what must be done to solve the problem. This is the exact opposite of the CP outlook, and yields a significantly different outcome! To get a clearer handle on the distinctions between task- and ego-oriented persons, and to find out which you are, take a look at box 4-1.

12. *Will sabotage others' progress.* The CP's battle cry often is, "The best defense is an offense." Rather than just pursue their own goals, CP's are so threatened by others' gains that they commonly spend some of their own energies tripping up their coworkers. In the short run, this negative strategy may work, but they don't know when to stop. Thus they frequently end up eroding their own progress as well.

    Depending on the CP's own value system and attitudes about right and wrong, his or her opposition may be open or hidden. If the CP's point of view is "Win at all costs," the interference may be very planned, open, and direct. But if such behavior violates the CP's conscious image of himself as good or righteous, the subversion may be much more subtle, and even may be subconscious. The behavior then gets heaped over with rationalizations about what's "right," "good," and "for the benefit of the organization." "Moth-

Box 4-1

## THE EGO- vs TASK-ORIENTED PERSON

Below are the characteristics of the ego- vs the task-oriented person. Where do you fit on the task-ego dimension? To find out, fill out the scale below. Add up your score and divide by 10 to get your average score.

| Task-Oriented | *Points*<br>1 2 3 4 5 6 | Ego-Oriented |
|---|---|---|
| Asks "What must I do or use to solve the problem?" | _ _ _ _ _ _ | Asks "Will I succeed or fail?" (often expects to fail) |
| Self-affirming, believes in self, confident | _ _ _ _ _ _ | Self-questioning, doubts self, worries |
| Separates self-worth from performance | _ _ _ _ _ _ | Identifies self-worth with performance |
| Accepts challenges, takes risks | _ _ _ _ _ _ | Intimidated by challenges, avoids risks |
| Tries new activities enthusiastically | _ _ _ _ _ _ | May limit self to what he or she can already do well |
| Takes responsibility | _ _ _ _ _ _ | Rationalizes, makes excuses |
| Flexible, open-minded | _ _ _ _ _ _ | Rigid, closed-minded |
| Cooperates, will share leadership | _ _ _ _ _ _ | Must have own way, be the leader and/or call the shots |
| Creativity-oriented, looks for new ways and opportunities | _ _ _ _ _ _ | Maintenance-oriented, protects what he/she has |
| Follows through | _ _ _ _ _ _ | Often lacks follow-through |

Average score of 2 or less = high task orientation. Average score of 5 or more = high ego orientation.

As you worked through this scale, you may have recognized certain traits in yourself that you have not previously put together into an organized whole. Hopefully this little scale has helped you to see more clearly your own "big picture." Only then can you most effectively determine where you are, what to strengthen, and what to improve.

erhood and apple pie" fueled the Spanish Inquisition, and it is no less a rationalization for treachery today.

To sum up, here's a handy checklist of the characteristics of the Competitive Personality, along with a rating scale. You can score yourself, or use it as a guide for sizing up others who cause you difficulty. By putting a check under the appropriate number for each characteristic, you end up with a Competitive Personality graph. Remember that we all possess some of these traits to some degree, so when rating yourself, be honest, and when rating others, be fair. Be as objective as you can, for it's important to view yourself and those with whom you deal as clearly as possible.

|  |  | Rarely or never |  |  | Almost always |  |  |
|---|---|:---:|:---:|:---:|:---:|:---:|:---:|
|  |  | 1 | 2 | 3 | 4 | 5 | 6 |
| 1. | Dog-eat-dog world view | — | — | — | — | — | — |
| 2. | High-flown comparative goals | — | — | — | — | — | — |
| 3. | Marketplace orientation | — | — | — | — | — | — |
| 4. | Insecurity about status | — | — | — | — | — | — |
| 5. | Suspicious of others | — | — | — | — | — | — |
| 6. | Insidious comparisons and worry | — | — | — | — | — | — |
| 7. | Minding others' business | — | — | — | — | — | — |
| 8. | Jealousy and hostility | — | — | — | — | — | — |
| 9. | Imitative behavior | — | — | — | — | — | — |
| 10. | Hypersensitivity | — | — | — | — | — | — |
| 11. | Ego-oriented | — | — | — | — | — | — |
| 12. | Will sabotage others' progress | — | — | — | — | — | — |

# How Does the Competitive Personality Think?

If you want to predict and influence another person's behavior you need to know more than *what* think. Far more important is *how* they think, how they view their world. This knowledge will be a key tool in coping with the Competitive Personalities around you. You are a part of their world, and how they view you will determine how they cope with you. Fortunately, when you know how they think, you can more effectively influence their actions.

Much of how they think is spelled out in the twelve traits we just outlined. Now let's consider a couple of underlying factors.

1. Life-style Goal. The life-style goal of the competitive personality is to be the *Most*. This is a broader goal than just being the best. The competitive personality wants to be the most adored, most wealthy, most honored, most powerful, etc. The variations on this theme are endless, and no two CP's neces-

sarily have to be the "most" in the same characteristic.

The scope of the goal may be modest. They don't usually have to be the "most" in the world or nation. Often the reference group is much smaller, so that CP's strive to be the most in their company or community, or their industry, or their circle of friends.

By definition, Most indicates a comparison. You can't be sure that you're the "most" unless you're on the lookout for where others are. Most does not allow for other contenders; they must be surpassed, even defeated. He or she who must be most can rest only when the other contenders have been cleared away, clearly beaten, or remain in their place. CP's are ever watchful of others, lest someone start to gain ground on them.

For example, Williams in our opening story had to be the "most" influential in his department, and in control. Sharon was OK as long as he could see that she would not challenge his position. That's why, from his point of view, he had to sit on her recommendations. As Sharon spoke up and others outside Williams' department began to take notice, Sharon became a challenger for the title of "most influential." At that Williams felt he had to act to crush the opposition. And act he did, but initially in very subtle ways. He needed to keep Sharon in her place or drive her out. As Williams became more openly difficult, however, he tipped his hand. In the meantime, he had Sharon very confused.

2. Assumed Scarcity. Much of the intensity we see in Competitive Personalities is based on their assumption that "the best things in life are scarce." True, there are many situations in life where there are numerous contestants but only one or a few winners, e.g., a tennis match, a formal debate, lawsuits, college scholarships, or a company presidency or CEO positions.

But the CP mistakenly puts other qualities under the rubric of scarcity. Money, Cadillacs, honor, recognition, approval, even love are viewed as scarce "commodities." The person who coined the phrase, "That's a hard act to follow," must have been a competitive personality! Why couldn't an audience give 110 percent adoration and approval, with a standing ovation, *every* act, without making a rating? Such an idea is beyond the scope of the CP's imagination.

If there are only measured amounts to be had, then the Competitive Personality, who must be or have the "Most," will have to beat out all comers. The perception of scarcity, then, fuels the CP's competitive drive. After all, the idea of "most" makes sense only when there is a perceived limited amount of something; "most" means nothing when the commodity in question, such as love or approval, is limitless or indefinitely renewable.

Now we see what perceptions spark the CP's need to complete. But how can a CP label you as a competitor even if you are not competing with them?

3. Cooperators vs Competitors. Kelley and Stahelski did some fascinating research on the competitive mind set. They discovered that there are two kinds of people out there: the Cooperators and the Competitors. These two kinds of people have fundamentally different ways of viewing others.

Joe is a Cooperator. He sees that the rest of the world is peopled by both Cooperators and Competitors, and can accurately pick up on others' cues accordingly. When faced with Kim, for example, whom he perceives wishes to cooperate with him, Joe can cooperate in return. When faced with Ed, whom he sees as competitive, he is fully capable of responding by vying with him. The lesson Joe learns from this, which influences his future behavior, is that some people can cooperate and others compete. Joe is flexible.

Jill, on the other hand, is a Competitor. As such, she views the world as rivalrous and sets up a definite self-fulfilling prophecy to back up her point of view. Here's how. When faced with another Competitor, Ed, she accurately recognizes his competitive ploys and competes in return. So far, Jill's perception is similar to Joe's. But when Jill is faced with a Cooperator, Kim, she mistakenly views Kim's bids for cooperation as a hidden competitive tactic. To gain the advantage, or in order not to be duped later, she begins to compete with Kim. Kim, accurately reading Jill's competitive cues, will compete in return. Jill's lesson? "See, I was right! Everyone out there is an opponent!"

Why does Jill misperceive cooperation cues? Because of a practice we all engage in to some degree called "Projection of Motivation." Humans have a natural tendency to view others as having similar motivations as themselves. With maturity and learning, we tend to temper that faulty notion somewhat, but the roots of it remain. That's why very honest people sometimes get duped; they don't expect others to deal crookedly with them.

The CP "learns" at a very early age that the world is competitive, and that he or she "must compete to survive." As the Competitive Personality pattern and world view develop, the CP maintains and strengthens the view that others are competitive in order to protect himself or herself. By assuming rivalrous motives in others, the CP can maintain his or her suspicion and be forewarned. The suspicion reinforces the self-fulfilling prophecy, which in turn arouses more suspicion.

The end result is that it may take a great deal of time and effort to convince highly competitive persons of your loyalty. If they perceive, correctly or not, that you are actually competing, they will oppose you in order to keep on top. Their opposition may be open or very little subtle, or anything in between. Do not fool yourself into assuming that their vying will be fair or honest.

Neither must their contention against you be personal! It is more likely to triggered by the fact that *you represent a perceived threat* than by a dislike of you as a person. The dislike may develop, (you can't really like someone whom you can't trust!) but it may not have been the cause of the trouble.

This distinction may be small comfort but it in important in understanding what's going on between yourself and the CP. You can eliminate a great amount of guilty feelings and self-doubt when you recognize that you might not be at fault for the opposition you face. It may also help clear up your confusion if you run into difficulties when your behavior is innocent and well-intentioned.

# How to Recognize the Competitive Personality

Since CP's don't wear armbands advertising themselves as such, recognition can be difficult. Direct competitors, Lions, may not be too hard to spot; their competitivness is very open. But even so you might be confused by thinking somehow that their behavior is caused by something you have done.

Williams, on the other hand, would have been very difficult to second-guess. He is an indirect competitor, a Fox. His behavior was very subtle and well rationalized. How could Sharon have known?

You won't always be able to know. In a work setting where there is a great deal of emphasis on and talk about market share, "beating the competition," and "strategy," it's even more difficult because many people are into the "competition" act anyhow. Distinguishing the Competitive Personalities from the rest of the competitors becomes that much more difficult. But there are some characteristics to look for. While these in themselves don't always reflect a competitive personality, if they occur frequently and in a wide variety of situations, it's a good bet that they identify a CP.

First, listen for the *language*. Is the person's talk studded with win-lose phrases? Does he frequently use comparative language, such as "more than" or "less than," "better than" or "worse than?" Does the frequently use "dog-eat-dog" types of phrases when describing the company, the marketplace, society, or their family?

Next, look at *attitudes*. Does she usually worry what others think? Is she often on the defensive? Does she put others down? Is she sarcastic? Does she cast blame on others whenever things go wrong? Tend to kill others' ideas before giving them a try or a serious analysis? Appear to elevate herself at others' expense? Does she come across as self-protective more than cooperative? Is she often suspicious or critical of others' motivations? Does she hold a grudge? Have a chip on her shoulder? Put undue emphasis on externals, image, or status? Is she chronically tense or depressed? Prejudiced? Envious? Does she show anger, disdain, disappointment, or become moody when someone close to her has a success or achieves special recognition? Does she show interest in you only when she wants something?

Look also at *behavior*. Does he use people? Does he seem to get much more than he gives? Does he play favorites or base decisions more on politics than on merit? Does he passively or actively block, hinder, or sabotage cooperative efforts or others' endeavors? Does he justify his behavior with thin, sometimes overly pious rationalizations? Do his "reasons" confuse you more than they clarify his actions? Does he impress you as phoney or "too nice?" Seem to have hidden agendas or ulterior motives? Is he excessively competitive? Does he spill competition over into noncompetitive situations? Start rumors or thrive on gossip? Excessively pressure himself others? Does his power seem more important to him than his contribution to the organization? Does he frequently jockey for power or position? Have difficulty maintaining long-term relationships? Continually act as if he is in a contest with some other person or department within the organization? "Keep score" of what he and others do, have, or say? Frequently exert energy on "getting even?"

As you can see, these attitudes and behaviors are destructive, especially when acted out within your organization. If you want to produce at your peak, you can't afford to get hooked into these peoples' games. Staying clear of these entanglements can be difficult if your coworkers fit the Competitive Personality mold.

The next two chapters will give you specific methods for spotting indirect and hidden competition, and ways of coping with the CP's and other competitive people and behavior that you face.

# Note

1. Kelley, H. H., and A. J. Stahelski. Social interaction basis of cooperators' and competitors' beliefs about others. *Journal of Personality and Social Psychology.* 16, 1970, 66–91.

# 5

# Defusing the Sneak Attack

S AM is new to the firm. With ten years in selling and a top track record, he's quite an asset to the sales department. He's bright and enthusiastic; he has his product line down pat, and now he's ready to meet with the president of ABC company—one tough customer. As he is about to leave for the appointment, Paul, an old-timer in the sales department, stops him. "Sam", Paul says, "Good luck with ABC today. If anyone can pull off a sale with that outfit, I know you can. I've been here twenty five years and am a top salesman, yet I couldn't do it! They just chew up sales-people and spit them out over there. Salespeople get no respect. But with your enthusiasm and brains, you should make out OK!" "Thanks, Paul", says Sam. Sam appreciates Paul's vote of confidence, but as he drives to his appointment at ABC he becomes more tense. This is more than pressure jitters; he feels defensive and unsure.

What was Paul doing? Was he just wishing Sam well, and throwing in a little personal griping or warning? Or was something more insidious going on?

Paul was actually negatively competing with Sam, but at a very subtle level. Behind his well-wishing was an attempt to undermine Sam's confidence. Sam knew Paul's record: top salesman for the last eight years, and over a quarter of a century in selling, mostly with this company. And if Paul couldn't land ABC's account, no one could. This is exactly what Paul hoped Sam would think! Paul's implication was that Sam was lost before he started, that Sam would go into the sales call feeling one down.

# How to Discover Hidden Competition

Negative competition can be rough to deal with even when it's open and up-front. But when it's veiled or hidden, it can become extremely difficult to detect, let alone solve. This is true whether you're finding yourself competing with a situational competitor or a CP. And it's the hidden and veiled competition that can do you the most harm.

Why? First of all, because it's sneaky. This makes it dishonest by definition. The goal of this type of competition is to get you to react in the desired way before you know you've done it, or to undermine you without your knowing what's going on or who caused it. In order to cope effectively, early detection is vital. Otherwise your confidence and performance may suffer. You may end up on stage, all alone, with egg on your face, not knowing if, why, or how you were set up, and worse, not being able to explain it so it makes sense to anyone else.

Second, veiled or hidden competition rarely comes from known enemies. More often than not the ploy comes from someone you didn't expect to be competing with you. That's what makes it "hidden," as was the case with Sharon in the last chapter, and with Sam. Recognition can be particularly difficult when the competitor is a friend, colleague, or close acquaintance. In those cases it's very easy to deny that competition is going on. "After all," you reason, "he's my friend. He wouldn't do that to me."

Hopefully not, but let's get real (without becoming paranoid)! Business today is riddled with power lords who think their main task is to protect their turf. Power jockeying and jousting are the national pastimes, while office politics and intrigue characterize life in these feudal courts. Serving the company's needs and giving it one's best are important too, but perhaps not as important.

Mergers, acquisitions, and takeovers—hostile or not—which are happening at such a high rate today, muddy the water even more. They raise insecurity and lower company loyalty. This breeds suspicion, contempt, and may lower productivity. In this context, turf protection becomes even more vital. People see their jobs on the line. What will they do? They become more competitive. They feel their survival is at stake.

Yet infighting and rivalry are never considered acceptable organizational behaviors. It's OK to compete like crazy with our competitor companies, but it's never OK to compete with each other except in some formal way such as through sales or production contests. Often such activity within the company is judiciously overlooked or even denied.

This creates an interesting and sinister paradox. Competitive behavior goes on, but since it can't be expressed openly it goes underground. The Healthy Competitor needs to see beyond the masks of everyday life to discover and deal with what is really going on.

Other motives for expressing competition in hidden ways are power and revenge. A hidden competitor feels he or she has an advantage that would be lost if his or her competitive actions were discovered. A technique exposed is stripped of its mystery and effectiveness. Also, the hidden competitors often just would not want to be caught doing it. If found out, he or she would become vulnerable for censure, or worse.

In warfare, and ounce of subtle infiltration is worth more than ten pounds of frontal attack. Espionage is big business today, not just between nations but also between companies. The gaining of "competitor intelligence" has become a sophisticated art in the warfare of business. Is it any wonder, given those demands and attitudes, that people use the same subterfuges to counter their personal opponents?

Corporate competitiveness derives from individual competitiveness and not the other way around. But when competitiveness occurs at the group or corporate level, that fact alone serves as support, justification, and fuel for individual competition, regardless of how much the organization may outwardly attempt to discourage or supress it.

It's a fact of life: once a person or company has been labeled "the opponent," or worse, "the enemy," the rules automatically change. Anything goes. Fairness goes, too—right out the window. In this special adversarial situation, then, we act as if the ends justify the means. We may get fairness or a sympathetic ear from an opponent, but don't expect it. If we do expect that, we may be riding for a fall.

Our society partially knows the ultimate danger of competition. In situations in which competition is promoted and structured on a limited basis, such as in sports, games, and the courtroom, we have developed a balancing set of ethics which we call "good sportsmanship." This is intended to stimulate honor and good grace, but ultimately its purpose is to keep the negatives of competition in check. In competition in daily life, however, the checks and balances system is much weaker, if not nonexistent. Therefore, caveat emptor! Let the partaker beware! After all, don't we usually agree that "All's fair in love and war"?

Remember also that when people are intimately involved with each other in a work, love, or other kind of relationship, they cannot remain neutral very long. They will cooperate and/or compete with each other, depending on their goals in the relationship. And the intensity of that cooperating and competing will grow as the intensity of the feelings in the relationship rises. But these feelings, particularly the competitive ones, are often not expressed directly. The hidden competitor, then, becomes very much like the duck who looks so cool and calm on the surface of the water, but who is paddling hard underneath. Ineptitude in discovery and coping with office politics and internal competition can seriously undermine, or even end, your career!

Getting control when coping with hidden competition is a three-stage process: recognize, analyze, then strategize. Recognition and analysis can be difficult, so here are some guidelines you can use to evaluate the situations you face.

## READ BETWEEN THE LINES

Many common, bothersome, workplace behaviors are actually samples of negative competition, but often are not recognized or labeled as such. Yet until you can see them for what they are, you will find it difficult to turn them around. A recent survey indicated that managers spend up to one-fifth of their time dealing with people problems. Most of these have their root in misdirected competition. The following list gives several examples.

Sexual and racial harassment

Labor-management disputes

Work slowdowns

Blocking efforts at negotiation

Poor follow-through

"Water cooler" syndrome

Gossipping and backbiting, tale-carrying

Power jockeying

Excessive turf protection

Excessive criticism

Refusal to listen

Skirting or refusal to discuss relevant issues

Excuse-making

"Refusal" to accept full responsibility for ones own actions

"Forgetting" to do certain tasks

Put-downs

Shows of superiority in order to impress

Inefficiency in spite of corrective measures

"Differing on issues" with a goal of hindering cooperation

Trying to be a superstar at the team's expense

Accidents due to carelessness or preventable circumstances

Some workman's compensation and insurance claims

## LOOK INTO YOUR OWN FEELINGS AND REACTIONS

Have you ever had a conversation with a person in which everything was pleasant, perhaps even jovial, but inwardly you felt uneasy? Ever have someone make an innocuous comment, or compliment, or joke, and later you felt you'd been had? Remember how you tried to put your finger on it but couldn't figure it out? Still at a loss, did you just give up, assuming that the problem was just in your head?

Guess again, and sharpen your radar! Barring excessive distortion on your part, the probability is ninety percent that someone says or does something to you that initially seems OK but makes you feel on edge, is competing with you on a hidden level, like Paul did with Sam. This is particularly likely when one or a few people tend to trigger this uneasiness in you more than others, or when the uneasiness leads to hurt feelings and the sense that you've been criticized or put down.

You can often discover the goal of another's behavior if you look at the initial emotional impact upon yourself of that person's actions or words. If, for instance, you felt hurt by someone else's comments, there is a good chance that person wanted to hurt you, whether or not he or she was aware of that motive.

There's a fly in the ointment that we need to attack right away, however. This "sixth sense," or ability to tune into your own feelings regarding others' behaviors *is* like radar. It can be so poorly tuned that nothing gets picked up, or it can be so finely sensitive that almost everything gets detected and interpreted at an emotional level. If you are a supersensitive person who is easily hurt, you run the risk of being overly suspicious of others' motives and reading too much into what they do. You must dilute this tendency with large doses of reality and caution if this "radar" technique is to work for you.

Here is a handy guide for guessing the other person's goal in an interaction, based on your feelings. Dinkmeyer and McKay outlined four "goals of misbehavior" for children,[1] and we find that adults often operate according to the same goals. In our context, these are "competitive goals," designed to put distance between people rather than draw people together as cooperative goals would.

Naturally, very few people would admit these goals openly. In fact, most people who operate according to these goals are usually not consciously aware of it. We've all acted in the service of these goals at one time or another. The question is one of degree. The more discouraged and competitive a person is, the more likely these goals will be underlying that person's daily behavior.

To use the guide, just consider your "gut level" reaction to an action or comment that made you uneasy. Locate it on table 5-1 and they read across for the hidden goal and the underlying belief of that behavior. Check this out with what you know about the

Table 5-1
COMPETITIVE GOALS[1]

| *Feelings and Your Reaction to Others' Behavior* | *Hidden Goal* | *Basic Belief Underlying the Goal* |
|---|---|---|
| Annoyed, frustrated, want other person to shut up or get lost | Attention | I can feel important only when I am the center of attention, when I one-up or upstage others |
| Angry, ready to fight, you feel your authority threatened, ready to give in | Power | I can feel important only when I can call the shots, dominate others, or show that I can't be dominated |
| Hurt, desire to retaliate or get even | Revenge | I've been hurt and I must get even, make them suffer, punish them through hurting them; this makes them weaker, and me stronger by contrast (This goal is often fueled by righteous indignation: "I'm giving them what they deserve.") |
| Hopeless and helpless, despair, "I give up," pity | Display of inadequacy | I'm afraid I can't suceed, so I give up and won't try; I'll frustrate all your attempts to coerce or motivate me (This is a rare goal among business achievers. But you may find it among lower-level employees. It is a result of high-flown goals and self-doubt. A key sign of this goal is when an otherwise highly competent person has one area in which he "just can't seem to perform.") |

person involved and the context of the situation. Do you notice patterns emerging? Remember that (a) depending on the situation and their perceived need at the time, people's behaviors and goals can shift, and (b) the goals lower on the chart will often carry elements of the goals above them. For example, a vengeful act or comment may also involve a display of power and quite often will attract negative attention. Later in this chapter, we'll discuss what to do about the competitive behaviors you discover.

## BECOME AWARE OF PSYCH-OUTS

Sport psychologists Tutko and Tosi advanced the concept of psych-outs with athletes,[2] but the idea is applicable to any competitive situation. A psych-out is a comment or action designed to undermine your confidence or get you hooked into competing in return. It usually acts as a red herring. It diverts your attention and energy from the task at hand, and if your opponent can throw you off track, he or she then has an advantage. Psych-outs carry the implicit message, "I'm OK, you're not OK."

Paul's comment to Sam at the opening of this chapter is a psych-out. There are many types of psych-outs, and those who use them are generally clever people. After all, it takes creativity to design a well-constructed ploy. In combatting them, you must be more clever. Fortunately, such cleverness can be learned.

Psych-outs, by definition, are a subterfuge. They have no power once exposed; therefore they will be disguised. Verbal psych-outs are often thrown into a conversation as an offhand remark that appears to be dismissible. This casual, "throwaway" language, however, can be full of hidden impact, which, of course, is what the psycher intends. Because of their sublety and finesse, the psycher's actions are easily denied or rationalized if you confront him. This makes it very difficult to combat these methods directly. The psycher can say, "Who, me? You must be crazy!" And if he plays his cards right, that's exactly how you'll look!

A well-designed psych-out will go right over the heads of casual observers, and if you confront the psych-out directly, others present will see you as supersensitive and are likely to defend the psycher. There's hope, however!

Naturally, awareness is the first key to successfully nullifying a psych-out. You can't fight what you can't see. So here is a brief catalog of some common types of psych-outs that you might encounter. Many of the factors cited below have a legitimacy of their own; they may or may not be psych-outs, depending on how they are used (the method, the context, the timing, and the intent of the user). Your initial gut feeling, or in some cases, like Sam's, your delayed reaction, can be a key to whether or not you were psyched.

Like voodoo, which is also a highly sophisticated psych-out, the power of the psych-out lies not in the technique itself, but in the impact it creates in the mind of the victim. It is highly common for people to psych themselves out, especially once they have become suspicious. When this occurs, they start reading in innuendoes, when none were intended. They worry too much, become supersensitive, second-guess, and waste energy.

If your opponent can get you to undermine yourself in that way, he's pulled off the greatest psych-out of all: he's made you your own worst enemy, and he can sit back and watch the fun.

One final note: awareness is critical to detect not only what is, but also what is *not* a psych-out. Now, here's the list:

- The Cold Shoulder. The psycher is more cool toward you than toward others. No direct hostility need be involved. You feel left out or shut out. If you look to see if your tie is on backward or your slip is showing, BINGO! The implication is that there is something wrong with you.

- The MBA. You hear about the psycher's latest courses, whether in-class or correspondence. She quotes (or misquotes) Drucker, Peters, Napoleon, or some other management or military guru to back up her point. To add real finesse, she may quote some obscure professor and act as if her source is as famous as Lee Iacocca. ("What, you've never heard of *him?*") Implication: I'm more educated than you.

- The Walking Thesaurus. As with the MBA, the implication is that the psycher is smarter. He throws around technical terms or the latest acronyms as if he has total familiarity with the concepts they represent. He appears to nourish every fiber of his being with alphabet soup. Usually, though, he's just putting on the style; his real knowledge is much more shallow. Talk a good line, sound like an expert, and you will rarely be challenged. That's his ace in the hole!

- Latest Info. This person can quote more statistics and facts than the *Guinness Book of World Records,* and usually does. Implication: I've got all the facts and figures. How can you compete with that?

- New Gizmo. She has the latest computer (usually at home), the latest software, or the latest equipment, which, she hopes can convince you, will give her the advantage. "How can I compete with that?"

- Grand Old Man/Grand Dame. Seniority, position, and age fuel this one. They know the most because they've been there the longest. "Around here we do it *this* way," studs their conversation. Demeanor is often smug. Implication: You're still the new kid on the block (even if you've been there twenty years).

- The Name Dropper. He appears to have more connections than a zipper! He has "friends" in all the high places (never mind that they never consult him or invite him out to dinner).

- "Now, Now, Dearie." This is the typical put-down of the younger woman by the older man, but it can happen regardless of sex and age. It reflects a patronizing or condescending attitude by the psycher that assumes the psycher's superiority.

- Free Advice. This person is always passing out free information, whether you want it or not. Implication. You need my help, so I'm the superior one.

- Mr. Nice Guy. This person is so sweet, butter would melt in his (or her) mouth. Why, you'd feel guilty if you had to compete against such a pleasant person (so he hopes).

- "It Doesn't Matter, It's Only a Game." The person appears not to take the situation seriously, thus lulling you into complacency. In the back room, however, she's sharpening her knives.

- Watch Out! The psycher tells you all the potential pitfalls and what-ifs of your action and plans. You need a really clear head and good vision to combat this one and to sort out fact from fiction.

- Overdone Praise. This person praises you in order to make you feel self-conscious. Here's *real* finesse: you get praised for something you routinely do well. The implication is that she doesn't think you handle things very well. Your good performance of a job you routinely do well is treated as the exception to the rule.

- The Muhammad Ali Special. The psycher distracts you by provoking you to want to defeat her. She may even get you angry. This is a red herring. She wants to get you emotionally wrapped up with her. She becomes superior when you choose her as the "one to beat." You risk slipping up and getting off of the task at hand, and letting your anger take over.

- "That Won't Work." The psycher is great at spotting all the holes in the Swiss cheese. By picking apart your ideas he is feigning helpfulness while undermining your confidence—implying his superiority. He can see faults you have overlooked.

- The Better Way. A high-finesse variant of That Won't Work. The psycher actually suggests improvements to your plans or ideas. Sometimes these "improvements" may really be sabotage, setting you up for a fall later.

- The Protector. The psycher will front-run for you, protect you, get others to go easy on you—as if you needed protection. Implication: I'm strong, you're weak.

- The Topper. Whatever you've done, she's done one better. She's the ultimate one-upper. Implication: I'm better; you're second fiddle.

- Super Supervisor. The psycher continually looks over your shoulder and may or may not offer advice. Implication: You can't do it on your own; you need my overview.

While it may look like I've covered all possible forms of interaction under the rubric of psych-outs, this list is far from exhaustive. Actually, many of these behaviors may be honest attempts others are making to help you. You can turn everything into a psych-out if you let your imagination take over.

Again, your feelings are a touchstone. If the interaction feels comfortable, the behavior is probably honest. But if it feels uncertain, or you feel insecure, poke around for hidden motives. Also consider what the other person might have to gain by tripping you up. Has he or she done this to you before, or to other people?

Watch out! You can also waste a lot of time analyzing! Let your amount of analysis be relative to the severity or importance of the situation. Don't get hung up on the small stuff. Better that your energy be put into the task at hand than into shoring yourself up against a possible attack unless the situation truly warrants it.

## TRY THE "TWO POINTS ON A LINE" TECHNIQUE

Psychiatrist Rudolf Dreikurs suggested a very effective method for analyzing personality, which he called "Two points on a line.³"

The technique was designed to help people discover the unifying theme of a person's life-style.

All behavior serves a purpose, and each person is a holistic entity. That is, a person cannot be truly divided against himself, even though it may appear that way on the surface. Therefore, all of a person's actions hang together somehow and reflect a common theme. If you can discover it, that common theme will make sense of most of a person's actions, making the person much more understandable and predictable.

The method is simply this: select the two most divergent behaviors you observe in another person. To use a graph as an example, these become the "end points" of a "line." Then try to determine one underlying theme, motive, purpose, or goal that would explain both of these behaviors or tie them together in a meaningful way. Any behavior makes sense when you know that goal or purpose, which becomes the "line" along which the rest of the person's actions and attitudes can be "plotted."

Granted, you run the risk of oversimplification, and without clinical training it may be difficult for you to make an accurate assessment. Yet the method can be very helpful in figuring out some of the broader motivations of those with whom you interact. If you are a manager or supervisor, using this method can help you to develop a frame of reference for the basic motives or goals of those whom you must direct, and can give you an entrée into situations where you must counsel them to improve their behavior.

Let's consider Bill Williams from the last chapter. If we were to draw his "line," with A and Z being the two most divergent behaviors Williams exhibited, what would those actions be?

A?_____Z?
Williams' purpose/goal

Lets call them:

Benevolent support_____Active harrassment
Williams' Purpose/Goal

What common theme might tie them together? What underlying motive might be common to both of them? Think it through. Go back and review the case study and look for hints. Also look at what Sharon was doing. Inadvertently her behavior served as a trigger for Williams' shift from benevolent supporter to undercutter. Try to find the connecting link yourself before reading on.

In Williams' case, the common motive was power or control. When looking at the scenario in power terms, the role of benevolent supporter placed Williams in a one-up position. From a power perspective, the giver of help is above the recipient because he or she provides what the other lacks. (This is part of the attractiveness of the "helper" role for many people, and part of the reason that unsolicited help sometimes gets rejected—because not "doing it myself" often reflects a lack of sufficient power. In our society, we call it "weakness.")

At the time Williams was so benevolent, Sharon posed no threat. She was quiet and efficient. When she was promoted, however, she began to step out of her quiet, passive role. Williams saw his power being threatened and he retaliated to maintain the upper hand. At this point, Williams was thinking like a protectionist, motivated by fear of loss of influence, and he began to compete in a destructive manner. Ultimately such maneuvers backfire: Williams' credibility was destroyed, not Sharon's.

Williams shows another feature of the Competitive Personality, by the way. He was fine until *he perceived* he was crossed. This is usually true, which often makes the underlying competitiveness hard to detect unless you are aware of the signals described here and in the preceding chapter. Even then it can be difficult. That's where the "two points on a line" technique can be most helpful—when you're feeling difficult vibes but can't put your finger on what's going on.

Here's another hint: many behaviors are motivated by their apparent opposite. Altruism is sometimes motivated by desire for power or recognition. Shy behavior is often motivated by a desire to be the center of attention, and possibly also for power. How can this be, you ask, when shy people often work hard to avoid attention? To discover the motive, look at the end result of the behavior itself, not at what people say or think. Isn't it often true that their avoidance methods actually draw attention to them?

Deanne, a pretty sixteen-year-old, was painfully shy. In groups she spoke not a word, sitting mutely on the sidelines while everyone else discussed the issues at hand. Then the room would fall silent and all eyes would fall on Deanne. Someone would ask her opinion. The question was met with defiant silence. She became the center, and she could wield the power. The others would then try to pry an answer out of her. This is the same Deanne who would repeatedly ask her mother which color blouse to wear with such and such skirt, and then when mother would give an opinion, would loudly, criticize her mother for such a stupid choice. Deanne set up power struggles in which she could be the center of attention and be in control.

Not all underlying motives are bad, of course. After all, we all operate according to private motives all the time. Power, attention, recognition, and most other motives are basically neutral. *How* they are expressed is the key. They can be used for useful or hurtful purposes, depending on the mind-set and goals of the user.

Now try another case, one from *your* experience. Is there someone you work with, perhaps, whose behavior confuses you? Here are the steps to the method:

1. Identify the two most opposite behaviors you have observed in that person.

2. Look for a common, underlying motive or theme that could explain both behaviors equally. Often one of the behaviors will be the open, raw manifestation of the motive, and the other behavior will be a veiled or hidden expression of it, as in Williams' case. There may be more than one motive that can satisfy both behaviors.

3. Look also at the *context* in which these behaviors occur. This can provide a useful prediction as to what stimuli will trigger the behavior in question.

Here are some common underlying motives or goals, including those in table 5-1. They are not mutually exclusive, and many of them can promote positive as well as negative behaviors.

power

recognition, status

attention

security, protection, safety

revenge

selfishness

jealousy

control (either "I will be in charge" or "You can't control me"—
two sides of the same coin!)

accumulating wealth (this is often a variant of power)

excitement

self-actualization

Being important (this is often a variant of power)

being on top

avoidance of responsibility, Display of inadequacy ("I'll get you
to leave me alone by showing you I can't handle it")

You may have noticed that love, cooperation, and union with
others are not on the list. These motives, when they are truly honest, do not generally lead to conflicting behaviors and therefore
would not require this analysis. When positive behaviors show up
at one end of your line, however, and a negative behavior shows
up at the other end, it's a good guess that some deception is afoot!
Here's your line; give it a try.

Behavior_____Polar Opposite Behavior
Common Motive

How did you make out? If you got stuck, don't worry. It's often
hard at first to analyze subtle behaviors, even when you know some
of the signs to look for. With practice you'll be able to find the
common motive more easily.

Once you've figured out who your competitors are and what
they're up to, your main task is to cope with them. How do you
respond to the competition you face? Check out the next chapter?

# Notes

1. Dinkmeyer, D. and McKay, G. D. *Systematic Training for Effective Parenting: Parents' Handbook.* Circle Pines Minnesota: American Guidance Service, 1976, 14
2. Tutko, T. and Tosi, U. *Sports Psyching.* Los Angeles: J. P. Tarcher/St. Martins, 1976, 169–180
3. Dreikurs, R. *"The holistic approach: Two points on a line."* In Education, Guidance, Psychodynamics, Chicago: Alfred Adler Institute, 1966, 18–24

# 6

# Dealing with the Competitive Personality

NUMEROUS books and articles have appeared recently about how to deal with difficult people. A "difficult person" is one whose actions cause repeated problems.

Most of these publications identify and label numerous "types" of difficult people. R. M. Bramson[1] writes about Complainers, Super-Agreeables, and Negativists, among others. Cutting the pie another way, Eric Berne, in his classic, *Games People Play,* characterizes numerous maneuvers of difficult people, such as "Wooden Leg," "Now I've Got You—You Son of a Bitch," and "Rapo."

Whether you're looking at types of people or types of negative games, it helps to remember that the people who cause chronic problems are all cut of the same cloth, and are variations on the same theme: they all demonstrate Disorders of Competition. Perhaps more precisely, they manifest Disorders of Cooperation because *this* is the activity that is so hard for them to engage in. In short, they all show aspects of the Competitive Personality.

It is beyond our scope to type people and describe how to deal with each type. The topical reading list at the end of the book will guide you to this information. Here we will simply explore basic guidelines for handling the Competitive Personality and hidden or negative competitiveness. These general guidelines will help you regardless of the type of person or behavior you are dealing with.

There are many ways people typically respond to competition. Here are a few of the common ones:

The Rhinoceros. He snorts and charges headlong into his opponent, kicking up a lot of dust and often leaving incredible damage in his wake. Unfortunately the rhino is a shortsighted animal who doesn't often see clearly what he's charging. He is also easily and unnecessarily provoked.

The Toy Poodle. We once had a little chocolate poodle named Muffin. He always greeted our guests at the door. But if someone of whom he was afraid came, he'd back up down the entrance hall, barking as he went. In the dog-eat-dog world of business, the "toy poodles" often act the same way, retreating from a confrontation or a competitive situation.

The Fish. The poor, unsuspecting fish! She bites into the bait precisely because she doesn't see the hook. Then, when she gets hooked, she flip-flops, trying to free herself. If she gets hooked well, she stays hooked, and the rest is history.

The Mole. At the first sign of threat, Br'er Mole goes underground, digging elaborate tunnels, destroying plant roots, and anything in his way. He undermines the garden making the ground above him unstable, even though you rarely see him. He's a difficult pest to catch. The mole regards practically everyone as a hidden competitor and will readily subvert the organization.

The Fox. When the fox sniffs out a competitive ploy, she goes to town! She uses all her wiles and cleverness to compete in return. She can be more open about it than the mole, sometimes making a direct advance. She thinks she's being clever, but she's actually a sucker getting hooked into competing.

The Elephant. Where does a ten-ton elephant go for a walk? Anywhere he wants! The elephant approach is the retreat to power. You may recall the old jungle movies where, when the natives get in the way, the elephant calmly stomps on them. This person uses power or a position of authority to squash the competition. This is a retreat because it is usually a first response to opposition, lacking planning and creativity, and generally leading to problems later. In the corporate jungle, stomped natives usually turn into moles.

All of these approaches to coping with competition have their drawbacks, as you can see. The common drawback is that they simply don't work! While some may achieve short-term results, they rarely solve the real problem.

The response that holds the greatest hope of success is that of the Strategist.

---

# Your Action Plan

Here's how you, as a Strategist, can cope with the competition you face. There are as many personal ways to cope with negative competition as there are competitive situations that need correcting. It is impossible to catalog all your options. Here are general principles that will help you to determine your specific tactics for dealing with the competition you face.

## DISCOVER WHAT'S GOING ON

You can't fight, or fix, what you can't see. If you feel uncomfortable, if you suspect a problem, sort it out. Trust your gut reaction, look for psych-outs, use the "two points on a line" technique. Look also for what situations, actions, or people trigger this competitive behavior. Take time to watch carefully what goes on day by day and analyze what you observe.

Remember that once you have determined that someone is competing with you, it makes their words and actions suspect, at least in the arena in which the person is competing. Also, don't overlook jealousy as a possible motive for the person's competitive behavior.

Look, too, at the surrounding issues. Check out the big picture, the total political scene in the company. Political maneuvers are rarely as all-encompasing when seen from above as when you're immersed in the political jungle itself. Tap into the office grapevine, get to know what alliances exist and who the key players are. Also, remember that the big picture is not only broad, but long. Find out your organization's future objectives, several years out. Most people do their job day-to-day, without analyzing these issues. Your having this information will help you set priorities and give you a distinct advantage. In terms of protecting yourself, coping with your competitors, and getting ahead.

One word of warning: look out for your own bias. If you're in a high-pressure situation, or feeling insecurity because your job is on the line or for some other reason, it's easy to become like the trigger-happy hunter who shoots at everything that moves. Don't make every shadow into a tiger. Insecurity clouds our vision. Be careful not to assume Competitive Personalities where they don't exist. The last thing you need to develop is paranoia. Remember, the ultimate goal is cooperation and contribution, not more suspicion. The more difficult your situation, the more careful and clearheaded you need to be in sorting fact from fiction. Like a good physician, don't apply the diagnosis until you have sure signs of an illness. Even then, check again. If you need to, check out your ideas with a trusted friend or coworker before drawing firm conclusions.

## CONSIDER THE SOURCE

Remember competitors' thinking patterns. Just because you may be the target doesn't mean that you're fully "at fault." While you may initially feel hurt or furious, don't jump to conclusions or react before sorting things out. The competitor may be acting out of his or her own bias or in response to a misperceived threat. It can help soothe the pain if you realize that, like beauty, misbehavior is often in the eyes of the beholder. Nonetheless the situation must be handled.

Before dealing with the situation, look to see what there is about you that may be triggering the reaction. Three things on your part may set someone else's competitiveness in motion: (a) your actions, regardless of how benign, (b) your image, how you dress, walk, and come across, and (c) your very presence, which would include sex, race, and ethnic origin. Check these out systematically. Start with your behavior. Consider the reactions you've been getting lately. Is there a realistic connection between your action and the other person's reaction? If so, you may have identified the crux of the problem. But even then it pays also to consider your image and your presence. If you can't link up your actions to the competitive reaction, even with the help of a trusted colleague or mentor, then the root of the problem is deeper.

Next, analyze your image. This includes not only your looks but also the impression you give others about your personality, e.g., assertive vs aggressive vs submissive. At this point, it pays to check out how well your image fits with the prevailing corporate culture. If you're out of step here it will affect how you're viewed and treated. How much you need to bring your image in line, and how much this spells "compromise" or "capitulation" to you is a very individual matter, but if you have an image problem, ignoring it can undercut your future.

Even if your image fits the prevailing culture, it still may provoke antipathy on the part of a Competitive Personality. If this is so, then the problem must likely rest with your detractor and you and he or she need to work it out.

If your actions and image are not the problem, you may be in a real bind. If it's your very presence that's causing the problem, then you're dealing clearly with your competitor's fears or prejudices. If sex, race, or ethnic origin are involved, you might have a case for harassment. All too often, however, people get flak just for being there. This is particularly true if they are highly qualified, productive, and assertive. Many managers, subordinates, and colleagues don't know how to work with a high producer, but they won't admit it.

When you analyze the issue of your presence, don't forget to consider the context. If you're new, and especially if you came into a situation during a merger, reorganization, shake-up, or rumors of same, the reaction of your competitor may become wholly understandable. If this is the case, it gives you a starting point in confronting the issue. If there is no contextual reason for your competitor's reaction, your situation is tougher.

## PREPARE YOURSELF MENTALLY

Gaining perspective and emotional distance is critical, especially in coping with hidden competition. These power games are played at the emotional level, and the goal, as stated earlier, is to undermine you, or get you hooked into competing. Steering clear of the emotional hook requires clear vision in discerning the barb embedded in the bait. That's why the recognition-analysis strategies are so important. Only when you can see the big picture, putting the pieces in context, can you be ready to disengage your emotions.

The next step in breaking free is to sort the wheat from the chaff. Determine what part of your daily experience is actual business and what is political gamesmanship, recognizing that office politics *is* a game, regardless of the fact that how the game is played may have important consequences. Treating it as a game, like chess, can help you to free up your ego. Believe that your worth as a person is a given, not dependent on others' approval, or on how well you performed today, or on the political climate of your organization. When your ego isn't bound up in the game, you have a broader range of options, including not to play.

Mental preparation also includes determining your stand. On what issues will you give in; on which ones will you stand firm, and refuse to negotiate? You also need to examine your ethics and values. Particularly important are your values about competing and cooperating. Are they crystal clear? At what point would you feel compromised if you got involved in what is going on around you? Clear values and ethical principles can be a necessary, welcome beacon on an often cloudy and stormy sea. Refuse to compromise what is important to you, and refuse to play negative games. Remember, getting hooked is something you can choose to avoid. So is allowing yourself to engage in a win-lose situation. Always look for the win-win option.

When preparing mentally for coping with competition, don't forget to hone your sense of humor. It can strengthen your armor when you're called upon to joust in the corporate fiefdom. A good laugh always helps to clear up your perspective when it gets clouded by work a day pressures. Humor protects you best when it's philosophical, recognizing that life itself is the joke, and allowing you to see the paradoxes of power jockeying and office politics as funny in and of themselves. Humor can hurt you—and your career—if you crack jokes at any individual's expense or put others down with it. Others will rightly view that style of humor as a feeble attempt to undercut the organization. They will laugh with you outwardly, but inwardly they will come to distrust you. After all, they wonder, "When will I become the next target?"

Humorist Walter "Buzz" O'Connell [3] calls "cosmic" humor—the philosophical type—humor's highest level. Cosmic humor is the art of bringing all existence into perspective, and recognizing that much of life is indeed a paradox, to be enjoyed as such. For example, we (hopefully) act every day as if whatever we do is of vital importance, yet we recognize that when our frail bodies are placed under the sod, life will go on, the earth will spin on its axis, getting along very well without us.

Cosmic humor is beautifully dangerous! When I fully came to grasp this paradox, it caught me up short. It caused me to assess the meaning of my activities in a much broader way, both in terms of breadth and direction. Was I doing anything that would *last?* Because of my new perspective, my life could never be the same. If you're like me, once you've faced the issue of the ultimate meaning of your life and activities, you'll find you've little time for jousting or jealousy. After all, work, like life, is too important to be taken too seriously.

No discussion of mental preparation can be complete without addressing mental self-programming and visualization. These skills are absolutely vital for the Healthy Competitor. Check the Resource List at the back of the book under "Mental Self-Programming" for recommended training materials. Audio cassette training is especially helpful for these kinds of skills.

## Solidify Your Own Position

This positive move is dealt with at great length throughout the rest of this book. Suffice it to say here, however, that you cannot build a tower of strength when you use as your foundation the bodies of your opponents. Build rather on your own strength and merit.

## Where Possible, Sidestep

Many political issues are red herrings, and the proper response is to ignore them. When someone tries to besmirch your character, ignoring it is often the best move. While countering the gibe is tempting, to do so may actually harm you. It might suggest that, if you take it seriously enough to defend yourself or otherwise respond, the false accusation must contain some truth.

Responding to competitive ploys wastes energy and time. Having an appropriate perspective and having developed a solid personal position may make countering unnecessary. Only you can determine if the energy required by a counter move is worth spending.

It often is, but before acting in a given situation, figure out whether the issue can be sidestepped. Many times your opponent will hang himself if you leave him alone.

## WHERE NECESSARY, CONFRONT

Problems of competitiveness rarely disappear on their own. If they cannot be sidestepped, they must be actively dealt with. Negative competitive employees are making mischief, regardless of how they justify their behavior. To that degree, they are undermining your company and thus cannot continue. How you procede, however, will depend on what triggers set the situation in motion, and the results of your analysis to this point.

Confrontation brings the issues out in the open. No longer can people hide behind thinly veiled excuses. Confrontation lets the game player know that *you* know what's going on. Psychiatrist Alfred Adler called this, "spitting in the soup." It's like the old boarding school trick of spitting in your neighbor's soup at meal time; the soup can still be eaten, but who would want to? This is what happens when a hidden ploy is unveiled; it can never work the same way again, and can never have the same meaning or payoff for the perpetrator.

Negatively competitive issues need to be talked out. Any direct confrontation will probably be met with defensiveness, however. In approaching negative competitors, you need to get your own ego out of the picture. Forget about "being right" or "getting in the last word." At this point the goal is to calm fears and bring in reason to reduce irrationality.

If you are approaching your boss who is the competitive one, you might present the discussion as if you are the one who might need to make a change, taking a low profile. This approach can also work for dealing with coworkers and subordinates. For example: "Mr. _____, I have a concern. I may be wrong, but I feel that there is a kind of coolness between us. I'm not sure what it's about, but I'd like to correct it if I can."

If the existing situation (such as a merger) is part of the problem, you might open this way: "Mr. , I know that there's a lot of pressure and uncertainty around here right now, especially with the merger that's about to take place. I'm concerned that this tension might be interfering with relations here in the office. I'd like to do what I can toward resolving it." From these openings, you can narrow down to the specifics.

Most negatively competitive people, and Competitive Personalities in particular, despite their bravado, are defensive and overly ego-involved. That's where the irrationality in their reactions comes from. Be careful, therefore, to preserve their ego and dignity. While this is just good human relations, it is especially important here, where a little, off-hand remark on your part may trigger an attack.

From your opening gambit and discussion, move toward negotiating an action plan that will attempt to solve the problem. Attempt to clarify the issues at the behavioral level—specific and definable actions—that are causing the problem. Show empathy and understanding, but keep the discussion behavior-based. Attempting to discuss attitudes is an invitation to warfare, and a possible EEO grievance. If you can work out a plan, monitor it to see that it stays in motion. Sharon's case at the end of this chapter is an example of this approach.

When you're the boss you have more control over the situation. Your goal should be to salvage and win the loyalty of recalcitrant employees. Try to make allies out of enemies whenever possible, helping them to channel their competitive drive in positive, cooperative directions for everyone's good. Here are some tips for turning competition around. They are offered here in the context of coping with competition, but they will be elaborated later in this book.

- Provide background training on Healthy Competition and positive cooperation. These values and behaviors will not evolve on their own, they must be nurtured.

- Confront the behavior directly, firmly, but diplomatically, emphasizing the positive value of the employee. This blows his cover, and shows him that his negative competition is actually hindering his advancement.

- Help her to establish a plan for improvement and monitor the plan.

- Attempt to discover competitive employees' personal goals and help them to redefine or align their goals with company goals.

These people want power. Can you show them that by "joining forces" with the overall company they can meet their goals faster, easier?

- Look for unique positive strengths in these employees and explore with them ways in which these strengths can be used and recognized.

- Emphasize, structure in, and reward teamwork wherever possible. Raise more Pigs (Positive interdependency Groups, that is)! See chapter 15 for details.

- Set a date to meet again to evaluate progress. Setting the date in two weeks to a month shows urgency and that you mean business.

- If this doesn't work, insist the employee get personal counseling or be terminated. (Some cases of personal competitiveness are so ingrained that counseling or psychotherapy is essential for improvement.)

- Above all, model healthy competitive and cooperative behaviors yourself, and be totally committed to the growth and encouragement process. Otherwise, you'll be seen as a phony.

# A Case Example

Remember Sharon? And Mr. Williams, her boss, who was a perfect example of a Competitive Personality? What should she have done to defuse the situation?

An outside career coach helped Sharon to see what her problem with Williams actually was, and she was advised to confront the issue on the basis of her "confusion as to what went wrong" between her and Williams. Her initial attempt was met with denial, as her coach told her she could expect.

She then cited, in as nonjudgmental a way as possible, some specific incidents of Williams' anger and non-follow-through. He hemmed and hawed—he was caught dead to rights, without an explanation. She pressed further, whereupon he responded that he thought her ideas were "insufficiently thought through" and "wouldn't fit in."

"If that's so," replied Sharon, "why is it that you appear to be attacking me personally?" Williams was sweating at this point. He shrugged it off as "a lot of stress right now" and never did own up to his competitiveness.

Wisely, Sharon preserved Williams' ego. She pinned him to the floor with her comment about a personal attack, but let him back up by accepting his stress excuse, using that comment as a springboard for working out a plan. She reiterated that "the *last* thing I want is to usurp your authority or position. Perhaps I could run future ideas through you first and we could work them out together."

This was Sharon's attempt to win Williams over, to defuse the competition and build an ally out of a former enemy. She played her hand very carefully, and stayed judiciously wary of Williams. Williams was indirectly "put on notice" by Sharon's meeting that she would not hesitate to confront him again if he began to violate their agreement to collaborate. Once Williams saw that Sharon would confront him directly, he believed that Sharon would go over his head if he stepped out of line.

In time, the edge between them softened. After they struck a bargain, an emotional load was lifted from both their shoulders and they could interact more freely. Note that Williams' basic competitiveness was never explicitly mentioned; that wasn't necessary. A behavioral solution, the agreement to collaborate on future ideas, set the ground rules for their relationship.

Some would think that Sharon was "weak" by not pressing Williams to the limit. Actually her low-profile solution was a long-term gain. While they never became true friends, they could at least work in harmony. Forcing Williams' hand would have been a sweet, retaliative, short-term victory, but ultimately would have lost Sharon the war.

Here's a general principle: your opportunity for advancement will be curtailed to the degree that your superiors see you as a threat. Assuming you do your job well, how they perceive you and how they advance you will depend on three additional things:

1. The degree of your boss's mediocrity, insecurity, and need to play C.Y.A. ("cover your anatomy")

2. How you handle the competitive pressure you face

3. The "competition" at your level.

Up to this point we have zeroed in on coping and self-protection methods. The balance of this book will spell out the rationale and strategies for healthy competition and cooperation which, when applied, will fortify you more.

Your ultimate goal is not to fight back, but to rise above.

# Notes

1. Bramson, R. M. *Coping with difficult people*. Garden City: Anchor Press/ Doubleday, 1981.
2. Berne, E. *Games people play*. New York: Grove Press, 1964.
3. O'Connell, W. Personal communication.

# 7

# How to Compete and Really Win

Down through the annals of time, there has been—and always will be—only one way to determine whether you win or lose. What do you think that way is?

Think about it. The answer is not as obvious as it might first appear. We'll discuss the answer, but first a story.

A young man decided that he wanted to be a marathon runner. He was in his early twenties, was physically fit but had no prior running experience. Neither had he been lifting weights or working out in a gym, although he stayed physically active and strong through his factory job.

He wanted to run in a major city marathon. He got checked by his doctor and was found to be fit. He hired a running coach to work with his feet, and he hired me to work with his head for quick peak performance. There was only one problem. He decided to be a runner when the marathon was only six weeks away.

By the fourth week he was running thirteen miles evey other day. His feet, form, and head were all in gear. On the day of the marathon, he was psyched up and totally prepared. He ran his best.

The next week he burst through my office door yelling, "I won! I won!" Knowing who the marathon winners actually were, I asked, "Won what?" "The marathon!", he shouted back, excited and out of breath. "Come on", I told him, "Your performance was miraculous, but you didn't get a prize!" "Oh, I didn't *win!* I finished in the second thousand, but I finished without stopping or quitting. I didn't hit the 'wall,' and I met my goal. That's what I meant when I said I won."

Now, do you know what the answer is to the opening question?

In the 1984 Olympics, a swimmer won the gold medal, but when interviewed, he cried and was very bitter. The medal was meaningless, because he had a private goal which he didn't meet.

Now you know. The one way to determine whether you win or lose is how *you define* winning and losing. Winning and losing is totally subjective. It does not depend on the outcome of any particular contest. As you can see from the examples I just cited, what counts for your self-definition as a winner or loser is not the actual final standing but what you make of your performance, how you interpret it.

# What Winning Means

My friend has a bumper sticker that reads: The U.S. Special Olympics—A World of Winners. And so it is in life—or at least it can be. The Healthy Competitor knows this intuitively, while the traditional competitor has never figured it out. The Healthy Competitor can modify his or her attitudes and definition of winning and losing, while the traditional competitor is more "contest-bound" in his or her thinking.

While my wife was on the phone to a distant friend, my son walked in from playing a baseball game. My wife put him on the phone to say "Hi," whereupon the first words out of the friend's mouth were, "Did you win?" So totally immersed are we in winning and losing that we need to look very carefully at what "winning" in the traditional sense means to us—and does to us—as a stepping stone to figuring out the new model of healthy competition.

Can you think of anyone who doesn't enjoy winning? I sure can't. While some may feel embarrassed by the public display they may get as a winner, and some may feel bad if they win unfairly, the inner satisfaction and ego boost we get when we win brings genuine pleasure. We all *want* to win. But do we all *have* to win, in order to feel good about ourselves, to validate ourselves? Again, this is a very individual matter. Let's look at winning in terms of beating an opponent, or winning a competition of some sort.

What traditionally happens when we win? We feel good. Perhaps we feel gooooood! Our adrenaline might be up, there's a thrill, moreso to the degree that the contest was difficult and challenging.

But then what happens? The glory quickly fades, and it's back to business as usual . . . or is it? We might be hooked—we might try harder the next time, the next win might be even more important. We've won one game, we've got to win the next to keep the record rolling. As each contest becomes more important, the pressure mounts, and the pleasure diminishes. Yet for many of us, competing and winning is like a drug, we get hooked on the winning high and feel compelled to go back for more.

Something else also happens. Not only do we incur others' respect, we also incur their envy. We become the target, the one to beat. Or else others feel inferior by comparison. Those who envy us don't wish us well; they secretly pray for our defeat, and may even work to bring that defeat about. At least they can enjoy catching us in our mistakes. Don't get me wrong. It doesn't always happen this way, but it so often does that it's worth mentioning.

But something else also goes on, insidiously, behind the scenes. The more we win, in the traditional sense, the more we *need* to win. The glory quickly fades and the win is good only for one time around. The next time the prize is again up for grabs. There is no such thing as a continuous win. Sooner or later a challenger will come along who can beat us, unless like some champion prize-fighters, we retire first. We can never rest on our laurels, we've got to keep at it harder and harder to keep ahead of increasingly stiff competition.

What emotion underlies traditional competition? Fear! The more we win, the more we need to win, the more afraid we become. Afraid to lose. Afraid to fail. Afraid of losing face in front of our friends, colleagues, superiors, even our families.

Paradoxically, this fear of failure is linked to the fear of success. The higher a person rises in the status hierarchy, or in the organization, the more public, the more weighty, the more risky her every action becomes. This catches the traditional competitor in a double bind: she is afraid to stand still, and she is afraid to move. She has to continue to try to get ahead, to win, but in each subsequent play the stakes get higher. Gone is the pleasure in competing once we entrap ourselves on this vicious treadmill.

So the more we "win," the more vulnerable we actually become. We fall prey not only to stiffer and more numerous competitors, but also to our own inner pressures and stress, which competition increases, and to the "law of averages."

You see, in traditional competition, we can't keep winning forever, but in healthy competition, we can!

This is a strange paradox, but the key to the riddle goes back to the opening question of this chapter: How do you define winning and losing?

# The New Method of Competition

Healthy competition has its roots in an entirely different base than traditional competition. Healthy competition—the new model—bears little resemblance to the cutthroat methods we currently practice. Healthy competition is not just a strategy or a set of actions. Nor has it much to do with glad-handed "good sportsmanship" (which is often just a euphemism for gracious losing). Rather, *healthy competition is a value system, a way of life.* It is the purpose of this chapter to explain the new model and to make these differences clear.

Let's compare the traditional model with the new model on several dimensions. Box 7-1 summarizes this comparison.

### COMPETITIVE GOAL: SUPERIORITY VS SIGNIFICANCE

Winning traditionally means beating the opponent. Carry that to its ultimate conclusions and you have war! The goal is to be above others, to be superior in a comparative sense. But winning in this sense is an external goal, dependent not only on what you do but also on the actions of your opponents. This puts the outcome out of your direct control. That's why people cheat—to increase their degree of control over the outcome. (The nature of traditional competition actually encourages cheating, by the way, in spite of our social lip service against it.) This lack of control over the final outcome adds to the personal pressure and stress one feels, especially as the stakes for winning and losing get higher.

Box 7-1

| MODELS OF COMPETITION | | |
|---|---|---|
| *Current Model Operating in Society* | | *New Model of Healthy Competition* |
| 1. *STRIVES FOR: SUPERIORITY*<br>Goal: winning<br>elite (status, one-up)<br>self-interest | vs | *SIGNIFICANCE*<br>Goal: achieving, contributing<br>excellent (status comes naturally)<br>group interest and self-interest |
| 2. *RELATIONSHIPS: WIN-LOSE*<br>power over, dominance<br>competitive<br>individualistic | vs | *WIN-WIN*<br>power through positive influence<br>cooperative<br>community |
| 3. *ENERGY DISBURSIVE*<br>center of gravity outside<br>lack of inner core<br>others set the pace<br>illusion of freedom<br>minds others' business<br>external control | vs | *ENERGY INTENSIVE*<br>center of gravity within<br>strong inner core<br>sets own pace<br>real freedom<br>minds own business<br>internal control |
| 4. *CONFORMITY* | vs | *UNIQUENESS* |
| 5. *EGO-INVESTED, SELF-AWARE*<br>worth relative, based on<br>  performance and approval<br>uses comparison to measure worth<br>work = problem (place where<br>  worth is tested) | vs | *EGO-FREE, AWARE*<br>worth absolute, given<br><br>uses comparison to learn and grow<br>work = opportunity (place of<br>  contribution) |
| 6. *"HOW AM I DOING?"* | vs | *"WHAT AM I DOING?"* |
| 7. *SATISFACTION: OUTCOME* | vs | *PROCESS* |
| 8. *ANGER (internal or expressed)* | vs | *CALMNESS* |
| 9. *STRUGGLE, IMPATIENCE* | vs | *FLOW, PATIENCE* |
| 10. *PSYCHOLOGICALLY SOFT*<br>feels insecure | vs | *PSYCHOLOGICALLY HARDY*<br>feels secure |
| 11. *TRADITIONAL WINNING*<br>excludes people<br>overcomes others | vs | *REAL, TRUE WINNING*<br>includes people<br>enables others |
| 12. *WORLD VIEW: SCARCITY* | vs | *ABUNDANCE* |

How well does this goal of beating others motivate peak performance? Only up to a point. My friend and mentor, Dr. Lars-Eric Unestahl, heads up the Institute of Sport Psychology at Orebro University in Orebro, Sweden. In this position, and also privately, he has provided mental training to thousands of professional and world-class amateur athletes over the years. Part of his program focuses on goal definition, and here he found interesting results.

When an athlete first enters Unestahl's program, he or she is asked what his or her goals are. Usually the athlete will say, "To beat so-and-so in the next competition." The athlete is then asked to visualize that goal. What happens? His or her performance improves—for about two weeks or so, and then it plateaus. As the athlete learns to shift the goal—focus away from beating others to a personal, noncompetitive standard for his or her own performance, such as "running the mile in 3.5 minutes"—performance improves even more, and continues to improve.[1]

As these findings indicate, there is a curvilinear relationship between performance and competitive goals. Performance in the service of a competitive goal (beating someone else) will rise to an optimum point. If the person concentrates too much on that goal, his or her performance will actually begin to worsen. Why this happens will be explained later when we discuss energy.

The traditional competitor, then, in attempting to one-up others, is looking for elite status. His interest is in himself, often at the expense of the opponent. While you may be engaged in a "friendly" competition, the very nature of traditional competition puts you at odds with your opponent. After all, you're trying to beat him. You would not want to give him any advantage. Your behavior and his are negatively linked. If you help him, you hurt your chances of winning. So much for "friendly competition." Down deep there really is no such thing.

The Healthy Competitor, on the other hand, strives for *significance*. He or she realizes that achieving excellence is more important than winning. All you must do to win is to edge out the opponent. You don't necessarily have to be excellent to do that. Therefore winning and excellence *sometimes* have very little in common.

In fact, people who focus primarily on winning will often stop when they think they've done enough to beat all comers. A second-grader was reading books for a county-wide school read-a-thon. He quit after reading forty seven books because he figured he was way ahead, even though he had several weeks until the contest was over. On awards day he was shocked into tears because he didn't win. Someone else read sixty seven books! The story of "The Tortoise and the Hare" has the same implication.

Of course, the Healthy Competitor wants to win and will work very hard and smart. But *how* he or she wins is of vital importance. His or her key emphasis in on achieving a standard of excellence. This is an internal goal, unlike winning. No other persons need to be involved in the perception of the goal, although they will be involved in the competition itself. The Healthy Competitor recognizes a vital truth: go for excellence, for achievement, make a lasting contribution, and the winning will take care of itself.

This is profound, but traditional competitors will consider it naive. That's because they are unwilling or unable to *trust* this principle. They are so busy struggling that they can't go with the flow of the full power of their resources. Shame on them, for they accomplish what they do in spite of themselves, whereas the Healthy Competitor maximizes his or her potential in efficient channels.

Are you beginning to see that the new model of competition is more "streamlined"? The Healthy Competitor has the edge in part because he or she has much less competitive stress and worry than the traditional competitor. This gives him or her much more energy for the task at hand.

When excellence is achieved and recognized, your status will come naturally. You will be recognized for your strength of character and/or the quality of your work. These factors have an intrinsic value about them, and are based on a rock-hard foundation upon which one can continually build. One-upmanship forms of status are, by definition, extrinsic. They depend not only on you, but also on how fa your competitors climb on the ladder relative to you. Hence these forms of status are always up for grabs, which creates anxiety. The Healthy Competitor builds a castle, while the traditional competitor plays King of the Hill!

## RELATIONSHIPS: WIN-LOSE VS WIN-WIN

The traditional competitor views the world much as the Competitive Personality does, although she may not be as extreme or as myopic in her vision. Nevertheless, the me-versus-thee mentality pervades her approach to competing. "After all, this is a contest," she thinks. "There can only be one winner, and it had better be me!"

If one's goal is to "win"—to beat the opponent—then a win-lose approach to competing follows naturally. Unfortunately, that mentality prevails wherever that person perceives a contest, whether a contest is really there or not. Remember, this is one of the pitfalls of highly competitive people: they tend to see a contest where one was never intended to be. I remember in college taking a microbiology lab exam. We came into the room and there were thirty microscopes all set up with specimens we had to identify. We were to proceed in order from station 1 through 30 and write down our responses. The student ahead of me would look at the specimen, and before moving on, spin the focus knob to make the image blurry for me, so I'd lose time having to refocus the microscope.

While not all win-lose behavior is unethical, it is often carried out at other people's expense. In a win-lose situation others are opponents by definition, and we discussed in an earlier chapter what happens then. The problem this creates for the traditional competitor is that he now must unavoidably fight the battle on two fronts, the first being to win at the task at hand, and the second being to keep the wolves at bay. How fast can you climb a ladder when you've got to spend time stomping on the hands or kicking the head of the person beneath you?

Which brings us to the issue of power. All human interaction can be interpreted in terms of power. The traditional competitor views power as a commodity, which she often feels is in short supply. Since others are opponents, her orientation is one of power-over: who is the boss? who's in control? She assumes that others want to wrest her power from her. While this may not have been a true perception at first, if she manages her power poorly she can actually create the opposition she wishes to avoid. Again, this is a vertical power dimension, over under. Dominance is the theme, and King of the Hill is the game, whether it is played openly or in veiled or hidden fashion. The corporate world is so full of power lords that I don't need to give you an example here; you see plenty of them firsthand every day.

Since they view power as a limited commodity and figure that their "opponents" are trying to unseat them, traditional competitors must engage in continuous power jockeying in order to maintain position. But even the best jockeys, if they had to remain in the saddle eight hours a day, would get saddle-sore—one more self-induced competitive stress.

Also, a me-versus-thee outlook promotes individualism, which, in turn, fosters the me-versus-thee outlook even more. People with this point of view, regard cooperation with suspicion lest a team member try to take over the lead or gain undue advantage.

The Healthy Competitor understands the social-embeddedness of humankind and capitalizes on it. She knows that support freely won is true power, while support that is mandated is an illusion. The Healthy Competitor, then, is a solid cooperator, a team player. Because she values and cares about others and their needs for their own sake, she looks for win-win solutions to problems. She would rather negotiate than mandate, and her leadership style is democratic rather than autocratic.

All competition is a show of strength. The question is which kind? Take one pencil in hand and break it. It snaps easily. Breaking two pencils is harder. Try to break a bundle of ten pencils. The Healthy Competitor knows that the greatest power in relationships, as well as in nature itself, exists in harmony.

The Healthy Competitor is committed to people power and sees people as the greatest resource. This power orientation, then, is power through positive influence. Is this "manipulation?" You bet it is! But it's of a much different nature than we normally think of when we use the term.

## ENERGY: DISBURSIVE VS INTENSIVE

We have only so much energy. Where are we investing it? It just makes sense that if we channel it in one main direction we will pack more wallop than if our energy is going in two or more directions at once.

We said earlier that traditional "winning" is an external goal, and that the traditional competitor often finds himself fighting his battle on two fronts. This is energy disbursive. There is less energy, less creativity, less impact when your energy is divided. You just don't have as much to put toward the task at hand. This adds to the competitive pressure and gives the Healthy Competitor an advantage. Why is the traditional competitor's energy divided? Where does it go?

First, some energy goes into worry and concern, particularly that others are better and will get ahead. Remember that traditional competition is built on comparison! In fact, there is the competition comparison cycle. You can't have competition without comparison. Once we start to compare, we often begin to feel competitive, with jealous feelings and rivalrous acts. Why? Because we want to be on top, yet when we compare, we often put others' heads higher than our own. This breeds more comparison and the cycle continues. It becomes a real problem when we start to compare our weaknesses to others' strengths. Most of us do this quite readily and regularly, but we think we're just checking to see where we are or how well we're doing relative to others.

To the degree that we need to see how others are doing in order to feel good about ourselves, we weaken our self-esteem and our "inner core," that complex of feelings and values that make up our self-concept and self-worth. Once we subject that inner core to comparison, we put our emotional center of gravity outside ourselves.

If we have a solid inner core and a firm, well-defined self-concept, the little tilts of life won't throw us. We'll bounce back because our emotional center of gravity is well grounded in a solid self-definition and self-reliance.

The more we compare, the more we place our center of gravity outside ourselves, the less we listen to our own inner voices, and the more we lean on and depend on others for approval in certain areas of life. Our emotional balance becomes more precarious. Traditional competition leads to following the pace of others, those whom we consider to be "successful" or "winners." Soon these others, our competitors, direct our actions, even though they are totally unaware of it. The traditional competitor thinks he's free, but in fact he is not. He is not free to not compete or not compare. He cannot stop trying to keep up with the Joneses. He is locked into an ego-invested, glory-seeking process that he cannot eliminate unless his basic mind-set changes. In other words, he has abdicated his own self-reliance

Letting one's emotional center of gravity drift outside oneself sets up an insidious cycle:[1]

1. When the focus of life is outside oneself, one's use of energy and resources is determined more by competitors than by oneself and one's own needs
2. This weakens one's sense of self-identity
3. Which increases feelings of emptiness and vulnerability
4. Which is compensated by engaging in more competition

When the focus is outside oneself, minding one's own business becomes an impossibility, so concerned is the individual with what his competitors are doing and where he stands in relation to them.

The Healthy Competitor, on the other hand, has his center of gravity well centered within himself. He has a strong inner core and a solid sense of self-identity. Self-concept and self-esteem are internally determined, and because of this he is self-reliant, free to set his own pace. He marches to is own drumbeat and has little need for invidious comparisons. Rather than having to keep up with the Joneses, he is free to *be* a Jones!

Because he is not hung up on externals and is internally controlled, he has real freedom of choice, to cooperate as well as to compete. He is free to mind his own business and to focus his full energy on the task at hand. True freedom can only come when comparisons are pushed aside and we hold no head higher than our own.

Thus, healthy competition is energy intensive. All one's resources can be mustered in one direction, on the task before you, without being split off into nonessentials. When someone once asked Marshal Foch how he was able to win World War I, he supposedly replied, "By smoking my pipe, not getting excited, and reserving all my strength for the task at hand."

## CONFORMITY VS UNIQUENESS

The traditionally competitive person is imitative. She follows the "winner," trying to unseat her and take over. If you have to keep up with the Joneses, then you have to go in the direction the Joneses go, and play their game, not your own. The instant you start comparing you set the object of that comparison as the standard for your self-judgment. This breeds conformity. It can do nothing else.

Marching to someone else's drumbeat, having someone else set your pace, is imitation by definition.

This imitation often stirs up so much actvity that competitiveness *appears* to stimulate initiative. But this is deceptive. Let's not confuse initiative with activity. Activity in the service of traditional competition, based on comparison, lacks internal direction. It lacks true inventiveness. Such activity may lead to "pseudoinventiveness," which is actually increased cleverness in undercutting the competition, but this is still geared toward an imitative goal.

Look at competitive advertising. In any given industry, many similar products compete for market share, with new imitators coming into the fray every day. Each claims to outperform the others, the advertising gets hotter and glitzier, but when we look at all the similar products on the shelves in the store, save for their external packaging, they are all very much alike. Do we really need another anti-wetness antiperspirant with aluminum chlorhydrate? Or do we just need one that really works? Where should companies' R and D energies be placed?

There's no limit to what we could do if we stopped playing comparison-conformity games and really let loose our creative potential. The world could not contain all the good that could be accomplished. Yet so strong is the illusion of competitive advantage, so powerful the trap of traditional competition, that we are afraid to let go, to risk maximizing our potential. So the traditional competitor stays stuck in the mire, continuing, as Deming stated in chapter 1, to create waste.

The Healthy Competitor breaks free! She transcends the boundaries of conformity, soaring into the stratosphere of her own uniqueness. The Healthy Competitor, whether a person or an organization, is free to take the forefront, to capitalize on her own mind, ideas, and actions.

True initiative and inventiveness depend on, and stimulate, independence of mind. This is the key element that pseudoinventiveness lacks. The Healthy Competitor doesn't imitate, she innovates, creates. True creativity is fragile, it can only develop and flourish in an atmosphere of freedom and independence of mind and action. Conformity, imitation, and comparison are the antithesis of inventiveness, regardless of how active and "creative" they appear. They ring the death knell of creativity.

The uniqueness the Healthy Competitor displays is deeply rooted in the solid inner core and spiritual center of gravity described earlier. Solid self-definition and self-worth fuel self-reliance, which is the bedrock of healthy competition, and the rest of the characteristics of the new model of competition, outlined later.

## EGO-INVESTED, SELF-AWARE VS EGO-FREE, AWARE

A review of the Ego-oriented vs Task-oriented person and the characteristics of the Competitive Personality described in chapter 4 would be helpful here. To sum up, the traditionally competitive person has his ego wrapped up in the contest, and in almost every other endeavor in which he is involved. To the degree that this is so, he confuses his worth with the outcome of his performance. Thus he is like a slave on the auction block. His worth is only as great as what he is able to produce. Our society, to its own detriment, strongly supports this attitude under the mistaken notion that it will motivate people to be productive.

Work, for the ego-invested person, becomes a problem. It is a place where one's worth is tested, which can raise the fears of failure and success and raise our stress level. It is true that many highly ego-invested people "thrive" on their work, but often this "thriving" is in illusion, reflecting a temporary feeling of satisfaction one feels only as long as one is winning or is ahead. Can one "thrive"in, system that produces increased stress and higher risk of heart disease and other stress-related disorders?

The Healthy Competitor, however, can truly thrive. Why? Because he gets his ego out of the picture. By being free of the pitfalls of traditional competition, he views his worth as a given. He accepts himself. It is no longer necessary to prove himself to himself, even though he still may have to prove himself at work.

Work, then, becomes not a problem, but an opportunity, a place to test new ideas and capitalize on one's uniqueness, to make lasting, valuable contributions.

The Healthy Competitor may face a real bind if he works in an organization that is not truly receptive to change. While most companies give lip service to creativity, few have a corporate culture that solidly supports innovation, except in a few traditional ways.

The political infrastructure in such settings actually subverts inventiveness. Such an environment will resist "radical" ideas, and the Healthy Competitor will have to be very strategic in how he copes with the competition and limits he faces.

Yet the basic attitude of the new model will work anywhere, and actually will relieve stress. What if we're blocked in attempting to champion a new idea or procedure? What really gets hurt? Our egos, that's what! This was stated earlier but is so important that it's worth restating here. The Healthy Competitor is (relatively) ego-free. He is not hung up in having to take a reversal so personally. While he may be attacked on the outside, inwardly his worth is not threatened because of his solid inner core. Of course, he may be disappointed and feel hurt sometimes, but he won't feel worthless or devastated, because his personal worth was never on the line, as it so often is for the traditional competitor. The Healthy Competitor, therefore, can take a defeat in stride, because he knows that, while he may have lost a battle, he has not lost the war.

Akin to the ego involvement dimension is the aware/self-aware dimension. Physically as well as emotionally, our awareness can be placed in only one direction at a time. You're tuned in either to what's going on around you, or to yourself. You can't do both simultaneously. Let's prove it with a little test. Turn on the television or the radio, or tune in to a conversation going on a nearby. Give the program or conversation your full attention. Concentrate on what is being said or done for a few moments. Then shift your thoughts. Think about your last success experience or the dream vacation you're going to take, or whatever. What happens to your ability to recall the television or radio program or conversation?

When you concentrate on the task at hand, giving it your undivided attention, you're aware. Then you start to daydream, or worry. You've become self-aware, you've tuned into your own thoughts and you've tuned out what's going on around you.

When I was a teenager I sometimes read the lesson in church. When I read aloud, sometimes my mind would rush ahead of my voice and I'd stumble over words. On a particular day I remember, I was reading very smoothly. My mind was on my reading—I was aware. Midway through the passage I thought about what would happen if my mind were to race ahead of my voice. At that instant

I shifted from being aware to being self-aware. What happened? You guessed it. I stumbled.

The traditional competitor is more self-aware because of the "contest bound" nature of his thinking. While he is acting, he is critically intent on his performance, getting hung up in how he is being evaluated. While not oblivious to evaluation and the opinions of others, the Healthy Competitor is much more free to be aware, to focus on the task at hand, because the evaluative/comparative aspects are put in proper perspective. He has learned where to put his energy for best impact. And you can bet your booties it's *not* into being self-aware. Incidentally, self-awareness as I've defined it here, is the root of "stage fright" in all its forms, and feeds into the fear that often underlies traditional competition.)

## "How am I doing?" vs "What am I doing?"

This is an extension of the previous dimension. The traditional competitor is never far from thinking in comparisons; Hence, "How am I doing?" is a primary question. The question is ego-involved and leads to second-guessing and worry. It is related to sensing one's position on the vertical ladder, which is so critical to traditional competitors. The question implies relativity and other-directedness: "How am I doing" in relation to what?

We all need to ask this question from time to time. We need to know how we come across so we can alter our moves when necessary. That's just plain feedback, and we need to take time to receive it. For the Healthy Competitor this question is a tactic; for the traditional competitor, it is a worry.

The Healthy Competitor is more inclined to ask herself "*What* am I doing?", focusing on the task at hand. The evaluation involved in the question is not one of relative personal worth, but rather of what is the best way to proceed, to get the job done properly. The feedback she seeks is not primarily aimed at validating her worth, but rather to see if her actions are properly directed and working. Since her ego isn't involved, she can accept criticism and advice as a useful tool to help her improve, rather than as a personal affront.

## SATISFACTION: OUTCOME-ORIENTED VS PROCESS-ORIENTED

This dimension harks back to how we define winning and losing. So often, for the traditional competitor, the goal is winning. Everything leading up to that goal—all the practice, study, planning, etc.—is geared to that end. If the person wins, then it all was worthwhile. But so frequently, if the traditional competitor loses, all the prep time and effort becomes a waste, worthless. He kicks himself around the block for wasting all that time, or for blowing his chance. Likewise, he delays until the outcome the gratification he could receive in the preparation efforts themselves. This is an unnecessarily rigid approach.

The Healthy Competitor has a much freer, perhaps even more joyful, outlook. Preparation time is meaningful and beneficial in itself. Winning, while it may be important to him, is really the icing on the cake. If he wins, it's wonderful, but if he loses, the loss is buffered into perspective by the realization that the preparation was a valuable learning experience which will help him to do better the next time. You see, the preparation can provide many satisfactions of its own, independent of the outcome. Thus the Healthy Competitor can enjoy his cake now, whether or not he gets any icing later on!

## ANGER VS CALMNESS

Anger and jealousy are usually never far from the surface with people who are highly traditionally competitive. They often have a mind-set of suspicion and a feeling that "life is unfair" if things don't go their way. Marry those ideas to the mind-set of comparison and placing others' heads higher than one's own, and you have a perfect seething cauldron in which anger bubbles and stirs. It's not hard to spot the anger and jealousy in much traditionally competitive behavior, especially social competition.

Healthy Competitors can remain much calmer in the face of pressure for all the reasons cited earlier in this chapter. They are mentally, emotionally, spiritually at peace and rest. They are secure in their power, in their knowledge, in their sense of direction, in their fundamental worth and self-esteem. They love themselves in a healthy, ego-free way, and would not seriously wish to trade places with anyone else. Physically they are relaxed, coping with stress well, resilient and generally in good physical and mental health. They are unflappable, tenacious, and active, like the experienced martial artists who can fly through a flurry of kicks, holds, and throws, and yet remain calm under fire.

## STRUGGLE, IMPATIENCE VS FLOW, PATIENCE

If your worth or value is always up for grabs, if you're playing King of the Hill every day, you want issues resolved quickly. You can't wait to find out if you're OK. Of course, given the nature and mind-set of traditional competition, the answer is never final. Add the ego-investment and you can see why life is a struggle for traditionally competitive people. But most of all, the struggle and impatience are created by the process of competition itself. Life becomes the contest, and we're all running in the "rat race."

But are we? Sometimes, paradoxically, we can faster, harder, by going with the flow and being patient. You can often change a tide by flowing with it rather than by butting your head against it. Part of the strategy lies in the timing. In the martial arts of judo and aikido, you go with, flow with, your opponent's energy. Similarly, flow and patience characterize healthy competition.

Flow and patience have to do with the direction, intensity, and timing of using energy. They are not to be confused with inactivity or an irresponsible attitude. Quite the contrary. The healthy Competitor is very active and tenacious.

Be a channel for the power that is within you. Don't block your own energy with your biases, preconceptions, and fears. Rather than to struggle with yourself to accomplish goals, let your goals and plans be a guide for your power to flow freely and effortlessly.

## PSYCHOLOGICALLY SOFT VS PSYCHOLOGICALLY HARDY

Recent research by psychologists Suzanne Kobasa and Salvatore Maddi has shown that psychological hardiness is a key factor in people who live high-stress lives by have a low illness rate. They handle stress better, both emotionally and physically. It's also fascinating to discover that this trait is not class-bound. The very poor who are psychologically hardy are as well stress-insulated as the rich who possess the same trait.

Psychological hardiness is more an attitude toward life than a set of behaviors. Distill all the findings and for characteristics emerge as the core of psychological hardiness:[2]

- Openness to *Change*

- Feeling of *Contribution* to and involvement in whatever one is doing

- Sense of *Control* over life events

- *Commitment*to stable and continuing social networks

These factors characterize the Healthy Competitor. But the traditional competitor is psychologically soft, regardless of how tough an opponent he may be. That's because the traits of psychological hardiness are the most difficult for him to bear. Let's see why:

- Change is viewed as threat to his position

- He often participates to gain power, position, possessions, or prestige, having little interest in the activity itself

- He is other-directed and views his own actions relative to others' moves

- He is suspicious, on guard for potential competition.

Psychological softness, then, is embedded in lack of trust in self and others and feelings of anxiety and insecurity. These are the traditional competitor's constant companions.


## EXCLUSIVE VS INCLUSIVE

Traditional competition excludes people. I must win over you, in spite of you. Traditional competition is designed to narrow the field, to eliminate the opponents.

The Healthy Competitor knows the real truth: to be a true winner, you must make others winners also. The Healthy Competitor is an empowerer and a solid cooperator. People are a fact of life. Whether they will help or hinder, be your allies or opponents, is in large measure up to you. Working through others makes your position stronger.

## WORLD VIEW: SCARCITY VS ABUNDANCE

The Competitive Personality holds a world view of scarcity. Scarcity is the mind-set that underlies all traditional competition. Of course, we encounter situations every day where there are more contestants than prizes. But the real problem occurs when the scarcity mind-set generalizes to include social factors such as status and personal worth. Then the implication is that there is not enough approval, admiration, or liking to go around. The scarcity attitude underlies the need to be Number One, or the "best."

The Healthy Competitor has a mind-set of abundance. New opportunities abound, new paths are waiting to be tried. Rather than scramble for crumbs of the existing pie, the Healthy Competitor looks for ways to create a bigger pie. Thus , she is free to give, while the traditional competitor, at least when she's in the competitive mode, is hung up with getting.

By now you've probably figured it out: healthy competition really isn't "competition" at all. It is taking initiative, striving for achievement, and doing one's best, with the realistic recognition that one must also position and protect oneself in the process from the unhealthy competitive ploys of others.

# Notes

1. Unestahl, L.-E. Personal communication
2. Pines, M. "Psychological hardiness." *Psychology Today*. December 1980, 34–35.

# 8

# The Spirit of Healthy Competition

T HERE are two S words spelled out in the last chapter that capture the spirit of healthy competition. They form the bedrock for all the strategies and tactics we will discuss in this chapter and the rest of the book: significance and self-reliance.

## Significance and Self-reliance

Be significant rather than superior. Be important rather than self-important. Achieve true significance and many of life's other benefits will accrue. Significance, as we saw in the last chapter, is not a question of status. It has nothing to do, necessarily, with earning power, or the price of your home, or the economic level or reputation of the community in which you live (although in our society truly significant business people often do well in these areas). Likewise, significance has nothing to do with the number of people or operations that you command.

Significance is a personal quality. A significant person exudes depth, power, sensitivity and high character. He or she has a deep, abiding respect and caring for others and their needs, is too big for petty politics, and is generous rather than jealous. He or she acts honorably and fairly, and makes major contributions in his or her own way. Gandhi, Churchill, FDR, Eleanor Roosevelt, Albert Schweitzer, Mother Teresa, Martin Luther King, Jr.—these are significant people. They had a vision and made their visions reality through their personal efforts and their ability to inspire others. They were Healthy Competitors, winners in the truest sense. These people are world-famous, but this is not a criterion for significance. Most significant people are unsung heroes. Their "fame" is very limited, but their contributions are real nonetheless—vital to their organizations, important to their communities.

The Healthy Competitor, in striving for significance, doesn't compete by straining to beat the opponent, but by making his or her own position unassailable—so solid, so vital, that it is impossible to be overlooked.

Remember Rudolph, the red-nosed reindeer? He was putdown, teased, ostracized. But when Santa asked Rudolph to guide his sleigh, he became a hero and went down in history, and apparently lived happily after. What would happen if Rudolph were working in Corporate America? If the CEO were to single him out for a major mission, how would his coworkers react? While he would get support from his friends, he'd also become the target of the envious.

The higher you rise, the more opposition you are likely to face, and the heavier the political power plays become. This is a fact of corporate life, and you will have to face it if you aspire to rise, whether you,re a Healthy Competitor or not. It would be folly to assume that because you're a Healthy Competitor the red carpet will be rolled out for you on the stairway to the top. In fact, if you refuse to play petty games, you will likely face more resistance. You just need to be bigger than the impediments they throw in your way. It is very difficult to attack a truly honorable and significant person.

Strategy is vital to a Healthy Competitor. Play your cards right and you will rise with greater support and more honor. But play you must, in some way. The Healthy Competitor is not naive, nor blind to political reality. He or she must be as adept as the opposition, but must place energy, first and foremost, on the essentials. And that gives him or her the critical advantage, the "competitive edge."

Self-reliance is the second S. "But," you say, "I *am* self-reliant. I work hard, I make my own decisions, I'm my own boss!" Of course you are. Most every reader of this book is, at that the level of decision-making. But I'm talking about *emotional* self-reliance.

Being able to choose based on *your* ideas and values. While highly traditionally competitive people are often very assertive and effective, they have not fully discovered their true inner selves. They are too dependent on other's, or society's, definition of success and how to achieve and measure it.

Healthy Competitors are self-reliant at the emotional level as well. They may choose society's definition of success, but they do so of free choice, not because it is foisted upon them through a spiderweb of invidious, ego-invested comparisons. Their measure of self-worth is internal, not external. Look hard at the Healthy Competitors listed above, and at those you know of or observe at the highest strata of corporate life. They're "driven" all right, but by a sense of mission, not by a relentless obsessive fear of failure. Look close and you'll find that they're tailored society's definition of success to their own needs rather than the other way around. They live deeply fulfilling, meaningful lives rather than shallow, empty, shell-like existences. Their competitive practices are streamlined, even though they may have to plow their way daily through a political jungle. While their lives are busy, even hectic, and they face stiff pressures, they are less stressed and more resilient. Therefore, they are physically and emotionally likely to last longer. That in itself is perhaps the best competitive edge of all! This is the stuff of true self-reliance!

Now you see why I said earlier that healthy competition is not just a fancy set of tactics or actions, nor is it another euphemism for "good sportsmanship," which is so shallow a concept by comparison as to be almost meaningless.

Now you see that healthy competition is a way of life. It goes to the root of our being, and of how we value and define our essence as well as our actions. Healthy competition is not perfection. Yet its principles can serve as a yardstick for our daily plans and endeavors. It is an ideal to be striven for, and which *can* be reached.

You can't have corporate renewal without personal renewal. It will be a great day when Corporate America wakes up to the fact that the corporation is really no better off than its people are. This book is for people, although corporations may read over their shoulders. The principles and methods written here for people will also work well at the broader, organizational level. Keep that in the back of your mind as you continue.

# The Formula for Healthy Competition

People like formulas. They pack broad principles into a quickly usable shorthand. They become recipes for living. Healthy competition can be expressed as a formula also. Here it is:

$$W = E^3 + C_1 + C_2 + P$$

Winning equals excellence plus commitment, contribution, and positioning.

If you look at all lasting, healthy wins at the political, economic, or personal levels, you will discover that they have involved all of these components. I define a "lasting, healthy win," at any level, as including not only power, but also strong loyalty on the part of the consumer, or employees, or the populace being governed.

Excellence, commitment, contribution, positioning—these four. But the greatest of these is excellence. That's why the equation shows E to the third power! Nothing beats quality. You can be totally committed and extremely well positioned, but if the quality isn't there your product or service will eventually flop. Today the world is extremely quality/excellence-conscious. A poor product in a glitzy package won't cut it anymore, whether that "product" is an item, a service, or a person. Yet, as Franklin P. Jones said, "A lot of people are too busy trying to get ahead to do a good job."

Sure, we all know some incompetents who are being protected by upper management. But unless you're sleeping with the boss, holding secret, sensitive information over the boss's head, or are the boss's close friend or family member, this isn't the way to go. Besides, these people become very vulnerable amidst the winds of change sweeping across Corporate America.

*The winning way is the quality way.* That's it! Hands down! Excellence must be your driving force. Make a significant contribution, fueled by the power of your commitment, and by all means position it well. So simple, yet so complex.

## LAWS OF HEALTHY COMPETITION

Backing up the formula for healthy competition are five laws. These paint the broad strokes; the specific strategies for achieving them follow.

*Law #1 Cream Always Rises to the Top, as Long as It Is Positioned Properly.* It has been said that "excellence is its own reward." While being excellent will warm the cockles of your own heart—as well it should—this statement is patently false at the broader level in Corporate America. There are two basic reasons why, which the Healthy Competitor must fully understand.

The first is that while honorable people applaud excellence within their ranks, it is sure to bring out the envy and resistance of the Great Unwashed. We've sent up the warning flares on this issue in earlier chapters, so enough on that subject.

The second reason is this: The news from the front lines is, sadly, that, while the Quality Revolution is picking up, "excellence" is not yet the main watchword across Corporate America. "Profit" is. American management has often been criticized for not seeing past the next quarter's balance sheet, and for sacrificing quality on the altar of the fast buck. We have yet to learn that quality and profit walk hand in hand!

According to Tom Peters, we Americans have been lulled into thinking that bigger is better, more is better. He states that we didn't win World War II with the superiority of our technology (the atom bomb excepted, perhaps), but with the fact that we just had *more*. Our weapons were not technologically superior to those of the Axis powers, he argues, but we had the ability to turn them out quickly in huge numbers. To confuse that with quality, however, is a big mistake.[1]

An acquaintance of mine supplies custom-tailored men's clothing. Recently he added shirts to his line. I asked him, "Where are your shirts made?" "China." "Do they make them less expensively?" I asked. "Heck, no!" he replied. "The Chinese and our American suppliers can produce for about the same price, but the Chinese shirts are better. They have better technology. I get only a 10 percent reject rate from the Chinese, but 27 percent or more from the American suppliers. The Americans just don't know how to make a shirt!" Indeed, to gain quick profit, quality is often given short shrift. Quality costs, but in the long run it pays off, as the Japanese have been teaching us by biting off greater and greater chunks of our international and domestic market share.

All this to say that, when you emphasize quality, you might be a prophet crying in the wilderness! I don't mean to be cynical, just realistic. You need to judge your own situation. The "quality" we're talking about is *you*—yourself as a person and the goods and/or services you produce. And if you want to get ahead, you must not, you cannot overlook how you position yourself within your organization. The road to success is paved with the carcasses of positioning errors, from the New Coke, to the Edsel, to individuals who have zapped their own careers through "fatal" corporate mistakes. Indeed, while quality is essential, positioning yourself may be a much trickier process, and one more critical to whether you succeed than the degree of excellence you produce!

*Law #2 Greatness and Meaning Come Through Contribution.* This seems self-evident, but it is often overlooked. I guess that's because making a significant contribution is not always easy. But something truly worthwhile is rarely a piece of cake. How well you rise, and how firmly you stand, depends on the nature and solidity of your foundation. Your best foundation is an important contribution from which others benefit. Only the givers last through the ages; the takers are buried along with their names.

*Law #3 Authenticity Is the Hallmark of the True Winner.* Whatever else he may be, the true winner is himself. To be phoney involves following someone else's drumbeat; to be yourself means that you're directing your own image and actions, as described in the last chapter. Many people hope to get ahead by patterning themselves on someone else. To the degree that they diverge from their own personal inclinations and personality, they assume added stress. After all, it's hard to play a role every day without letting down your guard. And don't forget, in spite of what Xerox may say, the copy is never as good as the original.

*Law #4 The Greatest Power Resides in Gentleness.* This is perhaps the toughest principle for many of us to swallow—we've been so trained in being tough. Tough is important in its place, but gentleness is more powerful.

Inner power has often been likened to water by Eastern mystics. Like water, power does its main work by moving around objects, not by battering into them. When you batter you only get resistance. So it often is with a frontal attack. Such a move is always dramatic but rarely cost-effective. Consider Picketts's Charge. Total wipe out. The American Civil War chalked up more battlefield deaths than America had in all of our other wars combined, from the Revolution through World War II. Why? Because brother fought against brother, father against son. The toll is always greater when both sides are us!

Now consider this: as you look back in your life on those people who most positively affected you, who had the greatest supportive impact on your life, how did they do it? What did they provide? Were they tough, or were they gentle? Case closed.

Gentleness is often irresistible. It meets a natural human longing. When I work with long-standing opponents in conflict resolution, they often end up with their arms on each other's shoulder. But that doesn't happen until they can drop their tough facades. Then, in moves of mutual gentleness, they begin to find each other, often recognizing for the first time that they both want the same things. But that still, small voice was drowned out by the din and clamor of their warfare. Gentleness doesn't smash through armor; it melts it, it wears it down. "Gentleness is having the power *not* to react when everything about the circumstance says you should."[2]

A scorpion once stood on the bank of a large river trying to figure out how to reach the other side. Finally a duck swam by. The scorpion called to the duck to give him a ride on his back. The duck was cautious and remained a little bit off shore. He said, "If I take you across, you'll sting me and I'll die." "Nonsense!" the scorpion called back. "I won't do that. Besides, if I did, then I'd drown too!" Reluctantly, the duck became convinced. He swam over to the shore, the scorpion climbed up onto his back, and the duck started to swim across the river. When the duck was about halfway across, the scorpion stung the duck and the duck became paralyzed and started to sink and drown. With his dying gasp, the duck asked, "Why did you sting me?" The scorpion, who was now also beginning to drown, replied, "Because that's what I do!"

Warfare is commonplace. Yet warfare is the opposite of wisdom. It is artificial. It's what we do. It's what we've been trained or forced to do. But it's not what we really want—or need.

The Healthy Competitor, who scores high on inner power, knows the true power of gentleness. He instinctively knows, or has well learned, that true inner power has no room for hate, only for love.

A friend of mine once said, "Where you don't find love, put it. Then you will find it."

*Law #5 To Win with Others, Keep Your Focus on (a) Yourself and Your Actions, and (b) Others' Needs.* Again, so profoundly simple, but so many traditional competitors have it backward! They keep their eye on their competitors and worry most about meeting their own needs. In the last chapter we saw the folly of that approach. These ideas will be fleshed out more as we continue.

I doubt that this list of laws is exhaustive, and you can probably think up others. There is one more overriding law I'd like to add here that was cited earlier in a different context. I'll give no explanation; just let it sink in:

Life is a game. It's too important to be taken too seriously![3]

# Competitive Fitness

While healthy competition is a far cry from traditional competitiveness, the new model of competition strongly promotes positive Competitive Fitness. We can define this as the ability to thrive, not just survive, in the face of increased competition; the ability to maximize your probability of winning and do so with less stress, and at the same time increase your value and contribution to your organization.

Proper Competitive Fitness involves:

- Putting competition and cooperation into proper perspective, with a healthy set of values regarding each, and having a workable model of how to complete and cooperate most effectively.

- The ability to understand, discover, and deflect hidden competitive ploys and political entanglements that could undermine your success and contribution.

- The ability to compete with finesse against true opponents and to cooperate with equal enthusiasm with colleagues, and the ability to recognize who is who.

- The ability to cooperate and compete honorably and flexibly, free of jealousy, envy, anger, or other negative emotions and behaviors, which undermine your success and personal well-being.

- The ability to mobilize all of your resources during the contest and yet let go of competitive feelings and behaviors when the contest is over.

- The ability to enhance your personal position and build a positive power base, at the same time improving cooperation and contribution.

- The ability to program your mind for stress-free competitive success.

- The ability to accept and respect your opponent's personal worth as equal to your own, without engaging in invidious comparisons.

- The ability to merge personal goals with broader company goals, to cooperate effectively with other persons for the achievement of these goals without undue suspicion and protectiveness.

- A belief and understanding of your true strength built upon a positive and solid self-esteem.

- The ability to empower others to achieve their goals, to become winners.

- The ability to relax

No discussion of Competitive Fitness could be complete without addressing a very vital, popular but problematic issue: competing with yourself

---

# Competing with Yourself

Many people are turned off by the pitfalls of interpersonal competition but don't want to let go of the idea of competing altogether. "Competing with yourself" appears to many to be a viable compromise. But is it?

"Competing with yourself" sounds noble, but it can actually be devilish, depending on how it is used. If it is based on the premises of traditional competition it can be destructive. Because it is seen as an ideal, however, it is all the more devastating. It is a wolf in sheep's clothing.

What do you do when you compete with yourself? Do you turn inward, against yourself, all the relentless pressure you would have otherwise mustered against your opponent? Do you drive yourself intensely, never being satisfied? Do you criticize yourself more than reward yourself? Do you focus more on your weaknesses than on your strengths? Do you push yourself to meet impossible goals? (We saw the results of Dr. Buckalew's research with Type A exercisers in chapter 1). If you are doing all these things you are deluding yourself. By "competing with yourself" you are actually competing *against* yourself. You've become your own worst enemy! You've been building your definition of success on self-hate.

"Competing with yourself," in its most basic sense, serves no useful purpose. Why must you set yourself up as your opponent? When you do so, the same rules apply to yourself that apply to any other opponent in the framework of traditional competition. You're wasting time and energy this way. Cut it out!

Healthy Competitors do not compete with or against, themselves. For Healthy Competitors this concept is a contradiction in terms and a red herring. Since they are not divided against themselves, with whom, then, do they compete? Certainly not themselves they may strive to surpass a past performance. They may push to meet a particular standard of excellence. But this is "achievement," "self-development," "the pursuit of excellence." Call it what you will,—it has nothing to do with "competition."

Competition against oneself is patently destructive. It implies "dividing" yourself, which wastes energy. It implies "beating" yourself, which undermines your self-esteem. If you need to compete with others, then you can't afford to undermine your own position by turning yourself into your opponent as well. Rather, for maximum personal advantage, you must do something entirely different. You must prepare to win.

# Notes

1. Peters, T. "U.S. traditions have been bigness, speed; not quality." *Baltimore Sun,* May 10, 1987.
2. Paul, S. *The Worrior Within.* Golden, Colorado-Delta Group Press, 1983, 109.
3. O'Connell, W. Personal Communication.

# 9

# Positive Strategies

To win, you have to *prepare* to win. So said John Avianantos, former head college football coach of the Scottsdale Artichokes. And how right he is: Why do you think the Boy Scouts, given their high values and many virtues, choose as their motto, "Be prepared"?

There are numerous strategies and tactics that will help us, as Healthy Competitors, to prepare to win. As we go through the list, you may wish to assess several things:

1. Am I using this method now?

2. How effectively am I using it?

3. How much am I using it? Do I need to beef up my efforts in this area, or am I doing it now to overkill proportions?

4. Am I using this method in the healthiest way possible for me? If not, what should I change?

5. What is the relative importance of this strategy to me personally, and in my work setting?

Carrying out these strategies in a systematic, balanced way will make you not only a very Healthy Competitor, but a peak performer. Not coincidentally, these two factors have a great deal in common. While the Healthy Competitor is a peak performer, not all peak performers are Healthy Competitors, and these individuals may be falling short of the true peak they could achieve.

# Ten Healthy Competitive Strategies

Following are the strategies and tactics that will help you "prepare to win."

## OVERLEARN THE FUNDAMENTALS OF YOUR JOB

Get back to basics. Often we pass through the basics so quickly that we never really learn them well. We're too interested in getting to the advanced material. After all, basic stuff is so boring!

Yet basics are essential. World-class target shooters will still spend many practice hours "dry-firing", or shooting an empty gun, so they can practice trigger squeeze, their stance and grip on the gun, and their sight alignment, and many other basics. Pro tennis players still spend endless hours practicing their basic backhand. Why? To develop what athletes call "the subconscious feel" of the perfect performance. In other words, they want their performance down-pat, so that in competition, they do things correctly automatically, and so their conscious minds are free to focus elsewhere. The heat of competition is no time to have to think, "How do I do this?" It all must happen on its own, like clockwork, because you don't have time to think!

The Healthy Competitor in business takes the same attitude. When you're "on stage"—say, in a sales call—it is not the time to work out the final details of you presentation or to figure out how to respond to a basic objection. You need your mind to be free to handle more complex issues, such as unique questions the buyer might ask. You need to be aware, so you can respond quickly and freely, not self-aware. At the moment you're self-aware, you're missing vital information from your client, or from the situation at hand.

*Exercise 1: Back to Basics.* List on paper five or more basic tasks that make up your job. Then rate your ability to pertain each task on a 1–5 scale, where 1 = forgotten how, 3 = moderately OK, but I'm not fully comfortable, and 5 = do it flawlessly, without thinking. Then for those on which you scored 4 or less, determine what needs to be done to bring them up to 5, and how and when you will go about it. (If you commit yourself to a reasonable time frame and put it on your calendar, you're more likely to accomplish your goal.

Remember there are four levels of learning for any skill:

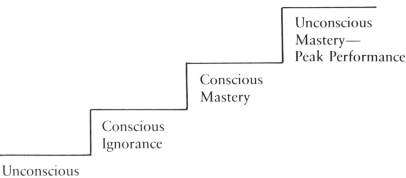

At the stage of Unconscious Ignorance, you don't know a given task and are unaware that the task exists or that you need to know it. At the next level, Conscious Ignorance, you realize that you don't know how to do the task. As you attempt to learn it, you reach the level of Conscious Mastery, where you practice the task step by step, paying attention to the details required to do it properly. Then you reach the stage of Unconscious Mastery, the stage of the subconscious feel of perfect performance. You can carry out the task without thinking. Your mind goes on autopilot. Even after reaching this stage, world-class athletes will return again to the Conscious Mastery level in practice, working to hone specific skills so they can perform even better at the Unconscious Mastery level in competition.

The fundamentals of your job, as well as more advanced aspects, need to be learned at the Unconscious Mastery level if they are to serve you reliably when the chips are down.

## KNOW THE "BIG PICTURE"

How does your job fit into your division? How does your division serve the company as a whole? How well does the company operate? What is your company's mission statement? Where is it going and how does it plan to get there. What are its goals for the next month, next year, next five years, next twenty years?

Get this information. It's vital that you know this. Most organizations, especially large ones with many divisions, are like flotillas: separate ships sailing in formation. Each ship has its own crew and captain, and the admiral receives data and gives commands from the flagship. Hopefully all the ships are in solid communication with one another. Often, however, they are not. In large organizations, communication is often lacking between divisions. Accounting may never talk to purchasing unless there is a need to talk about the budget, or order equipment, or discuss a particular bill. And so on.

Many managers, like ship captains in the flotilla, are so concerned with steering their own course and putting out daily brush fires that the big picture gets overlooked. If you take time to see and analyze the big picture, you automatically are at an advantage over many of your colleagues. If you know it and understand it, then you can provide input. If you don't, you are at the mercy of the interpretations and actions of those above you.

*Exercise 2: Discover the Big Picture.* Are your knowledge and vision of the Big Picture like a mural, or like a jigsaw puzzle with some pieces missing? Fill in the blanks. Gain access to the organizational chart and any other documents having to do with corporate goals, mission, objectives, etc. But don't just find out *which*, also find out *when* changes will be made, goals reached, etc. Even more important, find out *why* all these things are occurring. What is the rationale behind the big picture? Discover the rational reasons and the emotional ones if possible. Only then will you fully know what's going on.

## DISCOVER, AND TAP INTO, THE "POLITICAL INFRASTRUCTURE"

Every organization has two organizations, the "official" one, which exists on the organizational chart, and the "real" one, the political subculture, through which everything gets done. The leaders of the official structure may or may not have much power in the political infrastructure.

For your purpose as a Healthy Competitor, knowledge of the formal organization is useful, knowledge of the political infrastructure is vital. It is at the latter's hands that you will receive your coronation or crucifixion. Not knowing or taking seriously the impact of office politics has destroyed many a promising career. While it is at the formal level that your primary goals may be achieved, it is at the political level that your primary battles will be fought. So knowing the political infrastructure is just good old "competitor intelligence." Never, never, never underestimate its power, nor its volatility! While the formal structure might be rigid, like an ocean's barrier reef, the infrastructure may shift like a sandbar, flexing with the currents of change. Keep on top of these changes, tap into the informal networks, use the system to your advantage, but be careful not to get caught up in it. Never lose your main focus on the excellence of your achievement. But never assume that you are "above all that political stuff." You may refuse to play petty political games, but you must reckon with the political infrastructure nonetheless.

*Exercise 3: Your Political Map.* Draw an "organizational chart" of the political infrastructure. Who influences whom? Who are the informal leaders, the powers behind the throne. To whom must you go to get things done in each department, whose wheels must you grease? If you ask favors, what will you be expected to give in return? Go back to the beginning of chapter 6, to the section discussing different responses to competition. Who fits each of these categories? Who fits where in the Competitive Quadrant from chapter 3? (Had Julius Caesar done this, he might have lived longer!) Most important, who are your allies and who are your opponents? What styles do they use? How closely does your infrastructure chart mesh with the formal organizational chart?

## Know Your Industry, Inside and Out

It's easy to get so wrapped up with the home fires, especially when you have to keep putting them out, that you lose the broader perspective. Keep tabs on broader industry problems and how they're being solved. Look at industry advances and who's making them. Don't get so hung up on being loyal to your firm that you become nearsighted. If other firms are ahead of yours in some way, you need to know it, and to bring those lessons back home.

Many people take their membership in trade and professional associations lightly. Yet association conventions and house organs provide your easiest access to industry-wide information and to "competitor intelligence." While many go to the conventions and meetings for the fun of it, the Healthy Competitor goes as a sponge, to soak up and absorb all he or she can. Fun's important too, but the Healthy Competitor has his or her priorities in order.

Go to your key conventions, even if (and perhaps especially if) you have to pay your own way. But do some prep time before you go. Bone up on the association journals beforehand. See who's published what. If a particular article has major impact, and you need more information about the issues it addressed, plan to meet the author at the convention. You might even contact him or her in advance, introducing yourself and expressing interest in discussing the article and its implications. This will flatter most authors and they'll be happy to give you some time. Remember that most authors never get much feedback on their articles, and they will often be ecstatic if someone such as yourself has taken them seriously.

Every association has an executive director (title may vary) who is employed by the association to direct the association's affairs. Get on a first-name basis with that individual if you can. Do likewise with the association meeting planner and other key association committee heads. Since the association is a clearinghouse of industry information, being on friendly terms with them can gain you a direct pipeline to the latest scoop. Keep in touch between meetings, and be prepared to feel information into the pipeline as well as to take it out.

Here's a pre-convention planning checklist:

1. What are my goals for attending? What do I want to get out of it? (Be specific.)

2. What personal areas for my further development do I wish to highlight and work on?

3. What industry contacts do I want to make? For what objective? How should I approach them?

4. On what industry issues/advances do I need further information? What is the best way to acquire it at the convention?

5. What information and insight does my comply need that the convention might help me obtain for it?

*Exercise 4: Developing Your "Industry Dossier".* From what you hear and read, distill the key problems facing your industry right now. Zero in on key industry advances and find out who's making them. Make up a file on these issues and advances. Identify key industry leaders and resource persons, and plan to become acquainted with them.

## SPOT FUTURE TRENDS

This is perhaps the main reason for the strategies listed up to this point. You may not be the admiral of the flotilla, but you are sure to gain points if you can help navigate! You increase your personal value greatly if you can help guide your organization. If you can divine future trends from the current industry information you possess, all the better. Probably someone will have done that for you already in terms of projected demand, projected profit/loss, future world economic outlook, etc. Get that information, absorb and distill it, make it usable for your company, and have it ready to use when the time is right.

Also pay attention to trends *outside* your industry. Broader social, political, and economic trends will impact on your industry and your organization. Discover what those trends are and determine what that impact is likely to be. You may then need to think about contingency planning. This is an important area in which you might become an informal leader or in-house consultant.

*Exercise 5: Trend Mapping.* Outline or graph the industry-wide and broader future trends that will impact on your organization. Try to assess their degree of impact, and whether or not contingency planning is in order now. Translate this information into language that will help your company understand and act.

## IDENTIFY AND CAPITALIZE ON YOUR OWN STRENGTHS AND TALENTS

Given the nature of our society, which we've already discussed, most of us are more cognizant of our failings than we are of our strengths. We often tend to discount and censor ourselves when we think of our assets and talents. Worse yet, we're reluctant to talk about them for fear that others will think we're being snobs.

Healthy Competitors, however, have a clear understanding of (a) what their strengths, assets, and talents are, and (b) how these strengths show themselves in behavior. Not only do Healthy Competitors know their strengths, they believe in them. Here's the key: you can only truly believe in something if you've *tested* it! Therefore, capitalize on your strengths. Use them and develop them in a planned, goal-directed way.

Here's where authenticity comes in. While many people try to develop for themselves what the Joneses have, Healthy Competitors use their drive to beef up what they already possess. When I was in fifth grade, my art teacher told me, "When you paint into a new area, paint from where it is already wet, not from where it's dry or from where there's no paint." Bill Gove, a motivational speaker, puts it another way: "Go with what brung ya!" Develop and expand on the areas in which you're already strong, then branch out into related areas. This is a much better use of energy than starting over in a new direction altogether.

*Exercise 6. Strength Analysis.* List on paper ten or more of your strengths, talents, and assets. Job down every one that comes to mind. Don't censor the list. Then write down how each one shows itself in your outward behavior. Star those that are very strong, and check those that need more development or greater outward expression. Then list what actions you can take to maximize the very strong ones and develop the weaker ones. Hang on to this list. Review it regularly and add to it as you think of more things. You will also be using this list again in a different vein, in chapter 13 on personal positioning.

## ENGAGE IN SELF-MONITORING

Many top athletes keep a log of their practices, and also "Monday morning quarterback" their performances in competition. This is necessary to skill improvement. People don't learn from experience; they learn from how they use their experience.

The best way to use your experience is to examine it. Yet this can be painful if the performance was a flop or fell short of your expectations. Therefore, self-monitoring needs to be a loving, non-judgmental, dispassionate process. You want to analyze a particular performance noting both strengths that made it good and the areas in which it fell short, and the reasons why. This is not to form a basis for self-criticism but to create a useful blueprint for building a peak performance.

When doing self-monitoring, allow time to think through and sort out the factors affecting your performance. Get feedback from trusted friends and coworkers. Focus on the specifics, not on global, vague impressions. Do it regularly to keep on top of improvements, and never, never do it *while* you're competing. From the last chapter, you know where your mind must be during the contest itself. Self-monitoring, lovingly done, should be a regular part of your healthy competition fitness training.

What to self-monitor? Any important performance such as leading a meeting, giving a presentation, counseling a subordinate, giving a sales presentation. Anything that you need to do repeatedly and can benefit from doing better.

*Exercise 7: Positive Self-monitoring.* Box 9-1 provides a format for positive self-monitoring. You may wish to copy the format and jot down your answers to the questions. By doing this at repeated intervals for the same kind of performance, using the same format, you can quickly spot improvements and catch areas of performance slippage.

## SHARPEN YOUR CONCENTRATION

Top athletes, and top businesspeople, are studies in concentration. Most people don't know what concentration is, however. It is *not* forcing your mind to think. That's *straining*. Nor is it thinking about a given topic. That's *contemplation*.

Concentration is being aware rather than self-aware. It's being open and totally aware of the *now*. Past and future melt away. It means avoiding extraneous thoughts, such as worry and second-

Box 9-1

---

### SELF-MONITORING GUIDE

TASK: _____ DATE: _____

By self-checking, you fine-hone your skills, sharpening your strengths and surpassing limitations. Do it honestly, with love for yourself and all you have to offer.

---

| Current strengths, improvements<br>    (responses) | Current behaviors needing<br>improvement<br>        (responses) |
|---|---|
| Specific example(s) of excellent<br>performance:<br>        (responses) | Specific example(s) of performance<br>needing improvement:<br>        (responses) |
| What behaviors made it excellent?<br>        (responses) | What behaviors interfered with<br>performance?<br>        (responses) |
| What circumstances contributed to<br>excellence?<br>        (responses) | Under what circumstances, and/or at<br>what point did performance slip?<br>        (responses) |

---

*Goals for improvement:* (responses)

*Strategies and strengths I will use to make that improvement happen:* (responses)

---

guessing, and focusing on *what* I'm doing, rather than on *how* I'm doing.

In a competition, top athletes narrow their focus. They block out the score and the fans in the stands, even the opponent. They tune in totally on their performance—nothing else. This requires intensive training to learn to clear the mind and narrow the focus. Fortunately for our purposes, we needn't narrow our concentration that much. Yet the same principles and benefits of increased and narrowed concentration apply to us as to the world-class athlete.

Another aspect of concentration is seeing with "soft eyes." This is emphasized in certain forms of martial arts training. Seeing with soft eyes means being open and aware of everything in general, not focusing on anything in particular. It has nothing to do with "blurred vision" and seeing fuzzy images.

Perhaps the closest everyday experience we have with seeing with soft eyes is driving our car. While driving, we see everything. We're aware not only of what is dead ahead, but also of what lies in the periphery of our vision. Then something special catches our eyes. We focus on it and perhaps turn our head. At that instant we shift out of soft-eyed vision into a narrow focal point.

While soft-eyed vision and narrowing our focus appear to be opposites, both are examples of different forms of concentration. Both feature total involvement in the now and total awareness. Soft-eyed vision, though, lets us perceive a wider range of stimuli.

Concentration is best accomplished when we're relaxed. Relaxation promotes awareness, while tension promotes self-awareness and distraction into worry or self-doubt. To concentrate well requires practice. We are used to straining and contemplating, thinking that we are actually concentrating.

For our purposes, concentration is closely tied to effective listening, being totally aware of the speaker rather than judging or preparing our rebuttal. By clearing our minds of the cobwebs of our own biases and inner motives, we are free to take in significant amounts of data about the other person or the situation in which we're involved.

We'll come back to concentration again, in a different vein, in Chapter 10.

*Exercise 8: Sharpening Your Powers of Concentration.* There are several exercises you can use to improve your concentration. Here are a few of them.

1. Stare at the open palm of your hand. Focus on the details, the lines. Note the patterns. Flex your hand and observe the changes in the skin and lines. Focus on the feeling in your hand as you flex it. Do you tune out background noises and other distractions after a while?

2. Continue looking at your hand, but shift to soft eyes. You're now probably looking *through* your hand. It may look dis-

torted, and you see much more around you. Become aware of the details of what you see.

3. In a conversation with another person, keep continued eye contact, without "staring" of course! Clear your mind and listen. Listen with your eyes as well as your ears. Be aware of the details of the person's face and appearance without judging or forming conclusions. Tune out everything else. Shift to soft eyes and take in the whole context: the room, the furnishings, everything. Tune into the other person's feelings, attitudes, facial expression, and posture, without analyzing. Be there in the moment, totally participating, allowing yourself to "resonate" with the other person, feeling as he or she feels. That's true empathy. Don't think about the process and the steps you're taking. That will interfere with the process itself.

## Keep Your Eye on the Ball

Rod Laver tells potential tennis stars, "In concentrating, you have to wipe everything out of your mind but . . . the ball. Nothing but the ball. Glue your eyes on it. Marry it. Don't let it out of your sight. Never mind your opponent, the weather, or anything. Nothing but the ball. Make that ball an obsession. If you can get yourself into that trance, pressure won't intrude. It's just you and the ball."[1]

Tennis coaches advise focusing so totally on the ball as it's coming across the net that you see the fuzz on it, notice its spin and trajectory. Then and only then can you know best how to hit it to land where you want. If at the moment the ball comes toward you you are looking at your opponent, you will miss the ball.

Try this little exercise: Hold your thumb up, at arms distance in front of you. Focus your eyes on your thumb so that it looks crystal clear. Now, without shifting focus, what does the wall in front of you look like? Now shift your focus onto the wall, so that you see *it* clearly. Now your thumb looks fuzzy.

The same principle applies to us as Healthy Competitors, and is closely tied to what we just said about concentration. We can't focus on two tasks at once. Pick your target or goal and keep your energy and thought directed toward that. If you shift your focus to your opponent, you are likely to slip up. Muhammad Ali was a master of distraction. Before a fight he would grossly berate and belittle his upcoming opponent. When he got in the ring, all the opponent could think about was Ali, about beating him. But who won?

Likewise, when you're in a competitive situation is no time for self-checking or second-guessing. Save that for the practice session. Now its for real, and your only focus is the task at hand—*what* you're doing, not *how* you're doing. If your opponent can get you to shift your attention to self-evaluation, or onto keeping score, or onto thinking about *him*, he gains the upper hand.

Maintaining a task focus requires discipline, so easy is it to distract ourselves. Mental discipline is a key to healthy competition of any kind, both in athletics and in business. While the objects of that disciplined focus may differ, the basic process is the same. "Keeping your eye on the ball," for the business competitor, translates into "mind your own business," "stick to the task at hand," and "refuse to be distracted." This does not mean that you close your mind to others' input and new information, of course, but that you keep your priorities straight and stay on task.

*Exercise 9: Keeping Your Eye on the Ball.* Take a tennis ball, or some other simple object, and place it before you on the desk, about three feet away from you. Focus your eyes and mind totally upon that object until everything else around you ceases to exist. Notice every detail of the object—its shape, size, texture, any markings on it. Zero in on infinitesimal details. Now you have achieved Rod Laver concentration!

Next, take out a project that you are working on. Give it the same intensity of concentration. Get totally involved with it. Marry it. Love it. Immerse yourself in it so that nothing else exists. It's just you and the project. What happened? What were your thoughts? What was your energy like? Are you tired or energized? Chances are you had entered a peak performance state and gave it your absolute best.

In order to do this, you might have to insulate yourself. Have someone take your calls and keep you "unavailable" for the amount of time in question.

## PRACTICE, PRACTICE, PRACTICE

And when you're through, practice some more! Linda Frattiani spent four to six hours a day on the ice from age six until she won her silver medal in the Olympics, now that she's a professional skater she probably continues to do the same. The average Juliard music student practices as much. Not only do these people spend great amounts of time practicing, but they do it with tremendous singleness of purpose. They continue to practice the fundamentals as well as increasingly advanced technique. They also hone their skill through attention to increasingly minute details.

Do you as a business competitor need to practice as much? You don't have time. It's been said that the average manager, during the course of the workday, spends only about eight minutes on a particular task before switching to a new one! All the more reason to carefully prioritize your goals and activities.

Ofttimes the biggest games are not won or lost on the playing field, but on the practice field. The quality of your advance planning and preparation will be pivotal to your success. Remember, you have to prepare to win.

And what is the "Winning factor?" Relentless, dogged determination, highly specifically goal-directed, carried out in a strategic, stepwise, progressive manner. In short, *excellence in the service of mission!*

And what is the "Winning edge?" In football or in a race it may be an inch or so. In horseracing it might be a nose. In the Olympics it may be a hundredth of a second. The greatest races are rarely won by leaps and bounds, but by being small fractions ahead. The greater your lead, the more solid your advantage, of course, but so often it's the little extra push that makes the difference. While you're giving the extra push, however, your eye belongs on your goal, not your opponent!

*Exercise 10: Set up Your Practice Session.* Determine what particular aspect of your performance needs to be fine-tuned. Set up a specific, realistic time period to practice uninterrupted. It's better to do ten to fifteen minutes a day than to "promise" yourself an hour and never follow through: Set up a regular schedule and follow it.

Determine in advance your goals and objectives for each practice session. It needn't be complicated, but your practice should not be just a run-through. It should focus clearly on some aspect of your performance that you want to improve. For a target shooter, it might be consistent trigger squeeze. For a salesperson, it might be rehearsing the opening greeting and handshake in a sales call to get the proper enthusiasm and vocal inflection.

Determine what props or equipment you will need and get them. A video or audio recorder perhaps? A flip chart? Procure and set up all props in advance. Only with advance preparation can you maximize the benefits of your practice sessions.

An effective series of practice sessions is both integrated and segregated. You segregate out a small but critical aspect of your overall performance. Repeatedly practice it until you master it, then integrate it back into the total performance. Neither practicing the whole without breaking out the parts, nor practicing the parts without putting them together into the integrated whole, is as valuable as the integrated/segregated format. How much you use integrated versus segregated practice depends on your personal needs and preferences.

There is one basic underlying, overriding strategic principle to which everything in this chapter points: My friend, Arnold "Nick" Carter, VP of Research for Nightingale-Conant Corporation phoned me a couple of months ago to chat. He said, "I've been reading over your newsletter and your other ideas on healthy competition, and an idea hit me. What you've really been saying is that business and salespeople should *outserve their competition!*" Nick hit the nail on the head. Again, so simple but so important:

Outserve your competition!

# Notes

Tutko, T. and Tosi, U. *Sports Psyching*. Los Angeles: J.P. Tarcher/St. Martins, 1976, 135.

# 10

# Enhancing Your Inner Power

Following the strategies in chapter 9 will automatically help you to develop your inner power. Here are some additional methods that will help build your self-esteem and self-confidence.

## Building Self-esteem and Self-confidence

### SELF-AFFIRM RATHER THAN SELF-QUESTION

So often we have been trained to doubt ourselves, to second-guess our actions or our motives. Some self-analysis is useful, but it can be overdone. It can become cancerous and lead to "analysis paralysis." Also, we often magnify the bad and discount the good. The proper task is to highlight the successes and see what we can learn from our mistakes. The latter portion can only occur when we've forgiven ourselves for our trespasses. This is the essence of positive self-monitoring.

In addition, stop and "catch" yourself doing well. Take a moment to savor your success. Let its sweet aroma fill your nostrils and satisfy you wholly. Daily remind yourself of your powerful qualities, your talents and strengths.

This is positive self-talk. Give yourself frequent verbal pats on the back. Congratulate yourself. Give yourself a positive pep talk. Avoid self-judgment. Tell yourself you *will* succeed.

## TRUST YOUR INTUITION

Reason will take us only so far in making a decision. What leads us the rest of the way? Our emotions, our feelings, our biases—those things which we have been reluctant to admit to trusting.

You buy a new car. Perhaps it's a Chevy compact. Why? Good gas mileage, low maintenance, ease of repair. Good rational reasons. Why did you choose a red one? We end up making the final decision on the basis of "intangibles." That's our word for something we can't quite pin down, but that makes sense somehow. That's often how intuition works.

The Healthy Competitor hones her intuition. People with a high level of inner power are intuitive. They have a "sixth sense" as to what will work, what to do, how others will react. And they're often on target. Inner power is intuitive by definition. It allows you to anticipate action and circumstances, sometimes to gain an edge by acting first. Most important in a competition, it allows you to put yourself into the mind of your opponent. When you can see as she sees, think as she thinks, you have the upper hand. Understanding is power!

Often we tend to substitute rules and reasons for intuition, but one will not substitute for the other. Aikido is a gentle martial art involving gaining an advantage by flowing your energy and movement in harmony with your attacker's and then using leverage to take him or her down. The movements are beautiful and graceful to behold. In America, aikido is often taught move by move, step by step. Each part is taught and then the total move is put together and practiced as a whole. In Japan the instruction is different. You go to the mat with your instructor and he demonstrates on you. You are thrown, again and again. It is up to you watch, with soft eyes, to figure it all out with no prior instruction. You are forced to use your intuition, to sense, to make the necessary mental connections, and then to perform. All in a split second. It's a whole different mind-set. But such is the nature of inner power. For intuition to work, trusting is not enough; you must also train yourself to see, and to connect. And that, by the way, is the essence of creativity.

## ELIMINATE ANGER AND JEALOUSY

Inner power requires inner peace. Inner turmoil weakens you. Anger and jealousy actually undercut your strength, but many people don't seem to recognize this, at least as far as competition is concerned. In fact, some coaches and supervisors try to get their athletes and supervisees to become angry or envious of their opponents in order to increase motivation. On the surface, this makes a certain degree of sense.

When I was a kid, I watched Muhammed Ali on television before a fight, strutting his stuff and making degrading comments about his opponent. Apart from drumming up viewer interest in the fight, I couldn't figure out why he'd want to make his opponent madder at him than his opponent already was. Muhammed Ali knew the fundamental rule of anger: Cool's the rule, hot gets shot. Sure, anger increases motivation, but it reduces precision. Angry people tend to fly off half-cocked, and they make mistakes. In any contest, the cooler person has the advantage. He or she can compete more carefully and channel his or her energy more effectively.

There is another insidious problem with anger and jealousy. All the angry or jealous person (and one cannot be jealous without being angry) sees is the opponent. He or she becomes so emotionally wrapped up with beating the other person that he or she loses sight of his own actions and the consequences thereof. That's another reason why angry and jealous people make more mistakes. Muhammed Ali knew that if he could get his opponent to concentrate on mostly on *him* during the bout, Ali would have a tremendous psychological advantage. This is why many of the psych-outs described earlier work so well.

There is a third, even deeper, problem with these emotions. The jealous person feels one-down, incomplete. I can't be jealous of you unless I feel that I lack something that you have. I can't feel anger toward you unless I perceive that you hurt me (therefore I must be vulnerable) or challenged or one-upped me, or that I am not in sufficient control. These feelings put you into a position of felt deficit in relation to someone else feelings which you feel you must overcome.

Anger and jealousy are red herrings. They lure you off track. They sap your energy, drawing you away from the task at hand, causing you to want to beat out, or beat up, someone else rather than to enhance your own situation.

I commonly see jealous spouses in my practice. For example, a wife discovers her husband is interested in another woman. What does the wife do? She yells and screams, or cries and gets depressed. She berates her husband and makes his life at home miserable. Why? To punish him for his misdeeds and encourage him to want to remain faithful to his wife! She really wants her husband back, loving and faithful to her. Her hurt and anger are very natural, but by losing sight of what she really desires and by acting strictly on the basis of her anger and jealousy, she drives her husband deeper into the arms of his paramour. How natural, as we look at what goes on, but how self-defeating when we see the big picture. Somehow it rarely, if ever, occurs to these women to fight fire with fire—to use strategy—and attempt to make themselves irresistible to their husbands so they can win them back.

Why don't these wives see this? Because (1) they're too wrapped up in their pain and desire to get even, and (2) they perceive that they are one-down on the other woman, that the other woman automatically has the advantage. Inwardly their own self-doubt does them in.

This is how anger and jealousy work. They are both born of fear. Social competition involves anger, jealousy, and envy, almost by definition, and all too often structured competition such as sports and sales contests arouses these feelings as well.

Inner peace means letting go of your fear and anxiety. And that means banishing their handmaidens: anger, jealousy, envy, and the competitive mind-set. Anger and jealousy may be useful in fighting a war where you want to motivate yourself to kill (yet any combat vet will tell you how vital it is to remain cool under fire), but it has no place in business, sports, or any other worthwhile endeavor. The "business-is-war" mentality that exists today runs the risk of confusing these issues. The Healthy Competitor needs to get these issues and feelings straight.

When you start feeling angry or jealous, stop. Ask yourself what is really going on that led you to feel this way. Ask yourself what you really want for yourself. Look beyond revenge or the destruction of the other person. Rather, focus on the best desirable positive outcome, and once picturing that, plan and implement your strategy for making it occur. Don't underestimate your opponent, but be careful not to *overestimate* him or her either. Never forget that it's not what you do to your opponent that counts, it's what you're doing to and for yourself.

What's the best way to take care of yourself? Stay on track, deal carefully with your opponent, and if necessary, forgive him or her.

## BALANCE THE YIN AND YANG IN YOUR LIFE

Translated into Westernese: "Be all that you can be," "Integrate both sides of your brain." So much has been made of the right hemisphere-left hemisphere dichotomy that we often forget we operate best with a "whole brain," which balances both sides.

The Chinese consider the Yin side of us to be the "feminine" side, characterized by feelings, sincerity, intuition, pleasure, social interest and cooperation, receptiveness, maintenance, diffuse awareness, mediation, and a tendency to see things as a synthesis

This is counterbalanced by the Yang, or "masculine" side, with such traits as rational thinking, toughness, and inclination toward facts and figures, accomplishment, analysis, personal drive and competition, pursuit, construction, focused consciousness, and inventiveness.[1] In Chinese tradition these two sides are polar opposites, but everything depends on their being in a constantly changing balance.

We all possess both Yin (right hemisphere) and Yang (left hemisphere) functions, but traditionally one side is underdeveloped. In most men, and therefore in most organizations, the Yin side gets short shrift. But it doesn't take much analysis to figure out that the Yin side holds the key skills required to solve people problems, while the Yang side is great for handling data and nonhuman concerns. Also, is it any wonder now that Yang-heavy organizations are so internally competitive, and that many women coming into the workplace have to develop Yang skills to survive? Parenthetically, this makes women really tough opponents. When they start Yang-sided competing they do it with Yin-sided finesse and sensitivity that their male counterparts often lack.

The task is to bring Yin and Yang in balance. Work to develop the skills you lack. If you're Yang-predominant, consciously try to cut back a bit and substitute some parallel Yin skills, and vice versa. You can do it. The skills are there already, waiting to be recognized and developed. If you need help, quietly watch a person who is strong in a skill you want to develop. Don't be a copycat, but watch how he or she does it, and learn. Ask for help if you need to. (This is a Yin skill we all could benefit from increasing.)

People and organizations both must work to increase Yin skills if they are to compete effectively amidst the increasingly complex pressures and challenges that confront us. The Healthy Competitor who balances Yin and Yang has a decided advantage.

## DEVELOP YOUR "WINNING FEELING"

The "Winning Feeling", or the high performance state, is actually a specific state of consciousness in which everything seems to happen automatically. Your subconscious mind takes over and it seems like you're on autopilot. This automatic quality is the state's key characteristic, but there are several other characteristics. You experience a natural coordination of all bodily systems. Everything flows in harmony. You feel physically and emotionally free. You are totally absorbed in the activity itself. There is no thought of past or future, or how you're doing. You're totally involved in the present moment. Your concentration is increased and narrowly focused on the task at hand, and extraneous factors tend to be blocked out. A major league pitcher whom I performance-coached told me he totally blocked out the fans, the scoreboard, even the batter! His concentration was on the ball itself and the ball's destination.

In the high performance state, people sometimes experience changes in perception, especially in time. A race car driver said that he felt like he had "all the time in the world" to make a particular move. In reality, he had a split second. Peak performers also feel a sense of exhilaration. The activity is a mountaintop experience for them. Energy level is high and fatigue doesn't exist.

Other brain functions click in to the high performance state as well. There is a shift to a predominantly right-hemisphere mode. Planning and analyzing functions are reduced, or even blocked out. Instead, the peak performer operates on synthesis, seeing the whole all at once, automatically. She acts on intuition, which clicks in at the subconscious level: she just acts and it *works*, without thought, without planning. Because conscious thought is diminished, there tends to be an amnesia afterward of what actually happened. Oftentimes you can ask an athlete, "How did you execute that really complicated move?" She will say, "I don't know!" That's because she *doesn't* know. Her subcionscious mind knows, and that's all that matters at the moment. Many athletes report a diminished pain sensitivity as well. In this state people often do their absolute best, many times outperforming their previous attempts.

How do you achieve this state when you need it? This is the tricky part. You can't force peak performance; you have to *let* it happen naturally. In fact, force, tension, and premeditated demands for peak performance actually kill your chances of experiencing it. Rather you need to "program" it into your mind. This is what world-class athletes do. You can do it, too. For athletics, business, or any other purpose, the principles and methods are basically the same.

Top athletes use mental programming skills of some kind, regardless of what they may call it. Given two athletes of equal ability, the edge goes to the one who can control her mind, who can recreate the subconscious feel of perfect performance at will. This requires a set of skills separate from the ones required for the sport. The same is true for the business competitor. Learn these skills and you'll have the edge. You also get another benefit: you will learn to relax and, by so doing, decrease your stress level and your risk of illness.

At one time or another, you have experienced the high performance state with some or all of the characteristics described above. Perhaps you experienced it very recently, or a long time ago. It doesn't matter. Incidentally, the "winning feeling" refers to peak performance; it has nothing necessarily to do with traditional competition or actually winning anything. Athletes often refer to it as the "subconscious feel" of an exceptional performance.

## DISCOVERING YOUR "WINNING FEELING"

Think back to the last time you experienced the winning feeling in relation to your profession. Close your eyes. Get that time clearly in mind for a couple of moments, relive it, then jot down what you experienced under the following headings:

1. What you were doing at the time
2. Physical sensations
3. Thoughts you had at the time
4. Emotions
5. What cues or circumstances contributed to or set in motion the winning feeling
6. Jot down a brief summary of your particular "winning feeling"

You may wish to repeat this exercise several times with different experiences to see what patterns emerge. What you have been doing is taking the experience apart, to see what makes it tick. Question(5) is particularly important. The high performance state just doesn't happen. It's triggered. Imagining your past successes will help you get into your winning feeling. So will mentally rehearsing an upcoming event. Visualize it. See yourself performing flawlessly. The more you run through your winning feeling in your mind, the more readily you will be able to perform at your peak in reality.

Tell yourself that success is inevitable, that you will succeed, no matter what. Ingrain that message deep within your soul. It will build your confidence, strengthen your resolve, empower your actions. This belief—no, this *knowledge*—will liberate your inner power and create a self-fulfilling prophecy that makes your success more sure.

Now, win at *what?* Should you run off half-cocked looking for something to succeed in? No way.

There is another skill that will help you expand your inner power, one that will give you the staying power to keep succeeding, one that no Healthy Competitor can ignore. You've seen it in business. You've seen it in sports. What drives those people who make the most of their inner power? What keeps them going in spite of frustration? Mission. These people possess a sense of Mission which empowers their lives.

Consider this quote on success. It exemplifies the wholesome expression of your inner power:

To laugh often and much; to win the respect of intelligent people and the affection of children; to earn the appreciation of honest critics and endure the betrayal of false friends; to appreciate beauty, to find the best in others; to leave the world a bit better, whether by a healthy child, a garden patch, or a redeemed social condition; to know even one life has breathed easier because you have lived. This is to have succeeded.

Ralph Waldo Emerson

# Notes

1. Adapted from Foy, N. *The Yin and Yang in Organizations.* New York: William Morrow, 1981.

# 11

# Your Personal Mission: The Healthy Competitor's Lifeline

WHAT brings meaning to your existence? What brings you true joy? Take a moment to answer these questions, not with your head, but with your heart.

Perhaps you had a quick answer. Perhaps you need more time to reflect. Perhaps you don't know. Perhaps you thought they are trick questions.

If your first reaction was that they were "trick questions," you were right, in a sense. They're tricky in that they are really profound, yet look simple on the surface.

"This a book on competition!" you say. "What have these issues of 'meaning' and 'joy' to do with gaining a winning edge?"

Everything! I contend that unless you find true joy and meaning in competing, in excelling, that you really don't have the "winning edge" at all. True joy, true meaning. Not the short-term thrill of beating out your opponents. We know that doesn't last. Not the short-term meaning of a particular activity, but joy and meaning that has the power to infuse your life, that can move you to greatness!

Here's the catch: traditional competition cannot possibly yield true meaning and joy. If you're not sure, ask yourself this question: Apart from money and survival needs, what do I need? What do we all need?

Now ask yourself this one: Can a competitive environment, or traditional competition, provide for these needs?

Think about this. When you answered the opening questions, did your answer have anything to do with your work? Take a moment to answer the following questionnaire.

"I am currently practicing my primary occupation in the setting in which I am now employed because . . ."
(Please rank your five main reasons, with number 1 being the most important one.)

_____ The job is "a natural" one for me. I'm comfortable.

_____ I am good at what I do. (do not necessarily enjoy it)

_____ Others tell me I am good at what I do.

_____ I inherited (or stepped into my role in) the family business.

_____ Of the amount of money I now make.

_____ Of the good relations I have with my coworkers.

_____ This job is my key to increased status among colleagues, friends, and family.

_____ This job provides the possessions I want, e.g., fancy car, big house, pool, etc.

_____ This job provides financial security.

_____ This job has a big benefit package—e.g., insurance, pension plan, profit sharing, excellent vacation and sickness benefits, company car, etc.

_____ I thoroughly enjoy my work.

_____ This job gives me a chance to help others, to make a contribution.

_____ This job gives me power.

_____ Of the advancement potential up the corporate ladder.

_____ Of the advancement potential financially.

_____ Of pressure from family, friends, or other significant people in my life.

_____ I'm trapped. The salary and benefits are such that if I took another position I'd lose too much.

_____ I must have this level of income to pay my expenses.

_____ I have freedom to innovate.

_____ I can be my own boss.

_____ This job provides me a significant sense of personal meaning and identity (apart from status benefits).

_____ This is what my training and/or experience fit me for.

_____ I want to (have considered) change jobs, but once in a job you stick with it.

_____ Other (specify)_____

_____ Other (specify)_____

What did your answers reveal?

Norm Rebin, a professional speaker, tells that when he was a boy in western Canada, a famous speaker in that locality came to town. The whole town turned out for the speech, which was absolutely breathtaking. When the presentation was over, Norm went up to the speaker and asked him, "Why do you do it? Why do you go around and speak?" Norm probably expected to hear about the glamour, the fame, or the income. Rather, the speaker said, "Because I couldn't live without it!"[1]

"Because I couldn't live without it!" That speaker possessed an inner fire, an inner passion, which spurred him onward. Do you do what you do because you couldn't live without it? If so, why? If not, why not? The choice is yours!

What is that drives a person onward? What is it that makes a person come back for more in the face of adversity, stress, and defeat? Frankly, we can think of some negative reasons: perfectionism, guilt, neurosis, stubbornness, and stupidity will do it. But these don't count. What's the positive drive?

Will goals do it? Goals are extremely important motivators, and no Healthy Competitor would be without them. But there's something even stronger, more compelling than goals, without which goals can lack coordination and meaning.

That elusive something is a sense of mission. The healthiest competitors possess it, although they may not have taken time to specifically define it.

It's a rough life out there. We live in exciting times, but tough times in some ways. Look around. Depression is the number one mental health problem today, and depression is often mixed with anxiety. Adolescent suicide is up three hundred percent in the last decade. Valium, a tranquilizer, is the most frequently prescribed drug in the world. Tagamet, for ulcers, is the second most prescribed medication.

My neighbor once had a problem with her Labrador retreiver. It had some kind of "nervous reaction." She called the vet, who told her to give it a Valium and call him in the morning. When she told him that she had no Valium he became incensed. "What do you mean you haven't got Valium?"

Look at the business pressure we all face: mergers, acquisitions, leveraged buyouts, takeovers, power jockeying, turfwars, reorganizations at the broad level, jealousy at the one-on-one level. We've already dealt with how to handle this. But what ties your activities together? What's your best protection against burnout?

Your mission in life is your welcome beacon in a foggy, rock and reef–filled sea of confusion and daily pressure. It is the guiding light that keeps you on track, that provides coordination and meaning for your goals.

You want to rise above the level of daily pressures? You want to put the joy back into work and "competing"?

Then be a *mission-ary.*

What is a "mission?" We can define it as *a passion and commitment to a cause larger than yourself.*

When I was in college, I was considering becoming a missionary. To discover what I'd be getting into, I interviewed many missionaries and read the biographies of several more. As I looked at their lives and listened to their experiences, I noted six characteristics that the most successful missionaries had in common, six qualities that gave them the direction, drive, and staying power to thrive in the face of severe adversity:

- *Vision of human need and possibilities.* They have the ability to see something where now there is nothing. The mission is sparked with creativity and strong empathy.

- *Identification with a worthy cause.* They identify with something larger than themselves, which provides personal meaning.

- *Sense of one's own importance in promoting the cause.* This is not egotism but a healthy respect for one's role, talents, and capabilities. The greatness of the cause promotes a healthy humility.

- *Indestructable courage and commitment.* Do or die. These people possess the ability to hang in there when the going gets tough.

- *Onward-outward orientation and drive.* They look for new avenues and opportunities of service. They have an expansionist orientation quite akin to that of many entrepreneurs.

- *Never-ending hope and faith.* This is the quality that provides the spark for mighty deeds.

You may have noticed that the first letters of these six qualities spell VISION. No accident. All great endeavors begin with vision. Without it we are doomed to live in the darkness of our own shadows. Put all these qualities together, however, and miracles happen!

"Me a miracle-worker?" you may ask. "Yes, *You!* You, who you are right now, where you are right now. Our society does us a tremendous disservice by leading us to think that greatness and creativity are the possessions of only a very few—the rich, or the famous, or the powerful.

Greatness, creativity, miracles are the potential of us all. Deeds of greatness and miracles happen every day, performed by unsung heroes whose fame may never spread beyond their immediate family, company, or neighborhood. "Common people doing uncommon things." That is a definition which has been used for excellence.

We all have the power to do mighty deeds. But the engine that drives a mighty locomotive requires a little spark to get going. Otherwise it remains idle. That spark, for us, is our sense of mission.

No one has ever been spurred to action by reason alone. "Reason rides the horse of emotion," someone once said, and this is where your sense of mission in your life has its greatest impact,—in charging up your feelings, which then guide your actions.

Your mission ties your goals to your life, and gives them meaning and power. Your mission is your purpose for your work, for your life, for your very existence.

How do you discover your mission?

For some people this is not a problem. There are a few of us whom Earl Nightingale, who pioneered the audiocassette learning industry, calls "River People." River people become aware of their purpose at an early age. "They are born to spend their lives in great rivers of the most absorbing interest, and they throw themselves into those rivers wholly." Great artists and musicians, such as Mozart and Leonardo da Vinci often fall into this category. So do businessmen such as Henry Royce, who was the founder of the Rolls-Royce automobile company.[2]

The rest of us need to set ourselves to the task of discovering our mission "with the patience and assiduousness of a paleontologist on an important dig," says Nightingale. But what a fantastic discovery! Sir William Osler once said, "Find your way into work in which there is an enjoyment of it and all shadows of annoyance seem to flee away."

Regarding the miracles that derive from the mission, listen to the poet, Goethe:

> Until one is committed, there is hesitancy, the chance to draw back, always ineffectiveness. Concerning all acts of initiative (and creation) there is one elementary truth the ignorance of which kills countless ideas and splendid plans: That the moment one definitely commits oneself, Providence moves too. All sorts of things then occur to help one that would never otherwise have occurred. . . . A whole stream of events issue from the decision, raising in one's favor all manner of unforeseen incidents and meetings and material assistance which no one could have dreamed would come this way. . . . Whatever you can do or dream, you can begin. Boldness has genius, power, and magic in it.

Let's begin—boldly!

To discover your mission where do you look? It lies within you. Your mission lies at the vortex of your:

Talents, strengths | What gives Satisfaction

>MISSION<

What gives excitement | What gives Meaning

To find these things, look into your own life. Figure 11-1 depicts the areas in which you might look. Seeds of your mission and

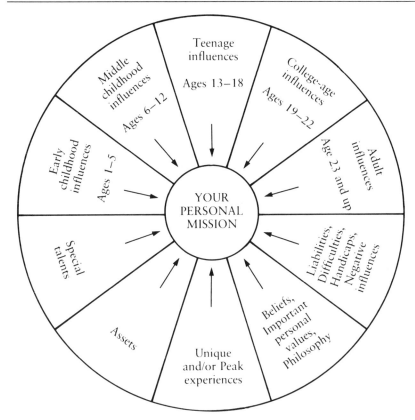

Figure 11-1. VECTOR ANALYSIS FOR MISSION DEVELOPMENT

purpose can be found in each of these areas. The top five vectors are the stages of your life. As you review them, your recall will be selective. Since mission discovery is your aim, you may well recall incidents that have some bearing on that mission, even though at first they may seem unrelated. What influences made the most impact on you? Why? What are the messages for you now? Do patterns or trends begin to emerge?

The bottom five are relevant characteristics and experiences. Does the liabilities vector surprise you? Often we are spurred to excellence more because of limitations and handicaps which must overcome, than because of the strengths we possess. Review these vectors. What patterns emerge here? How well do they fit with the common threads from the various stages of your life? What stands out that is significant, exciting, meaningful? What experiences or factors do you find particularly compelling?

W. Clement Stone, the founder of *Success* magazine, has outlined a four-step process for discovering your mission, for moving from the raw data phase to sorting out your specific mission:[3]

1. *Assess yourself.* Honestly appraise your strengths and weaknesses. (You've done this already, both in chapter 9 and in your vector analysis. Is there anything you've overlooked that you should add?)

2. *List your activities.* Jot down all the things you do, and the things you would like to do in your life. This may take several pages. Don't censor the list. Don't leave anything off just because it seems impossible. Nightingale says to pay special heed to those activities to which you feel drawn. "If it's the right work for you, chances are you've found yourself fooling around with it in your spare time."[4]

3. *Rate the activities.* Review your list and assign each activity an A, B, C, or D, with A being extremely important, B very important, C somewhat important, and D unimportant.

4. *Assign priorities.* Make a list of the A and B items only. Rank them, with 1 being the activity most important to you.

Stone says that if you've prioritized your list properly, item 1 should be your major purpose.

How can you tell when you've found it? Stone advises that if you listen to your feelings, they will tell you. "Psychiatrist Victor Frankl wrote, "Everyone has his own specific vocation or mission in life to carry out a concrete assignment which demands fulfillment." When you discover your mission, you will feel its demand. It will fill you with enthusiasm and a burning desire to get to work on it."[5]

You may not identify your major purpose on the first try. If you don't, then repeat the process until that purpose emerges.

You can't manufacture a mission. It starts within you and grows from inside out, where you discover it. Then it grips you and works its way from outside in. Lasting zeal can only blossom in the soil of personal meaning and faith. As the nineteenth-century poet of the Far West, Sam Foss, wrote:

Bring me men to match my mountains,
Bring me men to match my plains,
Men with empires in their purpose
And new eras in their brains.

Here are some additional questions you can ask yourself to help you crystalize your mission:

- What do you want to achieve with your life?

- What do you most want to contribute to society?

- What do you feel most compelled to do?

- If you had but two weeks to live and could do anything you wanted, what would you do?

- How do you wish others to remember you when you're gone? (As an exercise, you might write your own epitaph. This helps you to clarify what really counts.)

How sharply and succinctly did you answer these questions?

# Your Mission Statement

Perhaps the most significant document an organization can possess is a well-defined, mission statement or statement of purpose. It is the focal point of all the organization's activities and its reason for existence. It is the rallying point for motivating the personnel.

A properly executed mission statement will cause a company to rethink its operations in every area and level. It becomes the standard to live up to, the mission which must be made to happen.

This is what happened when George Patterson, president and senior partner of City Gardens, an interior landscaping firm in Newton, Massachusetts stated his company mission to his 135 employees: "I want City Gardens to be the best interior landscape company in the world. Second best is not worth the effort. Fairness, communication, and pride will get us there. Be fair to yourself, our customers, and the company. Communicate with your fellow workers and our clients. Do work you can be proud of."[6]

Organizations need mission statements; so do you! When you've discovered your mission, write it down. Then post it: on your desk at work, in the mirror of your bathroom, wherever you will see it. But most importantly, embed it in your mind, where it can begin to take charge of your actions.

Think your statement out carefully. Keep it short, simple, but powerful. Use emotion-laden words. Use superlatives. While your mission should be within your potential, it should have a magnetic, uplifting, larger-than-life quality about it. This may be a difficult balance to achieve, but try. Writing it out adds a sense of commitment and power to your statement. It is more compelling than just thinking of it.

(Practice Attempt)
MY PERSONAL MISSION IN LIFE:

_____

_____

_____

_____

Is this statement as powerful, as clear, or as brief as you want it to be. If not, polish it up and give it another try.

MY PERSONAL MISSION IN LIFE:

_____

_____

_____

_____

Does your mission, as you define it, relate to your work? If so, fine. If not, however, you may find your daily occupation shallow or lacking in meaning for you. You may go home at the end of the day wondering what you have accomplished.

For the Healthy Competitor who chooses to pursue or remain in a given line of work, there should be a very close tie between one's mission and one's occupation. Work should, ideally, be an outlet for your mission, a vehicle for bringing it to fruition, the arena where it can be manifested to its fullest.

If your present job is not providing that outlet, there are several things you may need to consider if you want maximum fulfillment in your life:

1. Can I bring my mission in line with my current job, or bring my current job in line with my mission? How? (This may be the easiest option, if it can be done without major surgery on your mission.)

2. Is there another position or opportunity in my organization that would be better suited to my needs and interests? (If so you might wish to pursue it. See chapter 13 on positioning.)

3. If you score a goose egg on questions 1 and 2, you may have to decide to:
   a. Jump ship—look for another organization that is compatible with your mission, or
   b. Stay put, and look for after-hours ways to fulfill your mission.

Whatever you need to do, suffice it to say that Healthy Competitors have a strong sense of mission operating behind their actions. It provides the drive, the persistence, that unstoppable quality that, in itself, gives them the winning edge.

Here is why so much "motivation" at conventions and in the office really doesn't work. One's inner chimes never get rung, so the "motivation," the hype, never sticks. True motivation can only come from within. Lasting zeal can only blossom in the soil of personal meaning and faith. That is the Healthy Competitor's significant advantage!

Yet a mission alone is like a dream without substance, like an automobile engine without the car to put it in. What gives your sense of mission the specific path or channel toward fulfillment?

# Goals

Goals flesh out the mission. They organize and coordinate the actions that bring the mission to fulfillment. They also save considerable energy. How often do people launch out on a new idea or project only to fail because their actions have been too haphazard. Uncoordinated activity is often worse than useless. It slows you down, wastes effort, and may actually put you behind.

Goals can be tricky, however, because once you set them you may actually achieve them! Therefore they need to be well-conceived, and certain pitfalls need to be avoided. Most Healthy Competitors in athletics and business have clearly defined goals. Most unhealthy competitors do, too. Two factors give the Healthy Competitors the advantage:

- Their goals are directly tied to their mission and provide the direct vehicle for its expression.

- They know how to wend their way through the goal-setting minefield so as not to get caught in unforeseen traps.

"Goal-setting minefield?" Isn't that strong language? Not at all. There are not many heavier albatrosses to hang around the neck of one's career than an ill-conceived goal! Rarely can one find more discouragement and demotivation (as well as confusion) than in the face of an unrealistically high goal. Failure to achieve the "big one" has crashed many people to the ground.

Here are some tips to help you maximize your goal-setting, goal-reaching potential:

1. Make your goal *personal,* not comparative nor competitive. In chapter 7 I discussed sport psychologist Lars-Eric Unestahl's findings regarding the motivation value of competitive personal goals. Competitive goals may bring out a short-term flurry of motivation, but in the long run they impede performance! Why? Competitive goals make winning relative, and therefore take some of your perceived control out of your hands. If your goal is to "beat Tom Jones for the vice presidency," for example, the wording of the goal itself forces you to think about Jones, and that may entice you to worry about what Jones is doing.

   To say, "My goal is to become company VP" may sound like only a semantic difference, but it is not. It is a difference that goes deep into one's subconscious mind. The competitive goal programs you to compete in the traditional fashion, whereas the personal goal programs you to achieve.

A personal goal is structured toward meeting an objective standard or position. No comparison or competition is implied in the wording of the goal itself.

2. Make your goal *totally positive.* Use positive language only, no negatives. Language conditions us. As your goals are *worded*, so will they be understood. As they are understood, so will you act.

3. Make your goal *reasonable, reachable.* Pie-in-the-sky will only fall on your head, and cloud your vision! The word, "positive" has two meanings, and both apply: (a) positive as opposite of negative, and (B)positive as confident and sure you can achieve. Your goal should make you stretch— if it doesn't it's of negligible value—but it must be within your potential grasp, as your mission should be.

4. Make your goal *highly specific and well-defined.* This is especially important for performance goals. A narrow goal definition focuses and intensifies energy. Don't go after a bear with birdshot. Don't get too spread out. Remember that a key factor in healthy competition is the maximization and efficient use of personal energy. Mix a little of everything, and you get a lot of nothing!

5. Make your goal *personally meaningful.* By now this should be taken for granted. But, oh so often, people confuse "acquiring a deeply desired possession" with "personally meaningful." Nothing is further from the truth! So you finally got the gizmo you wanted for so long. Perhaps it was a boat, or an expensive car. That's wonderful. You enjoy using it. But does it provide real happiness? This is much different than fleeting enjoyment. In my New Way to Compete seminars, I ask, "You wanted a new car. That was your goal. How long does it make you happy?" The answers are always "for the short-term." One person carped, "Until I have to make the first payment."

True happiness can only derive from personal meaning. Danny Thomas once said, "All of us are born for a reason, but all of us don't discover why. Success in life has nothing to do with what you gain in life or accomplish for yourself. It's what you do for others."[7]

6. Strive for *goals of giving* over goals of getting. This is what Danny Thomas was saying. True satisfaction is directly related to the contribution you make. A gift is of no value until it is given. Most of us are concerned with what we get. This is normal. The important question is *how* we get what we want. The Healthy Competitor is very aware of, and fully believes, the wisdom from the old prayer, "It is through giving that we receive." This isn't cutesy religious or sentimental pap; it's a iron-clad law of living!

7. Make your goal *powerful*. Word it so that it arouses deep desire to increase your goal's power even more.

8. Make your goal *visual*. Visualize it. Create in your mind a scene of you already having met your goal and enjoying its benefits.

9. Develop *long- and short-range goals*. A long-range or broad goal can be broken down into short-term, easy steps. Set time limits, e.g., three years, one year, six months, one month, even weekly goals.

10. Dare to *dream*. Your daydreams, and your night dreams too, can reflect your goals and give impetus to them. Your dreams also add color and creativity to your goals, and motivate you to go onward.

11. Be aware of the *"approach-avoidance conflict."* Sociologist Kurt Lewin many years ago developed the concept of the approach-avoidance conflict. What it means is that the closer one gets to a desired goal, the more apprehensive she becomes, and the further away she is from the goal, the more she wants it. This is a general psychological principle. It is part of the dynamic that many salespeople recognize as "buyer's remorse:" someone makes a big purchase and immediately has second thoughts about it. Many people, perhaps most, experience the approach-avoidance conflict the closer they get to achieving a major goal. If you know what it is in advance, you will recognize it and not be dismayed or confused by it if you experience it. But how do you tell

the difference between the approach-avoidance conflict and actual valid misgivings that you begin to recognize. Carefully listing all the realistic pros and cons of achieving your stated goals can help you sort this out.

12. Act as if it is *impossible for you to fail,* as if you possess all the powers and talents necessary for success. If your goal is properly conceived and defined, you really do!

Make a list of your major goals, tie them to your mission, word them powerfully, and assign time frames for completion. Review and refine this list frequently, keeping your mission and your goals in the forefront of your mind.

# Notes

1. Rebin N. "Power, Passion, and Principle of the public platform." address to national convention National Speakers Association, July 1986
2. Stone, W. C. "The river of success." *Success!* September 1987, 80.
3. Ibid.
4. Ibid.
5. Ibid.
6. Roman, M.B. "The mission: Setting your vision in words is the crucial executive act." *Success!* June 1987, 55.
7. Thomas. D. Quoted in *Bits and Pieces.* Issue unknown.

# 12

# Building Charisma and Your Power of Positive Influence

POWER is mysterious. It's supposed to be. A good magician creates an aura of mystery and awe. We know that all his magic is explainable, but not knowing the explanation makes the "magic." As Peter Johnson, corporate strategist, once said, "Technique explained is no technique." Ever try to get a magician to tell you how he does a particular trick? A herd of bull elephants couldn't stomp it out of him: For the magic to work, the magician had better know what he's doing; you had better not!

Power is like that. So is charisma. We observe it in action. It looks so natural, so effortless. For a few, it is. Some people are naturally charismatic. They seem born with just the right looks, just the right style. It all seems to fall into place for them. A few others couldn't wield an ounce of power if their lives depended on it.

For the 95 percent in between, however, "style" can be learned. That's right! There's a technology to social power, certain tricks of the trade. If you learn them and practice them, you will be more effective at working with, motivating, and leading people. You will be more effective at eliminating opposition.

What is charisma? John Wayne, George Washington, Franklin D. Roosevelt, Dr. Ruth, Winston Churchill, Dolly Parton, Robert Redford, Ronald Reagan, Barbra Streisand, Charlton Heston, Mother Teresa, John F. Kennedy, Eleanor Roosevelt, Hitler, Lenin,

Gandhi, Muhammad, Jesus: all these people had, or have, charisma. Charismatic people come from all walks of life. They hold different professions. Most are not "famous" in any sense of the word, although some others are. What do they have in common? Looks? Sex appeal? Size or shape? Personal style? Flair and polish? Ability to give a stirring speech in public? The answer: none of the above.

For all practical purposes, charisma is *the ability to attract, influence, and motivate people.* Nothing more, nothing less. "Style" helps, but which style? There is no common charismatic style. Then which style? *Your* style. The style you have, the style you polish, built on your inner power, demonstrated by (a) your methods and actions, and (b) your "presence." Your inner power is the root of your charisma. Without the inner power, style is just tinsel: glitzy but without substance. It won't last. For the purposes of this chapter, your inner power is assumed to be well-developed. By following the guidelines in this chapter, your inner power, as well as your social power, will be enhanced.

## Dynamics of Social Power

Power is complex and has been described in many ways. Boil it all down, however, and you come to one single root or basis of any organizational power: cooperation. He or she who has power, who is a good leader, is able to generate cooperation. That is the only practical yardstick by which true organizational power can be measured. One may be the boss, but if she cannot achieve cooperation from her employees, what true power does she have? No other form of power is as potent or as durable. She may be able to coerce others, but they will eventually rebel or sabotage. She may be able to instill fear, but then the power lies not in the person but in the fear itself. When people finally refuse to be afraid, the power of the fear-maker vanishes.

Threats and fear produce compliance. Never confuse compliance with true *cooperation.* Compliance can be likened to the submissive behavior of a vanquished people. They obey, but their heart is not in it. True cooperation comes from within. It does not require a great deal of sustained external pressure to keep it going. Cooperation is the only form of power that really counts, the only form you can depend on. Other forms of power are an illusion.

It is difficult to achieve true cooperation, however. It requires taking time to understand and to convince others. Other forms of power—those that occur through fear or fiat—are much faster and easier to obtain, but more difficult to keep.

There are two overall types of power which we must consider. They are distinctly different, not only in their tactics, but also in their basic philosophy. They are Pressure Power and Presence Power.

## PRESSURE POWER VS PRESENCE POWER

Pressure power is our traditional conception, the format around which many of our large organizations were built. The military is also a pressure power system. Cooperation can, and sometimes does, occur in pressure power organizations, but this is not the norm. Rather human power relations in pressure power organizations is based on a vertical, hierarchical structure of bosses and underlings. Naturally, however, not every hierarchical organization subscribes to a raw pressure power philosophy. The primary pressure power method is power-over or command/demand where the goal is dominance. The power base in raw pressure power is fear— fear of punishment or of loss of reward. The fundamental motivational question is, "How can I *make* them perform?

This is an impossible management question. One cannot make another person perform! Even compliance and obedience involve cooperation, at least at the behavioral level. The power to say "no" is irrevocable. There have been many instances down through the ages where people have been literally martyred because of their refusal to comply with what they considered to be "impossible" demands, from the early Christians in the Coliseum to victims resisting a mugger. It has always been true: government exists only by the consent of the governed. Presence power recognizes and capitalizes on this fact; pressure power has never learned it.

But as the winds of change sweep across Corporate America, inflexible institutions will decay and eventually die. Pressure power will be forced to shift. The new breed of American achiever will be much highly selective in choosing the type of organization in which he or she will work. Old power bases will need to flex in order to retain good people. In this area, American Individualism is firmly coming of age. The new achiever will not stand still for a workplace that does not meet, or even recognize, his or her personal needs and goals.

Presence power embodies the new age. Companies and individuals who develop that power now will have a decided competitive edge. Decentralizing authority, "flattening the pyramid." and the "reverse pyramid" approaches to management are all bids in the direction of presence power, although ultimate presence power goes much further. The primary power method is power through positive influence; the goal is to win them over. The power base is willing cooperation and teamwork. The ultimate management question, the only one that really works, is, "How can I *encourage* them to perform?"

Encouragement is the only true motivator for true cooperation. Not cheap rah-rah pep talks, nor shallow "you can do it" pats on the back, nor empty praise. These do not provide lasting encouragement, although they may spur an increase in short-term productivity. Encouragement evokes genuine caring, concern, and faith in others, and in their willingness and desire to perform if their needs are met. Encouragement is the stuff real charisma is made of!

True encouragement empowers people. It enables them to expand their strengths and capabilities, and hence their self-esteem. Managers with presence power provide channels for growth, for input, for increased decision-making and participation. In so doing they solidify their own position.

Let's turn now to how you can maximize your presence power in your own work setting.

---

# Maximizing Your Impact in Your Organization

Every organization has a "climate" or an "atmosphere." This is created initially by the personalities who work there and the circumstances that affect the organization from day to day. In time, however, this climate appears almost to have a life of its own, shaping in turn the behavior of the people who work there. The political infrastructure is a large factor in the organizational climate as well.

To maximize your positive impact and bring on positive change, your style and actions need to properly match the needs in your organizational climate, whether the organization is the one in which you work, or one in which you volunteer. Good leadership is essential in every case, even when everything is running smoothly.

Having expert knowledge and your ability to engender cooperation as a facilitator/empowerer are your key strategies when there are no problems. If there is turbulence in the organizational atmosphere, however, your specific strategy will need to change. He who has the most positive impact is the one who can most flexibly tailor strategy to the needs of both the situation itself and the people involved.

Geier, Downey, and Johnson have done significant research on the tactics which best impact on organizational climate variables. They identify six Impact Modes:

1. *Information Impact Mode*—Exerting influence because of the special knowledge and skill you have and can provide

2. *Magnetic Impact Mode*—Exerting influence because others like, trust or identify with you

3. *Position Impact Mode*—Exerting influence through the position or rank you hold

4. *Affiliation Impact Mode*—Exerting influence with others who need assistance in reducing high levels of anxiety caused by excessive demands on their skills and knowledge ("How much you care")

5. *Coercive Impact Mode*—Exerting influence through the rewards or benefits you can provide, or through being able to punish or take certain benefits away

6. *Tactical Impact Mode*—Exerting influence with others because of your recognized ability to organize and process a series of actions, activities, or functions to accomplish results. (How you execute):

They found that each of these impact modes was particularly helpful in dealing with a specific type of organizational dysfunction. They demonstrated that:

1. Information Impact Mode provides *enlightenment* when the climate is characterized by *ignorance*. In such a climate, information processing and dissemination systems are not operating well. The organization appears disorganized. Information vacuums can yield conflicting demands and expectations. Organizations are more likely to experience ignorance at times of rapid change and internal shifts.

   *Tactics to use:* focus on fact over emotion, provide necessary information, provide training and effective information processing systems, clarify issues

2. Magnetic Impact Mode provides *hope* in a climate of *despair*. There are many variations on this organizational theme, including hopelessness, low morale, and a depressive feeling. Varied events can lead to this climate, which is characterized by reduced work and output. People often see no way out.

   *Tactics to use:* motivate others, rally, inspire others to outperform previous levels, build enthusiasm, spell out others' unexpressed visions and dreams

3. Position Impact Mode provides *continuity* in a climate of *instability*. An unstable organization appears to be in a state of uneasy flux. Everything seems to be falling apart. In such a climate it is easy for people to do their own thing because of the apparent power vacuums. Power jockeying and conflicts frequently occur.

   *Tactics to use:* communicate through the appropriate channels, run the organization by the book, insist on using the proper chain of command, insist on adherence to policy and procedure, impose a monitoring system to provide control

4. Affiliation Impact Mode provides *security* in a climate of *anxiety*. In this environment, suspicion and mistrust reign. Responsibilities are fuzzy and the stress level is high. This type of environment frequently arises out of high levels of intense,

cutthroat competition. The direct causes of the anxiety are different and not easily identified; hence, the high levels of suspicion. (Author's note: Often the roots of the tension of lie within the nature of the competition itself, which is taken for granted and therefore not questioned.)

*Tactics to use:* attempt to develop unity and cooperation, show concern for others and their needs, recognize people's hopes and fears, stress common tasks and purposes, encourage and help others to find and implement their own solutions

5. Coercive Impact Mode provides *direction* in a climate of *crisis*. Crisis occurs in the wake of change that people are unable to cope with given their current skills and expertise. Reorganizations, acquisitions, mergers, and takeovers can precipitate crisis. Denial, apathy, and anger tend to show themselves, in that order.

*Tactics to use:* establish goals, targets, and standards for performance, use threats of punishment if necessary, establish rewards and make deals, show approval or disapproval, establish clear expectations

6. Tactical Impact Mode provides *order* in a climate of *disorganization*. Daily events do not run smoothly. It takes too much effort and frustration to get things accomplished. It's usually easy to see the symptoms of disorganization: people and processes seem to bump into each other, complaints accrue, production and service are slowed.

*Tactics to use:* set up strategies and procedures, diagnose possible problems and set up mechanisms to handle them, create systems through which goals can be accomplished, check up on how processes are being carried out and on how human resources are being utilized[2]

These tactics are generally appropriate to the climate situation described above. Your specific situation will require custom tailoring. Yet without an adequate diagnosis, your treatment plan will not be as effective. Using "The Climate Impact Profile System"[c] by Geier, et al, from which the above information was drawn, can help you pinpoint your natural impact style and the style which you expect that your organization requires. This self-scoring, self-interpreting inventory can be of great help in preparing an impact strategy. It is referenced at the end of this chapter, with information on how you can obtain it.

To attempt to modify an organization's climate does indeed require a systematic approach. The following steps should help.

1. Get a clear diagnosis of what is going on. Use the above six climate descriptions as a starting point. Does your organization fit one of these categories, or does it fit into more than one? What are the specific difficulties? What are their causes.

2. What skills or processes are required to solve the problem, to eliminate the causes?

3. Over which causes/problems do you have any direct influence? Which of your skills match the needs of the situation?

4. What other resources need to be involved? Which other key people need to come on board?

5. What is your vision of the end result? Assuming you are successful, what will the organization look like? How will you know when you've achieved this vision? You need behavioral criteria of success.

6. Develop your action plan, to include:

   • Your specific recommendations

   • What you can and will do yourself

   • How you will motivate and involve other key people

   • A step-by-step order of activities, with a monitoring system to measure how they are being carried out

   • Your time frame for completion

   • How to cope with "political" resistance along the way

Climate modification is no easy task. You may need to start small, in one division as a test case. You probably will only succeed if you get support from the top. Never overlook the political ramifications of your activities and the hidden agendas of others involved. At the outset, figure out who your supporters and resisters are likely to be, and what their relative power is, and plan accordingly.

# Overcoming Opposition

The traditional ways of defeating an opponent are with a direct attack or deception and infiltration. On a personal level, there is a natural tendency to "retreat to power" which we discussed earlier. Either way, the usual approach is to crush the opposition. This usually drives the enemy underground and provokes the desire to rebel and get even.

The Healthy Competitor looks not to crush opposition but to neutralize it. If you can find healthy ways to undercut your opponent's power base by demonstrating through your own positive actions that his position is untenable, you have made an important inroad. Choose the path of negotiation. Attempt to win your opponent over. The Healthy Competitor makes allies out of opponents whenever possible.

Conflict can be creative and vital to your organization. View it as a tool, an opportunity, rather than as a threat. Granted, "conflict resolution" can be a gut-wrenching experience sometimes, but often the outcome can put all parties ahead.

There was a division manager who had problems of backbiting and power jockeying in his division. The second-in-command position in his unit had been vacant for almost one and a half years. His attempts to achieve cooperation fell on deaf ears. An outside consultant showed him that a main problem was that he was seen by his employees as not sufficiently forceful and lacking in respect for them. There was a credibility gap between him and his staff.

This man was emotionally mature and dedicated to resolving the problems. It was discovered that the credibility gap centered on three or four key employees, one of whom was a supervisor. These key players spread their dissatisfaction among the other employees to gain support. Generally they had succeeded, and now they presented formidable opposition. What was the division manager to do?

He could "clean house," but this would kill his chances for improved credibility with the remaining staff. Instead he set out to build staff trust. He declared that no employees would be fired. He openly admitted his faults, but told the employees that he did respect them. He asked them for help in seeing how he could improve. He reiterated his vision for the division, which was actually very much like the visions his employees had. He began to work on calming his anger outbursts and set up one-on-one "conflict resolution sessions" with his key opponents. These were mediated by the consultant and focused on getting the barriers to cooperation out on the table. The emphasis was placed on mutual forgiveness and "where can we go from here?" to better work together and support each other. Figuratively, he put his head on the block, and not without effect. His employees began to see his improved interest in them and noted his courage in admitting his faults and asking for their help. This move began indirectly to erode his opponents' power base, as did the conflict resolution sessions. Two of the key opponents were won over, while the others still held out a while longer. The pendulum had begun to swing and eventually all opponents were won over. The division manager noted a significant improvement in morale and cooperation. Training on coping with competition and effective team building was begun, and other administrative changes were instituted that employees viewed as positive.

The division manager succeeded in building trust and gaining support. His opponents' energy began to work for, not against him, as the employees started to "see the light".

The division manager did not discredit his opposition; he even suggested that they had valid complaints about some of his actions! To continue to oppose in that situation became increasingly difficult. Words alone, however, wouldn't have been effective. The division manager *demonstrated* his concern by putting himself on the line and following through on his attempts at change. This had the "subliminal" effect of demonstrating improved leadership capability, and tacitly proving that a new, tighter system was emerging. By holding "conflict resolution" sessions, he was quietly warning,

"We won't let disagreement get out of hand. We don't permit barriers to grow. Most importantly, if you have a complaint, we'll deal fairly, but you will be accountable for getting it out in the open rather than resorting to tale-telling, gossip, and passive-aggressive competition."

The truly encouraging charismatic leader is committed to people power and win-win solutions to problems. Win-win solutions are rarely readily apparent, and the traditional competitive mode promotes win-lose. Therefore the charismatic leader must be a man or woman of vision, willing to see beyond the obvious, ready to transcend the limits of the situation wherever possible, and able to doggedly persist until the victory is won. On the other hand, if you absolutely cannot win, you need to be sensitive enough to know when to throw in the towel. Martyrdom and political suicide are never helpful. "Charisma" is as much a matter of strategy as of spirit.

There are several steps you can take to help you win over personal opponents:

1. Recognize and analyze their hidden agendas. Everyone has one. Hidden agendas are almost always be self-serving, concerned with solidifying or enhancing one's personal power or position. A negative hidden agenda is always competitive and reflects a competive attitude toward problem solving.

2. Commit yourself to problem solving rather than punishment. Go for a win-win wherever possible; go the extra mile to work things out rather than resort to administrative force or retaliation.

3. Look for what you and your opponent hold in common: goals, values, past experiences, vision for the organization. If you can discover a common meeting ground, if down deep you both want the same things, you're off to a good start.

4. Explore feelings and individual interpretations. Opposition is fueled by emotion. Once one is in an oppositional mode, he or she will interpret subsequent events in that light, to justify continued competitiveness. Get the feelings out on the table, privately and off-the-record, with a mutual agreement of no reprisal. Oftentimes long-standing feuds begin with a

misinterpretation, a side comment, etc. Frequently offense is taken when no offense is meant.

5. Compartmentalize disagreements. There may be some issues on which you will never agree. If so, then agree to disagree, and don't let that one issue interfere with the rest of your working relationship. A good working relationship is the ultimate goal, not "resolving" issues that won't be resolved.

6. Give each other permission to be open and to confront problems when they arise. There is no such thing as a "convenient time" to resolve an issue; to wait for a time that never comes only fuels the fires of hurt and discord. The longer you wait, the less likely the problem is to seem relevant, even though hurt feelings continue to fester.

7. Approach the other person in such a way as to let him or her save face. Say something like, "I have a concern about _____. I'm not sure I understand what you meant. Are you saying _____?" This opens the door to discussion with a minimum of defensiveness. It's easier for another person to address a possible misunderstanding than to cope with an accusation.

8. Open a confrontation with the three magic words. Psychiatrist Rudolf Dreikurs always trained counselors to begin interpretations or confrontations to patients with these words: "Could it be . . . ?" This allowed the patient a way out, to save face. It also implies that you're guessing rather than telling. No one likes to be told by someone else what he is up to. That's "playing psychiatrist," and is offensive to most people.

9. Strive for a mutual commitment to specific actions to help solve the problem. "Talking it out" usually isn't enough. Actions need to follow. By setting up an action plan, even if it's no more than an agreement to deal with issues when they arise, you have a basis for continued improvement. Always put your agreement in writing. You then have a "promisory note" that holds each of you accountable to follow through on your agreement.

10. Always treat your opponent with honor and respect. Also, be warm and friendly if you can do it sincerely. This dem-

onstrates that you are bigger than the issues that divide you and that you are too professional to harbor a grudge. This may do more than anything else to eventually turn around a recalcitrant opponent.

11. Pace things properly. How do you get a south-going horse running at full gallop to turn north? Very carefully! You tug the reins gently and the horse begins to turn before he knows it. Don't expect major improvements overnight. Your opponents may need time to sort things and to "sniff the air" to see if it's safe to let down their guard. Allow them that time.

You have developed your power of positive influence. You have goals and directions. You can make a difference! But to do it to best advantage, with greatest impact, you will need to create for yourself a viable position in your organization which will help you to meet your goals. Careful "positioning" is vital to your career, especially if you face tough competition. There's both a science and an art to it. To find out how to best position yourself from strength, read the next chapter.

# Notes

1. Geier, J. G., Downey, D. E., and Johnson, M. A. "The Climate Impact Profile System"© Performax Systems International, Inc. Minneapolis, MN, 1980. This is a self-interpreting, paper-and-pencil inventory. Performax markets these through distributors, of which the author is one. You may contact Performax to find the name of a distributor near you, or you may order directly from the author. See ordering information at the back of this book.
2. Ibid.

# 13

# Preparing for Advancement

THE old man sat in a solitary rocking chair on the porch of his little broken-down wooden shack deep in the forest. His long white beard hung to the floor and wrapped around his legs. Cobwebs were everywhere. They draped every corner, and connected the rocker and the old man to the floor and the wall behind him. The path to his door was overgrown with decades of isolation: the forest looked more like a jungle.

That's what the cartoon in the newspaper looked like. Underneath, the caption read, "He built a better mousetrap."

Such is the fate of many a good idea, and also many a potentially stellar career! Not for want of excellence, but because another factor was missing. Positioning. In chapter 8 we discussed the Formula for Healthy Competition, making the point that, so often today, excellence is not its own reward. Even with high levels of contribution and commitment, that fourth function, positioning, is often required to assure the victory. In fact, without a good personal positioning strategy, even the healthiest competitor can find himself up a creek without a paddle. Let's take that back. The *healthiest* competitor *won't* be without a sound positioning strategy.

Positioning is the vehicle of excellence. It gives wings, wheels, and direction to your excellent contributions. It is the means whereby you become recognized. And it goes without saying, recognition is vital to advancement. Without recognition, that old man in the cartoon could be *you!*

Of the four factors in the formula, positioning is also the most patently "competitive." One can be highly committed to excellent contribution and, in essence, turn one's back on power politics and the game of competition. This is competing without competing, doing one's best, meeting a personal standard. But for the formula to work, all four components must be in place. It is positioning that brings the Healthy Competitor back to the game, and, perhaps, back to reality.

We haven't even defined positioning yet. Why is it so vital? We live in the Age of Proliferation. Everyday there are more products, services, causes, even charities, bidding for our attention, and for our money. Our choices are multiplying, but our resources of time and energy, and perhaps capital, remain the same. We have only so much energy and time in the day. What do you think happens then? Right! More and more choices or opportunities means less time we have to consider each one. Therefore, all products, services, and causes have to compete harder for our attention. But something else more insidious happens. More and more potential choices get ignored. After so much overstimulation, we enter a phase of information overload and the mental computers shut down.

When the choices are fewer we can analyze them more carefully. As the number of choices increases, our precision in choosing decreases. We often procrastinate or make a hasty decision in order to put the issues to bed. We may even find that when faced with numerous choices, we become more irritable, and to the degree that those choices are important and/or more difficult for us, we may experience heightened levels of stress. We may smoke or drink more, get moodier, or use other unhealthy techniques to manage the stress. In the face of prolonged, serious choice making, we may even experience burnout. How do we stave off much of this stress? We limit the choices to which we pay attention.

Information overload leads to mental shutdown. You've experienced it. How many brochures for goods or services cross your desk each day? When you receive one or two, perhaps you will look at them. If you happen to have time perhaps you'll even read them. But if eight or ten hit you at once, particularly if they advertise similar things, what do you do with them? If your round file could eat, I'll bet it would have its hunger well relieved. This is part of the reason the speaking industry is booming. There are so many books, journals, and articles to choose from, people find it much easier to have a speaker distill the information and report it to them.

The question that every company is trying to answer in its marketing, then, is the "How can I make my product or service the *only logical choice* for the consumer?". Indeed, this is the goal of traditional marketing and selling. But it's not the ultimate question that you, as a Healthy Competitor should be asking.

Rather, this is the question you need to ask: "How can *the consumer* see that my product or services (or I, myself) is the only logical choice?" This is the question of positioning. The more competition there is out there for market share, the less of an opening there is into the consumer's mind. The positioning challenge is to find a niche in the consumer's thinking process, to get him to think of *you* when it comes to a particular product or service.

The same dynamic exists within your organization. With others competing with you for advancement, or to stay on after the reorganization or downsizing, how can you be seen by your boss as the *only logical choice* for the job? This is the task of positioning. It can be sticky, but it need not be cutthroat. There are ethical, positive ways to position yourself in this situation. The more difficult this goal, the more carefully strategic your planning needs to be.

The personal positioning process, then, is twofold: (a) creating in the mind of your boss, coworkers, or subordinates, the idea that you are the only logical choice for the job, and (b) making the right moves, so that when the right opportunity comes, you're ready. Obviously, these two factors are significantly intertwined. Let's look at each part of the process.

## Creating the Idea That You're the Only Logical Choice

The state sport of Maryland is jousting. Twentieth-century jousting involves riding horseback full tilt with a pointed lance under your arm. Your objective is to poke the lance through the center of a series of rings, decreasing in size, hung in front of you, one after another. It's quite a challenge!

Positioning is like jousting. As Ries and Trout, the developers of the positioning concept in advertising, say, "Cherchez le creneau. 'Look for the hole.' Cherchez le creneau and then fill it."[1]

Positioning is like jousting, and just as difficult. You need to find that small window in your prospect's mind, a weak spot, a spot of need, a spot not already filled with something or someone else. In our communication-saturated society, this is no simple task. Yet armed with the principles and techniques of positioning, you can gain a competitive edge.

Positioning, Ries and Trout tell us, is not something you do to a product, which, in this case, is yourself. Rather it is something you do in the mind of the prospect. This is a critical point. The goal is not to tout all your good qualities, but rather to make a lasting impression. In so doing, less is more. Your message needs to be simple, direct, and powerful in order to break through the information clutter that we all muddle through every day.

Once an impression is formed, it's difficult to change it. If your initial impression is a bad one, you may never be able to alter it. Changing another person's mind once it is made up is virtually impossible. Therefore it's often best not to make your move until you've worked out your strategy.

In positioning yourself for advancement, there are many variables with which you must contend:

- Figuring out which "holes" exist in your prospect's mind (If you're bucking for promotion, the prospect is your boss. If you're a team leader, your prospects may be the team members, other team leaders, and of course, your boss.)

- The needs and interests to which your prospects respond

- The position you currently hold (Don't worry! You hold one, whether you're aware of it or not, and it probably has nothing to do with your job title or the organizational chart.)

- The formal organization and the political infrastructure

- The type and amount of competition you face

- The position you want to hold

To complicate matters even further, there are two types of positions or "roles" to consider: formal and informal. Formal roles are job titles, rungs on the ladder of the organizational chart. This is what you get when you're promoted. Informal roles, on the other hand, exist in the political infrastructure and may have no direct bearing on the organizational chart. Informal roles more directly reflect how you're seen. They are most often earned (often by default) by your daily behavior rather than ascribed, as formal roles are. This is not to say that formal roles are not "earned," but the power in a formal position is backed by the formal organization, and is attached to the role itself rather than the person who holds it. When planning your positioning strategy, you need to consider yourself in respect to both types of roles.

# Making the Right Moves

Figure 13-1. THE GOLDEN MOUNTAIN OF SUCCESS

Right now you stand on the Peak of the Present. As you look out, you see the Golden Mountain of Success. You want to scale *that* peak, but there is no bridge that will take you there. You must trek out on your own, carving your path through the jungle that lies between the mountains. The jungle is treacherous. It has traps and quicksand. It is a maze of dead-end trails. It is peopled with friendly natives and hostile tribes—and you don't know which is which. The jungle is so overgrown that once you are in it, the Golden Mountain is not always visible and it is easy to lose your sense of direction.

What do you do? Do you just take off and go for it? Or do you carefully strategize, reducing the unknown as much as possible and fortifying yourself with the proper information and equipment?

This is what the positioning process is like. The trek through the jungle will be dotted with forks in the road. Only a clear "road map" will enable you to minimize error, reduce wasted time and effort, and avoid potential disaster.

Reaching the Golden Mountain is a two-step process: preparation and implementation. It is for the want of adequate preparation that many positioning attempts get waylaid in the jungle and never reach the summit.

The next portion of the chapter will provide you with a preparation process exercise that you may wish to follow step-by-step. It will fortify you with vital personal information and prior knowledge of the jungle.

The goals of this exercise are to help you gather and sort out necessary personal and competitor information, and to enable you to narrow down and to zero in—to develop the *specificity* which is the backbone of your position. Only when you have clearly defined your position and your objective are you ready to implement.

This exercise is divided into several parts. The first part is a preliminary self assessment.

# Positioning Preparation

*Exercise 1: Assessing Your Current Situation.* Answer the following questions as completely as possible. Don't move on to Exercise 2 until you have completed this exercise.

1.  *Who are you?* How do you define yourself? What kind of person are you? What are your likes and dislikes? How much stress are you willing to tolerate? What sacrifices are you willing to make to reach the Golden Mountain?

2.  *What are your strengths, talents, assets?* You probably outlined these in chapter 9. If so, why not bring the list out again and add to it? Don't censor the list. Also ask close friends and associates what they perceive your strengths to be. You might get a whole list of new ideas!

3.  *What are your limitations?* This is not meant to be a list of "faults." What, within yourself, could hold you back, personally or financially? What are the chinks in your armor? What personality factors could undermine you?

4. *What position do you currently own?* How are you seen by those around you? This is more than job title. How are you currently regarded? Don't answer this one in isolation. Get input from supervisors and trusted coworkers. Don't be shocked if you get some surprises. This question is vital. This is your starting point from which you must launch. If this position is strong, good for you. If not, you may need to make some repairs before moving ahead.

5. *What position do you wish to own?* What is your ultimate objective? This is your vision of the Golden Mountain. It may involve a formal job title, or an informal position. The position may be national or worldwide in scope, such as Charles Garfield's recognized position as the guru of Peak Performance, or much more local, such as a position in your own company. It may also be a position you wish to hold in your industry, or an informal one in your company, such as "the expert on employee benefits." In order to answer this question to best advantage, you need to review chapter 11 on your personal mission. Your desired position should naturally reflect your mission and goals.

6. *Who are your competitors?* This will depend on the scope of your desired position. If it is a national one, you may have many competitors you don't even know about yet. If you're aiming for a specific formal or informal position in your own company, city, or industry, the task of discovering your potential opponents is easier because the field is more restricted. List these people and/or groups; you will be using this information in the next exercise.

7. *What are your resources and power bases?* What have you got going for you? Who's in your corner, whom can you trust to help you? What physical and final resources are available to you? What groups will back you? What support do you have above you, below you, and at your own level? Are you *sure?*

8. *What is the scope of your network?* Is it large enough? Does it include the right people (i.e., those who can be influential in helping you achieve your desired position. Who the right

people are is relative. Do you have network ties both in and outside your company?

9. *Have you a mentor? Have you a career coach?* If so, is he or she the right one? Be careful that the mentor(s) you have now will not become a potential competitor as you move forward. More on mentors and career coaches later.

10. *Do you currently fit your desired position?* Does your dress, image, vocabulary, personality, expertise, and goals adequately reflect the position to which you aspire? If you were suddenly thrust into that position right now, would you be credible? This is important. Many times people are denied entre into desired positions because the boss or others in power don't think they would "fit" or "look or act the part" or "could carry if off well." If your image needs sprucing up, now's the time to do it.

Now you may wish to do a "force field analysis." Create a chart like the one shown and list in it those outside forces or factors in your current environment that can help push you on your way. Then list those that can hinder your progress. You can summarize those items from previous questions and add here any additional forces you think of.

| Propelling Forces | Barriers |
|---|---|
| (responses) | (responses) |
| | |

Congratulations! You've climbed step one of the preparation ladder. You have a handle on what you've got going for you and what obstacles you face. You have pinpointed your desired target. But you really have not yet worked out your final position. That's coming. First you need to supplement the information you currently have with one more significant set of data: Competitor Intelligence.

To maximize your chances of success, you need to know who your competitors are and how they operate. This analysis is important whether the competitor is a person or an organization, outside or inside your company. Do a competitor analysis for each major competitor.

Be careful to avoid bias. It is very easy, and sometimes tempting, to overestimate or underestimate the competition. Be careful to avoid generalizations in doing the next exercise. Be as specific and as factual as you can. You might have to do a bit of digging to get all the information you need. Do this exercise with a sense of respect for your competition.

| Competitor | Image | Strengths, Assets, Advantages | Weaknesses, Disadvantages |
|---|---|---|---|
| (responses) | (responses) | (responses) | (responses) |

You've now reached the second rung of the ladder. You've sized up the opposition that you will meet in the jungle. You're ready for step three. Here you will use the information you gleaned in Exercise 2 to begin to flesh out your own position a bit more. We are moving toward your unique specialty, but from a positioning perspective, this will not have much meaning in and of itself. Remember, the goal of positioning is to create an impression in the *mind of the prospect,* not in your own mind. Look for the hole.

*Exercise 3: Competitive Comparison.* Wait! Didn't we earlier advise against making comparisons? Yes, comparisons for *personal worth* are a no-no. Here we're comparing capabilities and practices. This is vital information to a healthy Competitor who, whether or not he or she *wishes* to compete, must engage in competitive activity while trekking through the jungle! Forewarned is forearmed.

Two tips for doing this exercise: First, get your ego out of the way. Otherwise you might get hurt, and, worse, your ego won't allow you to be objective. Second, consider yourself and your talents, strengths and assets *in relation to unmet needs in your area of interest and expertise,* keeping your competition in perspective. This factor is the key to the success of this exercise. The world is full of unmet needs. Which ones can you identify that *you* are most capable and desirous of meeting?

| Identified Unmet Needs | What I Can Do/Am Doing | What the Competition Is Not Doing | Holes I Can Fill |
|---|---|---|---|
| (responses) | (responses) | (responses) | (responses) |

Now that you have completed step 3, you're ready to refine your desired position to its most succinct form. You have listed your strengths and what you're capable of doing relative to the unmet needs you've identified. Now shift gears and think in terms of your *uniqueness!* This will derive out of what you can do or are doing compared to what your competition can't do/isn't doing. Obviously, if you discover that you are uniquely suited to excelling in some area that your competitors can't match or surpass you, all the better.

*Exercise 4: USP and Position Definition.* Every product should have a USP a Unique Selling Point, that sets it apart from, and hopefully above, its competition. Every salesperson should know his or her product's USP cold. You also have a USP and you need to know it and articulate it with ease.

Discovering your USP may be tricky. Before you go riding off into the sunset singing the praises of your strengths, consider this sobering paradox: While we are all unique, no one is indispensable. Sooner or later someone will come along to take your place. The more uniqueness you have to offer, the more carefully planned and executed your strategy is, the longer you can hold out. So defining your position and your USP carefully is critical.

Since you may be unique in several ways, to what should your USP be relative? To two things: (a) the utmost needs you plan to fulfill, which your competitor can't or isn't filing, i.e., the hole, and (b) your desired position. Your USP is the answer to the original positioning question: What qualifies you to be the only (or most) logical choice for the job? (The next part of that question is: "How do you create that idea in the mind of the prospect?" That's the implementation phase.)

OK. with all this preamble out of the way, what is your USP? Draw on any combination of the following to figure it out.

Your: strengths/talents

assets

experience/background

education/training

sex

ethnic or racial background

significant accomplishments/honors/awards

age (senior or youth)

geographical location (this is important if you are trying to position yourself as the special expert in a given community)

Licenses or certifications held

Disadvantages/handicaps upon which you can capitalize, turning them into opportunities.

Write out your USP in as clear and succinct a way as you can. In positioning, as in advertising, less is more. Make it simple, to the point, and powerful. Remember that to be unique for our purposes, you don't have to be the "only one in the world who can do. . . ." There is no such animal anyway, as any scan of the Olympic records will quickly tell you. Your USP should be narrowly defined, relative to the two factors stated above.

My USP: _____

_____

_____

_____

Now that you've defined your USP, the next step is to define clearly the nature and scope of your desired position. Until it's clear as crystal to you, it will be clear as mud to your prospect!

Nature and scope are both important components of your position. By nature, I mean whether you're going for a formal organizational slot (e.g., President of the U.S., VP of Marketing, etc.,) or an informal position that you hold within or external to your primary job or organization (e.g., expert on employee morale, communication facilitator, etc.) If you hold a viable informal position, then you are the "recognized resident expert" to whom people turn for consultation or help in a particular area. Many people establish such a position outside the job so as to boost their status inside the company and/or to prepare for a job change.

Next it helps to define your position in terms of scope: worldwide, national, state or regional, local, industry-wide, company-wide, division-wide, population-segmented (e.g., for women, for the handicapped, for minorities, etc.). Normally there is a direct correlation between degree of uniqueness and breadth of scope. If your unique asset is highly desirable and you are the first to apply it, you scope could conceivably be worldwide. To succeed on this scale requires megabucks and one heck of a support system! On the other hand, if numerous people do what you do, you could establish a niche in a particular industry or geographic location. If you're looking to establish your position within your own organization or industry, then the scope is more predefined.

To help you understand scope, here are some examples.

National: Tony Allesandra, expert on "Nonmanipulative selling" (Note: The world is full of sales trainers. Tony developed one particular aspect and parlayed it into a special niche.)

Charles Garfield, expert on Peak Performance

Tom Peters: "Excellence"

Industry-wide: Floyd Wickman, sales training and motivation to the real estate industry (Floyd's ideas and methods themselves probably are not unique, although he is a superb trainer and marketer. He trains nationally and is extremely well known to the real estate industry, his niche.)

Geographical: Jan Kantor, sales and management training in Ft. Myers, Florida (Again, topics are more generic, but he has heavily positioned himself in his home county.)

In-company: Ruth Zyna, Empowerer enabler, facilitator (Ruth works for a state regulatory agency. She has excellent human relations skills, and through careful planning as well as just being herself, she has become the "resident expert" on handling human relations problems in the office. "Empowerer" is a specific, informal position that Ruth determined to achieve.)

Paul Winston, attorney, expert on trusts (Paul works for a large legal firm. He has carefully researched everything he can on trusts, his favorite topic. Now even other attorneys in the firm seek his advice on sticky trust issues.)

Notice that the national positioning examples were all topic-based. The broader the audience, the much more highly specialized you need to be. When you narrow the scope, say to industry-wide or geographical location, you can become known for a broader range of skills, although well-positioned specialists are well received at these levels also. When you attempt an informal position within your company, however, the specialist mode is more likely to win. Generally, the following appears to hold true:

Highly specialized (and "unique") expertise works for a general, broad audience (worldwide, national)

Less specialized or highly specialized expertise works for a highly specialized audience (industry-wide, geographically limited)

Highly specialized (and "unique") works best for an in-company position

Think through your USP, strengths, mission, and goals. Write out your desired position, specifying realistically achievable nature and scope:

My desired position: _____

_____

_____

_____

In the next chapter we'll explore how to make that position a reality.

# Notes

1. Ries, A., and Trout, J. *Positioning: The battle for your mind*. New York: Warner, 1981.

# 14

# Implementing Your Advancement

Now that you have defined your position you're ready to plan the steps needed to make it a reality. Your strategy will depend, in part, on how you have defined your position. Your primary goal is not to beat out all comers, but rather to make yourself the only logical choice, to make your own position so solid, so entrenched as to be unassailable.

## Strategizing

The main thrust of this chapter will discuss techniques for positioning yourself within your company, and within your industry. These techniques apply to other levels of positioning as well. The order in which you implement the techniques, or whether you need to modify them, will depend on your particular needs and situation.

### TAKE NOTHING FOR GRANTED

Nothing can shoot you down faster than your own assumptions. If you're already "famous" or "well entrenched," don't rest on your laurels. Things change, and the Healthy Competitor is on top of those changes. When the wave comes in, you want to be riding the crest rather than being washed ashore. Vision is critical; so is timing.

Don't take your competition for granted either. You can count on the fact that, if what you want is worth going after, others will go after it, too. If they perceive your forward movement, they may start moving as well.

## MAKE LIKE A SEED

When a seed is planted, nothing sprouts for a while. But under the surface a great deal is going on. The seed grows. It takes in nourishment and puts down roots. By the time it sprouts, the plant has all its growth system in place.

Play your cards close to your chest. Prepare quietly. Get your strategy worked out and your support systems in place. Only then are you ready to make your move. This may sound self-evident, but surprisingly many people err in coming out in the open too early, only to find that someone else plucks the bud from their rose. How quiet you must be depends upon the amount and nature of the competition you face. Be careful, but also be careful not to become overly suspicious or secretive. It's generally not good to have others wondering—too much—what you're up to.

## DETERMINE WHETHER YOU ARE A LEADER OR A FOLLOWER[1]

A leader is one who already holds the key turf. He or she is already recognized as Number One—like Coca Cola. A follower, on the other hand, shares the field. He or she is recognized as Number Two or lower, if recognized at all. He or she is the new kid on the block. This is a critical distinction, because the positioning strategies of each are distinctly different.

Which are you? How can you tell? You are a leader if you got there first, or if you already hold your desired position unopposed, or if you can grab the desired position uncontested, or if you are currently the one most recognized in your given area of expertise in spite of the competition. If you can't say "yes" to any of these conditions, you are a follower. That's it.

You are probably a follower. In our New Way To Compete seminars, only one in twenty or twenty-five is a leader; the rest have opposition on the path to the Golden Mountain. Of course, the leader never holds the field alone for long. But he has the advantage because he holds the high ground. Keeping it requires different tactics than taking it.

If you are the leader, momentum, or the power of your position, will carry you along, at least for a while. Your task is to stay on the horse as long as you can, to parlay a short-term lead into a long-term advantage. Leaders can get stodgy with age. Don't make that mistake! Nothing in business is as certain today as change. To stay on top you must stay flexible.

As a follower, however, your task is quite different. Here's what Ries and Trout say you need to do to capture your niche.[2]

1. Unless the leader is tottering, never go head-to-head with him. This is particularly true if the leader carries political clout. If you can outclass or outmaneuver the leader, do so in your own way, but not in direct confrontation.

2. Avoid the "me too, but better" trap. So often a new product will come on the market claiming to be like an established product, only better. This is the kiss of death. Don't try to copy the leader. Rather, do your own thing, capitalize on your own strengths.

3. Look for a weakness or soft spot in your corporate structure or product or service area and build your strategy around that. The competitive analysis that you completed in the last chapter is vital here, and for the next suggestion.

4. Look for the "hole" and fill it. Look for what's *not* being done—something your competition can't or won't do. This can be the center of your unique position.

   There is one the temptation followers face, but watch out! Be very careful about "repositioning" your competition. In competitive advertising on television, one product is praised while its competitor is panned. The goal of repositioning the competition is to undermine a current idea, person, product, or project in the minds of others. You may reposition your opponents in several ways. The first is through out-and-out attack, à la Muhammad Ali. The next way is through direct criticism, such as "*That* won't work." A third way is through sowing seeds of doubt by dropping subtle hints that there is a flaw in your opponents' thinking, plans, or actions: "Joe has a real good plan here. He usually doesn't think things through enough to catch all the possible glitches, but I think he's basically got a good thing here."

These techniques may work on television, but they're dangerous! They can backfire on you! You can quickly be seen as catty, jealous, trying to act superior, or downright unethical. Others may develop these thoughts about you quietly, and on the surface pretend to agree or just listen. Rarely will they confront you. But that doesn't mean they approve. If they come to distrust you and your motives, wrap it up! You're through!

To reposition your competition at a personal level, always speak well of them or say nothing at all. Work on your own contributions and positioning. If you follow the Formula for Healthy Competition and apply it to a viable hole, the repositioning of the competition may take care of itself.

Remember where your energy needs to be placed! Actively attempting to reposition the opposition can divert valuable energy. Don't do it unless it is an absolute necessity—unless you can't achieve your goals any other way. You can't ignore what your competition is doing. You should figure it into your overall strategy, but avoid being an attacker.

Recognize whence your power comes. While you may be a very assertive, charismatic person, when it comes to positioning, *you* are not the source of your power. Your *contribution* is. The power lies in the service you provide, the tasks that you accomplish, as they relate to the hole that needs to be filled, the needs that must be met. To believe otherwise is ego-infusion and can court disaster. You must keep on your toes. Sad to say, but it's true nonetheless, the only place where you can truly say you've "finally arrived" is at your own burial!

## DETERMINE WHICH VEHICLE YOU WISH TO RIDE

According to Ries and Trout, there are six vehicles you can use to position yourself and your career:[3]

1. *Your company.* This is a good one if it's going somewhere. If you want to get ahead in your profession and your company can't help you get there, maybe it's time to think of switching. If you choose the company vehicle, you work to advance your company in any way you can.

2. *Your boss.* If your boss is a fast-tracker and well on the rise, you might choose to stick with him or her. He or she can pave the way for you. Work for the most assertive, creative person you can. Such a person can help you without fearing you. Many people figure that they can attempt to outshine a mediocre boss. Political suicide!

3. *Friend or mentor.* Cultivate meaningful but honest business friendships. The Beatles line, "get by with a little help from my friends" is not just sentimental drivel; it's a fact of life. Your friends, inside or outside the company, usually give you your best breaks.

4. *An idea (hopefully one whose time has come!).* This is a key vehicle, if you have the courage for it. It has been said that the measure of a good idea is the amount of resistance it receives. If your idea is utterly ridiculous, it will also be easily dismissed.

   But resistance, of course, is not the only measure of a good idea. The Declaration of Independence was a good idea. Hitler's Final Solution wasn't. To ride an idea to the top, you must prepare for conflict and ridicule. Also, the idea must be significant but succinct. If it is too confusing it probably will not fly. Simple but powerful, that's the ticket. Timing is also important. You may need to bide your time until your company, or the world, can handle your idea.

5. *Faith (in others and their ideas).* You can move ahead by supporting someone else and his or her ideas. You identify with that person, and as he or she moves ahead, you reap the benefits.

6. *Yourself.* This is the trickiest and most dangerous horse to ride. It is difficult, if not impossible to succeed all by yourself. Also, remember whence your power comes. Don't try to go it alone. "But how about the entrepreneur?" you may ask.

"Doesn't he or she go it alone?" Not on your life; not the successful ones, at least. They get plenty of help along the way.

## CONSIDER AN "OUTSIDE-IN" STRATEGY

Develop outside accomplishments of which you make others aware back at the shop. These serve as validation of your expertise, enhance your credibility, and bring honor to your company as well as to yourself (not to mention looking *very* good on your résumé!) There are two important outside areas you should consider targeting: industry recognition and community service. Which one will count more depends on the nature of the position you're attempting to achieve. Each can also lead to a secondary informal position of its own.

Industry recognition can be a spin-off of a particular area of expertise that you wish to parlay into a unique personal position. There are several possibilities for gaining recognition industry-wide. Some of these may be appropriate for you, while others may not.

1. Be a presenter at your trade or professional association's regional or national convention.
2. Get published. The best place is in a trade or industry journal your top management reads, but don't stop there. Other journals, both inside and outside your industry, are also candidates, as are local business or general interest publications.
3. Write a book. To have a book published by a major publisher is equivalent to a Ph.D. in your subject area. It is instant credibility. If you're nervous about going it alone, you might coauthor with a coworker.
4. Get broadcast media exposure. While we normally think of national television, don't discount your local radio talk show.
5. Earn industry awards. What merit awards are available in your industry? These are generally bestowed by trade associations. Find out how you can qualify, and apply if you meet the criteria.
6. Go for certification. More and more professions are setting up certification programs, again through major trade or

professional associations or other certifying bodies. Examples include CAE (Certified Association Executive), CPS (Certified Professional Secretary), CMC (Certified Management Consultant), CMP (Certified Meeting Planner). Is there such a certification in your industry? If so, get the criteria and plan to meet them.

Achieving industry recognition is really a matter of self-promotion. If this is the avenue for you, there's a lot you can do on your own. Jeffrey P. Davidson has written an excellent guide to self-promotion. (See the resource list at the end of the book.)

To provide true community service, it's not enough to belong to community organizations. You must also *serve* if you expect this type of involvement to enhance your position. Naturally, your involvement must be sincere or you can appear self-serving. Special service projects can be publicized in local newspapers. Some cities and counties give awards for tireless community service. Serving on the board of directors of a local charity can be extremely helpful. These activities can open doors to new networks with powerful civic-minded community leaders who often have broad industry connections.

## CONCENTRATE YOUR ENERGY

Don't try to be all things to all people. Those who try to solve every problem usually end up solving none. Choose your position carefully and narrowly define your niche. Where can you make your greatest impact? Balance this question with where you have the greatest opportunity.

## KEEP THEM AWARE; WIN THEM OVER

Without overkill, plan a program of regular memos or other notices to publicize your activities to key people in your organization. Another way of creating awareness is to ask for help or feedback. By getting input on your projects from carefully selected persons, you create the impression of a thorough, creative, go-getter. It's flattering to be asked for advice. If you ask others, you will be remembered.

Another "secret weapon" is the thank you note. When someone assists you, drop that person a line. Show your appreciation. It's a little courtesy that very few people ever observe. Keep it brief and to the point, but send it out right away, the same day you receive the help. Sales trainer Matthew J. Rettick, who advocates this technique for salespeople, states that he has received only three thank you notes from salespeople over the last seventeen years![4]

## PLAY YOUR CARDS CLOSE TO YOUR CHEST

Don't advertise your positioning intentions. Keep your game plan secret, except for your career coach (see below), and perhaps for your mentor.

Consider selecting a mentor. A mentor relationship should not be entered casually. The prime basis for selection is *not* the prospective mentor's position in the company, as important as that is. Rather, the first criteria should be trust and friendship. This is much more than a business deal. It should be based on a high level of mutual respect. The mentor needs to have a high respect for you and a sincere interest in helping you get ahead. It goes without saying that he or she should be sufficiently personally secure so as not to become threatened by your rise, and end up competing with you.

After mutual respect and position in the company, you need to consider (a) the person's power and reputation in the political infrastructure, and (b) the extent of his or her personal network.

What can you give back to your mentor? The best mentor relationship is give-and-take, both ways! Remember that, as you have, your mentor also has ego needs. The best ways you can give back are to pursue well what you are taught, and to grant your mentor special benefits of your expertise to help him or her also to perform better. In short, you and your mentor are a team!

Yet mentors have their limitations, one of which is that because they are a part of your organization, they may have some of the same blind spots you have, or be limited by certain political constraints.

Women may need to think twice about acquiring a male mentor. Male mentors often look upon female protégés as requiring remedial help. Male-female alliances may also be incorrectly perceived as having sexual overtones, which could damage her career. On the flip side, having a male mentor can help a woman break into the "good old boy" network.[5]

Should you have a mentor? Should you have more than one? This is a very personal decision. Not everyone needs one or would work well with one. Mentors can be very politically expeditious, but the prime criterion should be legitimate personal need, mediated by the availability of a highly compatible person.

## BUILD A SOLID NETWORK

Anne Boe, networking specialist, calls this the "manager's newest contact sport." Everything said above about mentors applies to your network as well. A network is like a bank account: the amount of interest you receive depends on how much you deposit. You can't continue to take from the network unless you give in return.

Who should be included in your professional network? In part, this will depend on your goals. Definitely it should include folks both inside and outside your organization. Include specialists in allied but noncompeting fields. A wide range of these people broadens your information and resource base. Customers, clients, consumers should also be included, as these people can give you vital information on how your firm's product or service is being received.

Industry contacts at the trade or professional association level should also be considered, as well as your industry leaders and pioneers, if you can connect with them. If the network is broad, you will not overburden any one or a few people. Keep in continual contact, and offer as much, or more, than you ask!

## *BE A MENTOR, AN EMPOWERER*

Perhaps this is one of the most important techniques of all. Empower others, help them to be winners, and your chances of winning increase. Take a true, caring, sincere interest. Become recognized as the one others can depend on when help is needed, but don't let yourself become burned out. You may need to be selectively available, or you may get used. However, if you want to win as a Healthy Competitor, give more than you get!

## PICK YOUR ASSOCIATES CAREFULLY

Mike Goodrich, president of the Goodrich Financial Group, raises another important positioning issue:[6] If you wish to advance up the ranks, with whom should you surround yourself? Many traditional competitors, afraid of who might be gaining on them, pick associates who are weaker than themselves. They hope that they will stand out as superior by comparison. This is an ego-based decision, one that is not good for the company or the manager. What really happens is that such a manager is creating mediocrity. One superstar can do a lot, but he can't do it all. If your are seen as indispensible because your colleagues and subordinates can't fill your shoes, you are likely to be left where you are.

The Healthy Competitor, on the other hand, being more ego-free, surrounds herself with people who are as skilled or even more skilled than she is. She knows the power of people, and by getting the best ones to work for her she benefits the company and makes herself look good through dynamic team contributions. Because her department is strong, she can be promoted without fear that her unit will collapse without her. The moral? If you build a temple to yourself at work, you might find yourself buried in it.

## TWO MORE POSITIONING PRINCIPLES

As you consider your personal strategy, there are two additional positioning principles to keep in mind:

1. *The Trailblazer Principle.* In pioneer days, the trailblazer would forge ahead into unknown territory, opening the way for others. When settlers started moving in, he would launch out again, keeping ahead of the migration.

   The one who is there first always has an advantage. Use your creativity, keep ahead of the pack wherever possible. Get the reputation for being on the forefront of change and growth, the first with the most.

2. *The Minnesota Fats Principle.* Billiard champ, Minnesota Fats, advised aspiring players, "When you take your first shot, always set it up so that you automatically roll into position for your second shot." The value of this principle is self-evident.

Of course, there is one key implication: that you succeed on the first shot so that you indeed get a second shot!

When trainer Tony Allesandra first began to market his training and consulting services, he offered his initial needs assessment for free. He'd fly in, carry out his study, and prepare his report, all at his own expense. Was this a big risk? Sure it was. But Tony always got the contract. He argued that, after he took the time and effort to get to know the company, the company would be more ready to hire him than to have another trainer/consultant repeat the process. Also, he figured, it takes a lot of self-confidence to give away all that front-end time. He was right. By doing the initial free analysis, he positioned himself well to get the final contract.

# The Career Coach

The career coach is your latest positioning and self-development resource. Most professional and Olympic athletes have personal coaches to help them cope with competition and play their game to their maximum potential. In fact, the better they become, the more elite their status, the more they need and rely on their coaches. Why? Because the higher they go, the more critical their moves become, the more important personal feedback becomes in avoiding mistakes. The bottom line: the coach gives them the competitive edge!

The higher you go in your profession, the more critical *your* moves become. And often the old ways of getting ahead are not as effective. Enter the "Career Coach!" He or she can help you diagnose and sort out your situation and opportunities, show you new strategies for coping with office politics and competition from other firms, show you vital stress management skills, help you work through major decisions, help you discover and capitalize on new opportunities, provide new tools to improve communication, and help you chart your goals and career path. Your career coach is your personal, behind-the-scenes confidant, consultant, and resource—all in the privacy of the coach's office or your home.

Since the coach works with you privately and confidentially, *you* get all the public credit. Several people have likened the career coach to a ghostwriter, while others see a strong parallel with individual sports coaches, such as in tennis and boxing.

*Your Coach's Role.* The Career Coach, being outside your organization, isn't bound by political concerns and can often be more objective. Also, because of the coach's background and training (which is discussed below) he or she can address a broader range of personal and career issues.

Your coach is not a mentor. Rather, his or her primary role is one of "cooperative coaching:" being a trainer, a listener, an observer, a motivator, and a sounding board. A good coach will help you discover your mission and assist you in mapping out your goals and strategies, and will monitor your progress. You will get objective, honest feedback without moral judgments.

Your goals and needs are always the specific foundation of your relationship with the coach. A career coach is committed to doing everything in his or her power to help you meet those objectives.

*What Background and Training Should a Career Coach Have?* First and foremost, an effective career coach should have a strong background in behavioral science and counseling. A master's in Psychology or an equivalent field is an absolute minimum; a Ph.D. is much better.

Second, he or she should have solid background in the latest high-performance and motivational techniques, and the ability to determine when and how to apply these methods to a business setting.

Third, your coach needs to be a good personal and organizational diagnostician. Insight into the nature of competition and cooperation in organizations, power politics, and organizational behavior is a must.

*How to Choose the Right Coach.* First determine your needs. This is often difficult, and many people are not always sure what their real needs are. The questionnaire in box 14-1 can help you. Once you've determined your needs, then you can direct the coach as to how he or she can most help you. Your coach can also help you define your needs more explicitly.

Now to find the coach. Unfortunately, there is no professional designation called "Career Coach"—at least not yet. The best place to begin is under the "psychologist" listing in the Yellow Pages. Of the various mental health professionals, psychologists are the most likely to have had the breadth of training and experience you need. To determine whether a particular psychologist or consultant is right for you, interview him or her. Most mental health professionals today are used to being questioned by prospective clients.

You may also wish to look under "Management Consultants" in the Yellow Pages. But here, too, it's wise to ask. Many management consultants take an organizational rather than a personal approach.

The author's corporation, Maximum Potential, Inc., has been doing career coaching for several years. Feel free to contact us for more information. If you live outside of the Baltimore-Washington area, feel free to call us for a referral in your area.

The career coach concept is revolutionary. This is forefront thinking, and serious, career-minded professionals at the cutting edge of success are availing themselves of this opportunity more and more every day. They range from presidents and CEOs all the way down the management and sales ladders.

Your career is important to you. It is too important to go it alone. Is a career coach the answer for you? Answer the questionnaire in box 14-1 and see.

# A Final Exercise

We've reviewed a number of tips and techniques regarding how to position yourself. Undoubtedly others have come to mind along the way. You may also wish to review the Additional Resources listed at the end of this chapter.

Now for your final exercise in this chapter: Map out your positioning strategy step-by-step with a timetable for implementation/execution. You might wish to run it by a mentor, career coach, or a close confidant in your network before finalizing it.

You now have your roadmap through the jungle. Best wishes as you scale the Golden Mountain of Success!

Box 14-1

---

### CAN I BENEFIT FROM A CAREER COACH?

Do you experience, or are you faced with, any of the following? If so, then perhaps a career coach is for you.

1. Organizational changes within your company (especially if they directly impact on you)
2. Acquisitions or mergers
3. Expansion into new markets
4. Diversification into new products or services
5. Increased competition to your firm from other firms trying to take over your market share
6. Increasing management or supervisory responsibility
7. Increasing leadership opportunities
8. A recent or soon-to-be-available promotion
9. A new boss, or leadership shake-ups above you
10. Changes in your role or assignments within your company
11. In-company competition and power plays, corporate intrigue, jockeying for position, turf protection—especially if you're on the rise, because often the higher you go, the worse it gets
12. Being blocked in your progress by internal feuds or informal political processes
13. Excess stress on the job
14. Increased media exposure and/or public speaking requirements
15. Increased production or sales quotas
16. A new project you must lead or participate in developing
17. "Quality Circles" groups or "Intrapreneuring" groups
18. Being a black, a Hispanic, or any other ethnic or racial minority, or being a woman or handicapped
19. A strong desire to advance in your company or profession, regardless of whether you experience any of the above

---

# Notes

1. Ries, A. and Trout, J. *Positioning: The battle for your mind.* New York: Warner, 1981.
2. Ibid.
3. Ibid.
4. Rettick, M. J. "Thank-you notes: Your secret weapon." *Master Salesmanship,* April 11, 1988, 1, 2.
5. Hurley, D. "The mentor mystique." *Psychology Today,* May 1988, 38–43.
6. Goodrich, M. Personal Communication.

---

# Additional Resources

Davidson, J. P. *Blow your own horn: How to market yourself and your career.* New York: Amacom, 1987.

Kravetz, D. J. *Getting noticed: A manager's success kit.* New York: John Wiley & Sons, 1985.

Newman, J. A. and Alexander, R. *Climbing the corporate Matterhorn.* New York: John Wiley & Sons, 1985.

# 15

# From Competition to Cooperation

Y OU wouldn't let "the man on the street" operate a giant crane without careful training, would you? Of course not! He pulls the wrong lever and things get destroyed. Competition has even greater potential for destruction in untrained hands. Yet we never think of that, for two reasons. First, in our society, no one wants to admit that he or she might not know how to best handle competition, so tied is competing to our egos. Second, because competition is the norm, because we're *supposed* to believe in it, few people will ever challenge a competitive system. If they ever said they didn't enjoy a contest or didn't like to compete, others might think they were crazy, or worst yet, wimps!

Yet more and more people are becoming aware of the potential destructiveness of traditional competition in the workplace. They see its results, but it is another thing altogether to turn it around once the cancer has begun. Is there a place for competition in the workplace? And if so, what will its effects be on cooperation and teamwork, which is, hopefully, your company's objective?

The answer depends on how we define competition. In chapter 2 we distinguished between two types of competition within organizations: structured (formally organized) and social (informal, spontaneous). There is no place for social competition in organizations where people must work together. Social competition invokes the rivalry, power plays, and superiority tactics that interfere with teamwork and productivity. A main problem with structured competition is that it often spills over into social competition, creating more rivalry.

In this chapter, then, we will address how to deal with structured competition—formally organized competitive events. Most managers who use competition believe that it motivates workers. In some ways it does. Let's explore how this can be so.

There appears to be a bell-shaped curve relationship between competitiveness and performance, as shown in figure 15-1.

Moderate competition, especially if it is structured in a healthy way, can generate a positive arousal and motivation. But as the competition becomes prolonged or more cutthroat, anxiety sets in and performance and productivity suffer. It is easy for competitive goals, i.e., beating the other guy, to eclipse performance goals in an intensely competitive situation. People become fearful and insecure, relationships are poisoned by rivalry. Stress and burnout are at high levels. In a state in which fear and suspicion reign, however, honest feedback is hard to find. People keep quiet and are less likely to point out the faults of the system, so the system goes on in ignorance, with those in charge thinking that it is working, or having no idea what went wrong.

Who is motivated by competition? Winners, that's who! A contest is only motivating to those who perceive that they have a chance

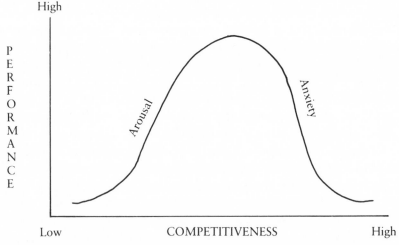

Figure 15-1. HOW COMPETITIVENESS AFFECTS PERFORMANCE

to win. As stated earlier, people who expect to lose are actually *demotivated* by contests, although they may pay lip service. After a while it gets pretty tiresome seeing the same faces receiving prizes at the awards banquet, and always clapping (halfheartedly) for the other person.

Traditional contests in which there is only one or a few winners often have the effect of pitting colleagues against each other. Rivalry may be expressed in joking ways, but it's rivalry nonetheless. Many times sales organizations will pit individuals against each other but think they solve the problems inherent in social competition by structuring the competition between "territories." Let's see if Southeast can beat Northwest, for example. This is a well-meaning attempt to make competition more palatable, but it does not solve the basic problems inherent in the structure of the competition itself.

What if we team up people? This is often done. Legend has it that, years ago, Sloan, then head of General Motors, walked onto the shop floor, wrote a number with chalk on the floor, and left. Supposedly he did this at the beginning of each shift. The workers finally figured out that the number on the floor was actually the number of cars produced by the previous shift. Production shot up quickly as the shifts began to compete with each other to see how many cars they could produce.

Posting scores between teams is a common motivator, but this and other team competitions in which groups vie against each other are still built on faulty premises that can backfire. Sure, individual or team competition will yield short-term increases in production, but what about the long haul?

Traditional in-company team competition is based on the "common enemy" hypothesis. A team will work together harder if there is a common opponent. This is usually true. But when the pressure is off, the motivation for teamwork is lessened. Why? Because it was built on the wrong premises. Motivation in a team needs to be intrinsic, born from within the team itself. Only then will it last. Competition, by definition is an extrinsic motivator, contrived from outside. It only works while the competitive pressure is on. In the face of competitive pressure people will *band* together, but will they really learn how best to *work* together? Effective teams rarely just happen. For best results, teams have to be carefully selected and nurtured. This is what team-building is all about, and it has nothing to do with traditional competition.

Is there a way to bring in the excitement of competition and still safeguard our people? Competition is an "incentive." So are bonuses, recognition, etc. Do these have to be tied to competition to be effective? There is an increased tendency in America toward performance-based pay, as opposed to traditional salaries that are not contingent on actual production. This is, in my opinion, a necessary move. But performance-based compensation does not depend on competition to be effective. Competition is *not* necessary for motivation!

But what about "competitive drive?" Where can it be channeled for maximum results? There are general principles that can guide you in structuring healthy competition. These may prove especially valuable if you have cutthroat competition going on now and you want to reduce it and redirect that competitive energy:

1. Never pit individuals against each other. If you do you will kill teamwork and increase rivalry. You will reduce efficiency, because this will lead to each person trying to do all tasks himself.

2. Avoid the "common enemy" motive, for reasons described above, even if the "common enemy" is another company. It is far better to instill a desire to win based on excellence of your own product or service than just to capture market share from someone else. Excellence is an intrinsic motivator.

3. Organize people in teams or work groups. This promotes division of labor and lets workers capitalize on their strengths and enjoy the support of others with complementary talents. Assign them and blend them carefully, according to their strengths. Then engage training in healthy competition/cooperation and team building to help them maximize productivity from the outset.

   Even the sales function can be organized this way. Some are better appointment-getters but they have trouble closing, while others are superb closers once they get in the door but have difficulty making the initial contact. Why not pair these types, or establish a contact or telemarketing function to set up appointments for your salespeople? Once you open the door to nontraditional options, all kinds of solutions come to mind.

4. Have your teams "compete" against an objective standard or quota, not each other. Every team that meets quota gets a "prize." This reduces rivalry and the "common enemy" syndrome. It allows for mutual support across teams. This approach can virtually eliminate in-group competitiveness because no one has anything to lose by cooperating. You can sweeten the pot by giving an added bonus to each person or team if every team meets quota. That promotes cooperation across teams even more. This system works for individuals as well, in situations where people are expected to perform as individuals.

Should every person or team have to meet the same quota? That depends on your particular situation. Sometimes having everyone perform to the same level is unrealistic. In such cases a handicap system or basing individual quotas on percentage increases as opposed to finite numbers might work.

A quota is actually a performance level and could be used for performance-based pay. Setting up quotas in terms of a contest is actually unnecessary but may be useful in situations that are otherwise competitive. Such a contest serves to shift competitive drive into a positive direction, while retaining a "competitive flavor." This opens the door to cooperation that would not be likely to occur otherwise.

A quota could be numbers of sales, or units produced, or it could be a quality standard. The ideal quota should combine both quantity and quality and be stiff enough to be a challenge. Are too many people meeting the quota too early? Then increase the quota. Don't resort to traditional competition.

# If You Want More Yield, Raise More PIGs!

PIGs? Positive Interdependency Groups, that is. A Positive Interdependency Group (PIG) is a group or team in which everyone's behavior is positively linked. If I perform well, you benefit, and vice versa. Contrast this with a negative interdependency group, in which performances are negatively linked. If you get ahead, my chances of advancement are hurt. What should I do in that case? The typical response is to undercut you, or at least withhold help. That's where traditional competition has failed. It creates a negative interdependency by forcing us into a win-lose paradigm.

A PIG, on the other hand, is a win-win proposition. The quota-based contest described above is an unfixed competition—everyone can win. PIGs go one step further by linking people's behavior. Here's an example.

Berol Chemical in Gothenburg, Sweden, is raising a fine herd of PIGs. The R and D and production divisions are set up on the basis of small project groups, each group in the division having a full complement of engineers and technicians. Sounds like a team; what makes it a PIG? Every six months the job of project leader is rotated. Everyone on the team will serve as project leader. (Individual rank has no meaning on these teams; individuals are assigned because of their specific qualifications.) This rotation helps pull the people together to help one another all the more. These project groups do not formally compete against each other.

Setting up "intrapreneuring" groups in large corporations is another method of raising PIGs. An interdisciplinary team is set up to work on all phases of a particular project or product, from design through distribution. Often the team is in full charge of the project budget and can receive a profit-sharing bonus from the product's sales. Intrapreneuring is a forefront organizational strategy that is too complex to consider here. For more information, contact the ForeSight Group, worldwide pioneers in intrapreneuring. ForeSight's U.S. office is at 277 Park Avenue, New York, New York 10172.

What makes a PIG different from and more potent than other groups, is that there is usually some administrative process and structure that puts all the people on the team into the same boat. There is some contingency plan built into the structure that links everyone's work toward the goal directly to that of his or her teammates. PIGs are also usually self-managed, and there are several ways this can be achieved:

1. Leader rotation, such as at Berol. This may promote a PIG but doesn't actually ensure it. This is an effective and important psychological move toward equality. It also subtly encourages each worker to think, "I'd better cooperate and help out because when I'm the leader, I want them to help me!"

2. Bonus shared equally by all members. The actual amount of the bonus can be made contingent on degree of profit, or number of units, or on the efforts of the members based on behavioral performance reviews. If one or two persons' work is not up to par, then the overall bonus is less, with each person getting less. Naturally, if you present this method to workers, you want to tell them the positive side: that everyone's bonus will be greater to the degree that each person demonstrates high performance.

3. Group-wide performance evaluation. This may have tricky personnel policy implications. What happens is that everyone on the team shares the same evaluation at performance review time. The same evaluation goes into everyone's personnel file, based on team rather than individual performance. Individual performance appraisals may be used, however, to determine the team performance. An individual's actual performance may be rated individually on some characteristics and team-wise on others. The intent is that the team evaluation has some impact on salary increases and other rewards that may be tied to the performance review.

4. Cross-training and job rotation within the team. This is a less "formal" method of creating a PIG, but it can have strong beneficial psychological impact. People learn firsthand the value, benefits, and frustrations of the jobs of their coworkers. They also feel that the company cares about them and is investing in them because a cross-trained worker is a more valuable, flexible worker. After cross-training, however, the employee should end up in a situation in which his or her primary strengths and interests are best utilized.

There may be other methods, specific to your organization, that you can use to create PIGs. The ultimate goal, however, is to promote an atmosphere of "group think" rather than a strictly individualistic orientation. Putting people on a team encourages them to work together. Making a PIG out of that team makes them realistically (and sometimes dramatically) interdependent. Most sports teams are PIGs by definition. Players all share the common prize. Their coaches drill them in interdependence. Achieving interdependence is not always easy. The superstar syndrone mitigates against it, and I have talked with several coaches who are dismayed at the difficulty they have in getting some individual athletes to cooperate as team players. Managers often experience the same problem.

The workplace PIG formally discourages the superstar syndrome by distributing all rewards and recognition equally among team members. In a PIG, peer pressure will help reduce negative competition and promote cooperation.

To some a PIG is a revolutionary idea. To many workers and managers it is a foreign concept. Highly individualistic people may see it as "socialistic," which, of course, it is not. It is a step toward social equality and human dignity at all levels in the workplace, and that is a vital goal which many companies need to address more vigorously.

Peer pressure, therefore, is not enough. Social competition within the PIG, or any other work group, needs to be officially discouraged and nipped in the bud when it arises. Don't wait for a "proper time" to confront it, for in a busy company a "proper time" never comes.

One of the best ways to handle the superstar syndrome or other forms of social competition is to address the issue openly when the work group is organized or teams are reshuffled. Address it as a "potential problem that may arise." Indicate that competition is not appropriate and that it goes against the team and company goals.

Remember, competition will not eliminate itself and members will not cooperate effectively just because you say they should. For many people, letting go or redirecting social competitiveness or working as an effective team member is not easy because it is not natural. They need to learn new skills in these areas, and they are not likely to come together quickly or well without training. Training in healthy competition is a vital base for team-building. Often team-building ignores the competition issue, and then people wonder why the team isn't working.

Many people will espouse a verbal commitment to cooperation, and will tend to deny competition problems. Many of the companies who say "We don't have a problem with competition" are actually riddled with it! It's just not chic to admit it. Don't wear the same blinders. Saying you believe in something and making it work are two entirely different issues! If you cover all bases when you start, you'll have less to do later. Start out right and avoid having to change course mid stream. Don't delude yourself. Even if you are setting up a new program you are still using "old " people. Even if they're young or new to your company, they come to you with their prior cultural training, which often must be reshaped.

# Transforming Negative Competition into Positive Cooperation

A stranger once drove into a small city. Becoming lost, he stopped and asked a pedestrian how he could get to the civic center. The pedestrian thought a moment, started pointing and rattling off directions, but then said, "No, that won't work." After doing the same thing several times, he told the stranger, "You can't get there from here!"

Isn't that what we feel like sometimes? How do we get the eagles to fly in formation? With competitive problems, cliques, private alliances and factions, difficult people, hidden agendas—can we ever build unity? It's so easy, when we're up to our necks in alligators, to forget that our original mission was to drain the swamp!

Teamwork is vital; so is excellence. Negative competition is a breeding ground for alligators and so must be drained away. But how?

People are people. You'll never eliminate social competition completely. You can't turn competitive people into noncompetitors. You can, however, teach them Healthy Competitor tactics to help them rechannel competitive drive in the proper direction.

You can do numerous things to transform your situation. The tactics you use, and in which order, will depend on your organizational climate.

1. Model healthy competition and positive teamwork yourself. There is no substitute for this. People will not follow a leader who does not practice the principles and actions she wants others to adopt. Most people have heard empty promises before. If they see you "walking the talk," they will respect you and may be quite eager to follow. But first you may have to prove yourself through your actions. Use the skills from chapter 12.

   Let's assume you'll score high on this factor, then what?

2. Determine your organizational climate and choose the proper impact strategy (chapter 12). This will be the channel, the manner, through which the rest of your actions will take place.

3. Determine your ultimate goal or objective. Get a vision of it. A vision is a sense of what your organization will look like at any given time in the future. Determine also the time frame for making this occur.

4. Determine what process, structure, or system will best get you there. Will it involve PIGs, Quality Circles, or your current structure? Will you cross-train or rotate leaders? How will you deploy people?

   You may wish to bring in key people for this (and for suggestion number 3), those who will have important roles in the "new order." Or perhaps, if the number is small enough, you will want to get all the workers involved. Cooperation rises when those who are going to be affected have a voice in determining the structure that will affect them. Don't forget that "key people" can come from all ranks, from CEO to janitor. All groups involved should be represented. *Important:* If you are bringing together those who are traditional opponents, a conflict resolution process may be needed at this point.

5. Fully orient all those involved before making a change, spelling out clearly the expectations for the group and the ben-

efits for participating. Let them ask all their questions and express their reservations. This orientation should be motivational as well as educational. "Such an obvious step," you may say. It is so obvious that it is often overlooked when companies restructure!

Change is not just a technical process. It's also an emotional one. People need to feel comfortable about it if they are to be maximally productive.

6. Focus on goal alignment to align workers' personal goals with company goals. This can be done as part of healthy competition/team-building training and works nicely if done in a retreat setting, off of company grounds, where people can come together more as equals and sort out these issues.

7. Confront negative competition directly, and hold people accountable for their behavior. People are less likely to make mischief if (a) there is no payoff in it, (b) there are tangible, positive benefits for cooperating, (c) there is an "open forum" of some kind to deal with hurts and grievances as they arise, before they get out of hand, and (d) they know that they will not be able to hide behind or rationalize away their behavior but will be called to task instantly if they start to disrupt. No one wants to have to explain his or her misbehavior!

8. Institute a system that rewards cooperation and discourages traditional competition. People are very adaptable in that they will behave according to what the system rewards and punishes. The tricky part of this, however, is that this behavioral compliance with the system operates at all levels at which the system operates. If the system openly encourages cooperation but at a hidden level rewards competition, you will encourage sneaky, hidden competition, and are likely to get it. If the system rewards competition at the emotional level or social level, you will get competition, no matter how hard you try to encourage cooperation. Make sure, therefore, that the system you set up is congruent, rewarding cooperation at *all* levels.

Most managers, when attempting to reorganize or restructure, rarely take this necessity for congruence into account. In a close-knit work group or PIG this congruence is vital and cannot be overlooked.

9. Consistently reward coooperative effort. Give the team plenty of public recognition for its accomplishments, with all members being recognized equally. Reward it informally as well. Give encouragement and positive feedback frequently, and then some.

10. Dig in for the long haul; there is no quick fix. Conflict resolution takes time. So does turning around negative competition. It must be done slowly and in an atmosphere of trust. Remember that the competitive mind-set is guarded and suspicious. They're watching you, they want you to "prove" your way is better, and then they may throw up all sorts of resistance, attempting to program you to fail. The hidden competitors, the passive-aggressive ones, are often the most difficult because they are not easy to spot. Sharpen your detective skills and review the material in this book on hidden competition.

There are three vital principles to keep in mind about competition when trying to turn it around.

1. When a conflict cannot be resolved by rational means there exists a hidden agenda, which is competitive by definition.

2. Whoever is not with you is against you. There's no neutrality when people are coping with common issues that directly affect their lives.

3. "Unresolved issues" are only the arenas where competition takes place. When labor and management fight over "benefits," for example, the benefit package often isn't the real issue. The real issue is competition at the relationship level: How do you see me? How am I valued or not valued? etc. The competitive history of the people involved is also part of the problem.

Persistent negative competition is always a *relationship* problem, and until some process is instituted to heal that scism, little lasting change will occur. That's why negotiations often break down, agreements are not followed through, or disputes continue to flare up. You don't solve the problem tossing the opponents a bone. Hardheaded management types may not wish to hear this, but you can't legislate lasting cooperation. There is no substitute for caring, understanding, and mutual respect—the only true win-win solution. The only antidote to war is proactive peace! Diversity without Division is Divine!

## To Compete or Not to Compete

We're back to the original paradox: Healthy competition is not really competition at all! In the last section we talked primarily about establishing cooperation. Internal contests use a short-term competitive model to achieve long-term cooperative goals. This is admittedly tricky whenever a "contest" enters the picture. Here are some guidelines.

1. Never insert a competitive framework if things are already functioning well without one. As indicated elsewhere, such situations usually involve fairly small organizations. Even so, that doesn't mean they don't need motivating from time to time. Find another motivator; never use a contest.

2. If the situation is fiercely competitive, switch to a quota contest and put people on teams rather than having them compete directly. *You* assign the teams. Don't let the "team captains" pick. (That becomes a popularity contest similar to the hell many of us went through when sides were chosen in gym class!) You may wish to phase out contests altogether for such a group, especially if there is a large percentage of Competitive Personalities within the group.

3. If you assign people to teams for contest purposes, do the following: (a) match them based on their strengths, (b) break up cliques, (c) run the contest for a short period of time, and allow some rest before the next contest, and (d) rotate team members from contest to contest. This keeps interest up, creates new challenges, decreases inter-team rivalry (which may occur in spite of a quota contest—just calling something

a contest can trigger the Competitive Personality into action!) and discourages new cliques from developing.

Remember what kinds of contests are the most positive, fun, and exciting? Those that are short-term, have little to do with our basic self-worth and self-image, and have little if any real impact on our egos and our lives. The more relevant and serious contests become, the more pressure they create. As we said earlier, that pressure is extraneous to performance and actually may impede it. People can get nervous and sometimes hostile and jealous; they also may cheat!

Here is where we have gotten confused. We look at nonrelevant contests as fun, and then think that it is competition itself—all competition—that is fun. That's why we think any contest should motivate us. No way!

There is no question that a contest at work, where recognition and money is involved, is relevant and serious. And there is also no such thing as a nonrelevant, nonserious contest to the Competitive Personality. That is why contests must be handled carefully. Their greatest problem is the negative impact they can have on self-esteem. When structured competition spills over into social competition, competition has been taken personally and the outcome becomes interpreted as a measure of worth.

To compete or not to compete? Follow the old grammar rule about punctuation: "If in doubt, leave it out!"

# 16

# The Ecstasy of Winning, the Agony of Defeat

WE love to win; we hate to lose. Given our cultural programming, that's natural. While winning and losing seem poles
apart, they share one thing in common: the Healthy Competitor
needs to put both of them into perspective! How we handle each
one is vitally important to our self-esteem.

Some wins are necessary, some losses intolerable—such as an
international military conflict. Generally, however, the importance
of winning and losing is relative. It's much more vital to win a war
than to win a football game. As the stakes get higher, as winning
and losing become more critical, it becomes very easy to lose
perspective.

The Healthy Competitor strives to win with the same intensity
and zeal as the traditional competitor. When she plays or works
on a team, she gives her all. Assuming honorable behavior from all
concerned, the main difference between the two types of competitors is the *meaning* of the win or loss.

## Losing

What happens when we lose? We may feel bad. We may lose face.
Pangs of jealousy may set in, along with anger—at others for beating us, at ourselves for not doing well enough. We may even feel
humiliation and embarrassment. There may possibly be a sense of
grief. Others may see us as less competent; worse still, as "losers."

They may make wisecracks or in other ways put us down. When we lose is a splendid time for others to act superior. Even if they're "only kidding," it still hurts. It's very hard to lose at something into which we've invested heart and soul. How then should we cope?

It goes without saying that you act with dignity and good sportsmanship, holding your head high. If someone criticizes you afterward, you might say something like, "Thank you, I'll consider that for the future." Giving explanations to a critic after a loss will seem like making excuses, whether or not that is actually what you're doing.

Harassment is not uncommon, unfortunately, even among adults. Women who lose to men may be especially vulnerable, not only to men's comments but also to other women who, watching from the sidelines, secretly made the woman contestant their standard-bearer. The loss is always tougher when others try to make you feel that you've let them down.

When you're competing, whom are you really representing? It's important to get that clear, because often "spectators," with their own private agendas, will try to lay their on expectations and feelings of hurt of your loss on you. They try to make you feel guilty or at fault for their disappointments. Be very careful not to fall for that trap!

Debbie Thomas, a U.S. figure skater in the 1988 Olympics, was our hope for the gold medal. The press built her up in advance, adding to the already tremendous pressure on her. We don't know for sure, but possibly she felt that she was carrying the honor and hopes of the whole United States when she skated onto the ice. In addition, she was *expected* to bring home the gold. Had she not been saddled with these expectations it may have been easier for her to bear the loss of first place (she finished third). Debbie must have known while out on the ice that she would not capture the top spot. When she came off at the end of her routine, she mouthed the words, "I'm sorry," probably directed at her coach. It was a sad moment. She obviously felt horrible, but the moment was even sadder because, in spite of errors on the ice, Debbie did not know that she had nothing to be sorry for!

If you do your best and you lose, you've nothing to be sorry for! Refuse to apologize, for no apology is necessary! Others' hopes and dreams regarding your performance are theirs, not yours. They may try to lay them on you, but you do not have to accept that burden. This is where emotional self-reliance enters the scene! It's prudent to remember, especially in the agony of defeat, that your self-worth is a given and unassailable; it doesn't have to be proved to anyone, regardless of what others may say. Your worth, and hence your self-esteem, is not based upon your performance in any one situation.

Remember our discussion of invidious comparisons? One of the main problems with comparing is that we often wrap our whole essence, our entire value as a person, around one small personality or status factor, or one performance: "If I don't excell in this one area, or if I don't win this one, I'm no good." Unfortunately we can get plenty of help from others in feeling like a loser! But that's *their* weak egos showing. It's always a sign of a weak ego when a person needs to elevate himself at your expense. Remember that. For when you lose; *you* most likely will feel like the weak one.

Never accept the assumption that losing equals weakness! Here again, as a Healthy Competitor, you daren't lose perspective. You are the same person after the loss as before. Only temporary, surface circumstances have changed. Don't confuse a temporary, relative setback with an absolute statement of your capability. This may sound obvious, but we have been culturally conditioned to perceive losses in absolute value terms.

Don't magnify this loss relative to your other losses or victories, don't blow it out of proportion. It is only one in a series of contests in which you will engage in the course of your life. Maybe this contest was more important, perhaps the stakes were higher. Even so it still was only one event. Life goes on. Look ahead.

Look to the satisfactions you gained in the process of preparing and competing. The Healthy Competitor draws strong process satisfaction, whereas many traditional competitors feel that, if they lose, all the preparation counts for naught. Ask yourself: "What did I learn? How did I grow? What can I do better now and tomorrow because of my preparation for this contest?"

When the hurt has diminished, lovingly subject your performance to a self-monitoring review as described in chapter 9. Zero in on details. Analyze not only what went wrong, but also what went right. Review your strengths. Relax and mentally rehearse the improved performance.

"Losing" is a lonely feeling. Involving your trusted friends helps you recognize that others still care for and value you. Ask their support at the time of the loss, and ask for others' help and feedback in the performance analysis process as well.

You notice I have not mentioned being "defeated." You are never defeated! There is no shame in getting knocked down. You can get up; you can make a comeback. The best way to use a loss is as a challenge to excel even more the next time. Keeping your perspective in the areas I have described helps you keep your balance in the time of loss. You can do this to the degree that you keep your ego-involvement to a minimum. This takes real practice beforehand, however, because contests tend to magnify ego pressures, putting additional, unnecessary weight on your performance and on the outcome.

The best way to cope with loss, however, is through prior preparation through learning and living the new model of competition. Adopting those values, attitudes, and strategies at practice time, building up your emotional self-reliance and Competitive Fitness, will enable you to handle yourself all the better when the chips are down.

Another tip: There are plenty of real contests that you will have to face. Another way of coping with a loss is to determine if you really "lost" at all. Was there even a contest? With surprising frequency, contests are internal, private agendas. We make an event into a contest in our own minds because of its importance to us, or for our own hidden reasons. While it may be "life and death" to us, others may not perceive it as a contest at all. If this is so, you haven't really lost.

# Winning

Perhaps you're saying, "I can see why it's important to cope with losing. But what's there to cope with about winning?"

Plenty! Perhaps winning causes more insidious damage than losing. Earlier in the book we spoke of the addictive quality of winning. It creates a slowly-building dependency, somewhat like alcohol and drugs. The more we win, the more we need to win and the more we come to depend on the "winner's high" to maintain our self-esteem. It's just as important for a person who wins to detach his emotions and ego as it is for a person who loses. I'm not against winning. No way! Loving to win is OK, provided that: (a) loving to win doesn't gradually turn into an emotional need to win, and (b) the desire to win does not exceed the desire to excel. When winning becomes more important than achieving, the door is open for all kinds of mischief, and for significantly added stress.

The Healthy Competitor must never lose sight of the Formula for Healthy Competition, and must never forget that the main task is to excel, to achieve. When this is done well according to the formula, the winning will take care of itself.

The minute winning becomes the goal, added pressures arise. A new ego dimension has been added, one that often mitigates against peak performance. Playing to beat the opponent is a very different experience than playing as an art form, doing your absolute best for the sake of excellence and contribution.

As you continue to win, the pressures continue to mount. Each subsequent contest, then, has increasingly higher stakes and stress precisely because of the self-imposed demand to keep winning. Once you've established yourself as a "winner," you have to keep "on the roll." You earn greater visibility and also become the target for others: you're "the one to beat." How do you cope?

Ego-detachment is critical. Give in to the competitive pressure to have to win and the fun and excitement diminish relative to the burdens. There is hardly a heavier albatross to carry than being a consistent winner. Winning is fun. Keep it at that.

Develop your process satisfaction; let winning be the icing on the cake. Too many people who consistently win become complacent. They expect to win, so they don't have to work as hard. "After all," they figure, "why should a horse who is winning change stride?" This takes some of the creativity, as well as some of the freshness and joy, away from the endeavor. Paul Harvey once said on a telecast that "every great nation that is no longer great, has died by suicide!" By keeping yourself committed to your mission, and by continuing to grow and advance, you avoid the complacency and also the undue competitive pressures that can do you in.

There is another reason for ego-detachment. Winning can go to your head. It is not true that everyone loves a winner. A gracious and humble winner, however, is pleasing to behold. A winner who is on an ego trip is just plain obnoxious! Part of the problem with fame and success is that it appears to ruin relationships. That's why many famous people, beneath the facade, feel so lonely and unhappy. Those celebrities who are truly happy have never forgotten their roots, and have worked at maintaining key relationships.

Do fame and success really kill relationships? Because of the envy factor, they can strain a relationship. But it's *people* who destroy relationships. It's not fame nor success that does the damage, but how people adjust to them how people *use* their fame and success. The lonely ones are those who use fame and success to vaunt their personal superiority. They become seen as snobs. Their friends wonder what happened to them. "Success has spoiled them" they say.

Will success spoil you? Not if you continue to care, treating others cooperatively as equals. If you use your fame and success in the service of contribution, in the fulfillment of a beneficial mission, you will actually gain friends and admiration. Remember that true success is not measured by the dollars you have earned, but by the lives you have touched. Look at Lucille Ball and Bob Hope. Now compare them to Howard Hughes!

Yes, winning, more than losing, has the power to make you or break you!

Which will it be?

# Resource List for Further Reading

## Competition Itself

Kohn, A. *No Contest: The Case Against Competition*. Boston: Houghton Mifflin, 1986.

Ruben, H. *Competing*. New York: Lippincott & Crowell, 1980.

## Competitive Personality, Interpersonal Games

Beecher, W. and Beecher, M. *Beyond Success and Failure*. New York: Julian Press, 1966.

Berne, E. *Games People Play*. New York: Grove, 1964.

Bramson, R. M. *Coping with Difficult People*. Garden City, New York: Anchor/Doubleday, 1981.

Evatt, C. and Feld, B. *The Givers and the Takers*. New York: Macmillan, 1983.

Horney, K. *The Neurotic Personality of Our Time*. New York: W. W. Norton, 1937.

## Women and Competition/ Coping Strategies

Hardesty, S. and Jacobs, N. *Success and Betrayal*. New York: Franklin Watts, 1986.

Harragan, B. L. *Games Mother Never Taught You.* New York: Warner, 1977.

————. *Knowing The Score.* New York: Signet, 1980.

LaRouche, J. and Ryan, R. *Strategies for Women at Work.* New York: Avon, 1984.

Madden, T. R. *Women vs Women: The Uncivil Business War.* New York: Amacom, 1487.

# Jealousy

Barker, R. L. *The Green-eyed Marriage.* New York: Free Press, 1987.

Beecher, M. and Beecher, W. *The Mark of Cain.* New York: Harper & Row, 1971.

Cohen, B. *The Snow White Syndrome.* New York: Macmillan, 1986.

# Anger

Keen. S. *Faces of the Enemy.* San Francisco: Harper & Row, 1986.

Laden, M. *Escaping the Hostility Trap.* Englewood Cliffs, New Jersey: Prentice-Hall, 1977.

Madow, L. *Anger.* New York: Charles Scribner's, Sons, 1972.

# Inner Power/Charisma

Brown, M. *Attaining Personal Greatness.* New York: Morrow, 1987.

Dinkmeyer, D. and Losoncy, L. E. *The Encouragement Book.* Englewood Cliffs, New Jersey: Prentice-Hall, 1980.

Leonard, G. *The Ultimate Athlete.* New York: Viking, 1974.

Riggio, R. E. *The Charisma Quotient: What It Is, How to Get it, How to Use It.* New York: Dodd, Mead, 1988.

Robbins, A. *Unlimited Power.* New York: Simon & Schuster, 1986.

Paul, S. *The Warrior Within.* Golden, Colorado: Delta Group Press, 1983.

# Assertiveness

Alberti, R. E. and Emmons, M. L. *Your Perfect Right,* 2d ed. San Luis Obispo, California: Impact, 1974.

Bloom, L. Z., Coburn, K., and Pearlman, J. *The New Assertive Woman.* New York: Delacorte, 1975.

Bower, S. A. and Bower, G. H. *Asserting Yourself.* Reading, Massachusetts: Addison-Wesley, 1976.

# Leadership/Influence/Team-Building

Beckhard, R. and Harris, R. T. *Organizational Transitions,* 2d ed. Reading, Massachusetts: Addison-Wesley, 1987.

Buchholz, S. and Roth, T. *Creating the High-performance Team* (K. Hess, Editor). New York: Wiley, 1987.

Conklin, R. *How to Get People to Do Things.* Chicago: Contemporary Books, 1979.

Kotter, J. P. *The Leadership Factor.* New York: Free Press, 1988.

Shea, G. *Building Trust for Personal and Organizational Success.* New York: Wiley, 1987.

# Positioning/Self-advancement

Davidson, J. P. *Blow Your Own Horn.* New York: Amacom, 1987.

Newman, J. A. and Alexander, R. *Climbing the Corporate Matterhorn*. New York: Wiley, 1985.

Ries, A. and Trout, J. *Positioning: The Battle for Your Mind*. New York: Warner, 1981.

# Power in Organizations

Bachrach, S. B. and Lawler, E. J. *Power and Politics in Organizations*. San Francisco: Jossey-Bass, 1980.

Cohen, S. S. *Tender Power*. Reading; Mass: Addison-Wesley, 1989.

Cuming, P. *The Power Handbook*. Boston: CBI Publishing, 1981.

Kotter, J. P. *Power and Influence*. New York: Free Press, 1985.

# Mental Self-programming

Bry, A. *Visualization*. New York: Barnes & Noble, 1972.

Donald, L. and Holloway, E. *Self-hypnosis to Self-improvement*. Muncie, Indiana: Accelerated Development, 1984.

Olson, H. A. *Champion Mind Power* six-cassette self-training program). Reisterstown, Maryland: Maximum Potential, 1985. (See ordering information.)

Singer, J. L., and Switzer, E. *Mind Play: The Creative Use of Fantasy*. Englewood Cliffs, New Jersey: Prentice-Hall, 1980.

# Sport

Orlick, T. *In Pursuit of Excellence*. Ottawa: Runge, 1980.

Tutko, T. and Tosi, U. *Sports Psyching*. Los Angeles: Tarcher, 1976.

Unestahl, L. E. (editor) *The Mental Aspects of Gymnastics.* Örebro, Sweden: Veje Publishers, 1983.

# Ordering Information

If this book has helped you and if your organization could benefit from speaking, training, or consultation by Harry Olson, Harry would like to hear from you. Contact him at:

Maximum Potential, Inc.
1 East Cherry Hill Road
Reisterstown, Maryland 21136
301–833–3452

Products mentioned in the text

*The Climate Impact Profile System* (paper and pencil self-scoring inventory) Published by Performax Systems International, Inc., 12755 State Highway 55, Minneapolis, MN 55441. Available from your local Performax distributor or from Maximum Potential, Inc.

*Champion Mind Power* (six-cassette mental self-training program). *The Champion* (Quarterly Newsletter on Healthy Competition/Cooperation.) Available from Maximum Potential, Inc.

Contact Maximum Potential, Inc. for further information or to order the above products.

# Index

# About the Author

HARRY A. OLSON, Ph.D., is a psychologist specializing in healthy competition and peak performance.

For over twelve years he has researched competition in sports, business, and personal life, and has developed a new model of competing that maximizes winning potential while reducing stress and improving relationships. He has "competition coached" many business and sales people, as well as professional and amateur athletes.

Dr. Olson is a popular lecturer and trainer on competition, office politics, and peak performance, providing training to corporations and individuals in America and abroad. He is president of Maximum Potential, Inc., a performance consulting firm located in Reisterstown, Maryland. He also maintains a private hypnosis and psychotherapy practice.